5

ENGLISH in Common

with ActiveBook

Richard Acklam and Araminta Crace

Series Consultants
María Victoria Saumell and Sarah Louisa Birchley

ALWAYS LEARNING

PEARSON

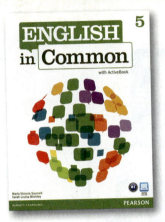

English in Common is a six-level course that helps adult and young-adult English learners develop effective communication skills that correspond to the Common European Framework of Reference for Languages (CEFR). Every level of English in Common is correlated to a level of the CEFR, and each lesson is formulated around a specific CAN DO objective.

English in Common 5 has ten units. Each unit has twelve pages.

There are three three-page lessons in each unit.

A Unit Wrap Up ends each unit.

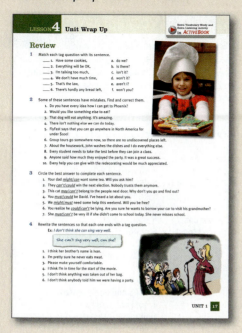

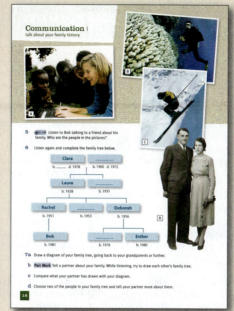

Back of Student Book

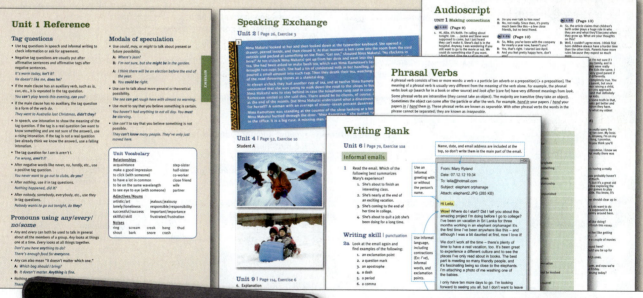

- Each Student Book contains an **ActiveBook**, which provides the Student Book in digital format. *ActiveBook* also includes the complete Audio Program and Extra Listening activities.

- An optional online **MyEnglishLab** provides the opportunity for extra practice anytime, anywhere.

- The Teacher's Resource Book contains teaching notes, photocopiable extension activities, and an **ActiveTeach**, which provides a digital Student Book enhanced by interactive whiteboard software. *ActiveTeach* also includes the videos and video activities, as well as the complete Test Bank.

Contents

READING/WRITING	LISTENING	COMMUNICATION/EXTRA VOCABULARY STUDY
Reading texts: • an article about what makes a good friend • an article about birth order and personality • an article about teens and texting **Writing task:** write informal notes and messages	**Listening texts:** • phone messages • a conversation about friendship • a radio show about a family of jugglers	**Communication:** talk about your family history **Extra Vocabulary Study in *ActiveBook*:** two word phrasal verbs
Reading texts: • an article about changes in attitudes toward work over the years • excerpts from the novel *The No. 1 Ladies' Detective Agency* **Writing task:** write a formal cover letter for a job	**Listening texts:** • a radio show about the Rock Gardens of Chandigarh • a report on survey results • job and program entrance interviews	**Communication:** carry out an effective interview **Extra Vocabulary Study in *ActiveBook*:** collocations with prepositions
Reading texts: • a review of the movie *Troy* • a newspaper article about the "good old days" • two letters to the newspaper editor **Writing task:** write a short story about a heroic figure	**Listening texts:** • a radio interview with an expert on China • a discussion on important technological inventions	**Communication:** talk about lessons learned from the past **Extra Vocabulary Study in *ActiveBook*:** forming nouns from other parts of speech
Reading texts: • a blog about a solo sail around the world • a magazine article about Outward Bound **Writing task:** write a blog entry	**Listening texts:** • summaries of different outdoor adventures • a conversation about the themes in the movie *Million Dollar Baby* • descriptions and a comparison of two photos	**Communication:** exchange information on familiar matters **Extra Vocabulary Study in *ActiveBook*:** distances and dimensions
Reading texts: • an article about the rags to riches life of Chris Gardner • an excerpt from the novel *The Memory Box* **Writing task:** write an email describing someone	**Listening texts:** • a conversation about photos taken in childhood • a monologue about past abilities • a summary of a book plot	**Communication:** state and defend opinions in informal discussions **Extra Vocabulary Study in *ActiveBook*:** idioms describing people
Reading texts: • a magazine article about living in the jungle • a article from a travel website about Bhutan **Writing task:** write an informal email describing an experience	**Listening texts:** • descriptions of the weather • a Q and A about trekking in Bhutan	**Communication:** exchange detailed information **Extra Vocabulary Study in *ActiveBook*:** expressions with *go*
Reading texts: • an article about the movie *Super Size Me* • an article about indulging pets **Writing task:** write a formal letter of complaint	**Listening texts:** • a description of a traditional holiday meal • a radio report on celebrity memorabilia • conversations with service providers	**Communication:** use persuasive language to get satisfaction from a service provider **Extra Vocabulary Study in *ActiveBook*:** prefixes
Reading texts: • a training brochure on leadership • a newspaper article about the pressure of getting into the "right" preschool **Writing task:** write a report about the results of a survey	**Listening texts:** • a work appraisal • descriptions of people • a radio call-in show	**Communication:** give and seek personal views and opinions **Extra Vocabulary Study in *ActiveBook*:** three word phrasal verbs
Reading texts: • a story about a famous crime • an article about the man who was the basis for the character of Sherlock Holmes **Writing task:** write an article about a crime	**Listening texts:** • a funny story about a lawsuit • a conversation about a foolish thief • an interview with "Sherlock Holmes" • an account of a famous financial crime	**Communication:** speculate on the reasons for a problem **Extra Vocabulary Study in *ActiveBook*:** newspaper headlines
Reading texts: • an article about using hypnosis to stop bad habits • an excerpt from the novel *Brave New World* **Writing task:** write a persuasive essay	**Listening texts:** • descriptions of unusual mental states • conversations about hypnosis • a radio interview with a consumer affairs expert	**Communication:** express personal preferences **Extra Vocabulary Study in *ActiveBook*:** commonly misspelled words

How much do you know . . . ?

1   Read the passage. Match each underlined word or phrase to the grammar below.

According to (**1.**) the ancient Greek historian Herodotus, (**2.**) in the 7th century BC the king of Egypt, Psamtik I, decided to conduct a (**3.**) scientific experiment. Using his absolute power over his subjects, (**4.**) he took two newborn babies and handed them to a shepherd, with instructions that they were to be (**5.**) brought up in total isolation. Most importantly, no one was to speak in the babies' presence. Psamtik wanted to find out what language the children would speak if left to themselves. He thought that the language they produced would be the (**6.**) oldest in the world—the original language of the human race. After two years, the shepherd heard the two children (**7.**) repeatedly pronounce the word "becos." This was identified as meaning (**8.**) "bread" in the language of the Phrygians, a people then living in central Turkey. From this experiment, Psamtik deduced that the Phrygian language (**9.**) must be the first ever spoken. Nobody now believes Psamtik's (**10.**) conclusion—a few commentators suggest that the infants (**11.**) were imitating the sound of the shepherd's sheep, but no one since (**12.**) has had any better success in discovering what man's very first spoken language was like.

____ **a.** present perfect   ____ **e.** article   ____ **i.** adjective

____ **b.** past continuous   ____ **f.** preposition   ____ **j.** adverb

____ **c.** noncount noun   ____ **g.** count noun   ____ **k.** pronoun

____ **d.** phrasal verb   ____ **h.** superlative   ____ **l.** modal verb

2   Find and correct the grammar mistake in each sentence. Compare answers in pairs.

1. They've been to Brazil last year.
2. This cathedral built in 1590.
3. I was reading in my room when I was hearing a loud crash downstairs.
4. My grades this year are a lot worst than last year.
5. You work for IBM, aren't you?
6. If I'll have time, I'll paint my bedroom this weekend.

3a   Complete the word webs with phrases from the box.

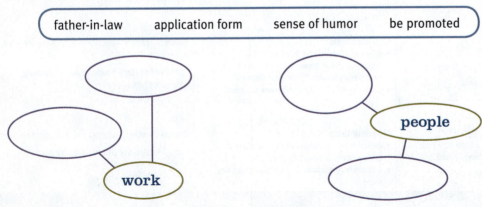

father-in-law   application form   sense of humor   be promoted

people

work

b   Underline the main stress in each word and phrase.

Making connections

Warm Up

1 Look at the photos. How do you think these people are connected?

2a What do these words mean? Use them to describe the photos.

> step-sister   half-sister   co-worker   acquaintance   partner   wife

b Read the sentences. What do the underlined phrases mean?

1. I don't think I <u>made a very good first impression</u> on your parents. They didn't seem very interested in me.
2. The first time we met, we <u>just clicked</u>. It was amazing. We started going out soon after.
3. We <u>have a lot in common</u>. We like doing a lot of the same kinds of things.
4. My sister and I don't really <u>see eye to eye</u> on much. We've always argued—even as children.
5. She thinks about things in the same way as me. I really <u>feel on the same wavelength</u> as her.

c **Pair Work** Who do you "just click" with? Do you always "feel on the same wavelength"? Why?

Reading

1a **Pair Work** What are three important characteristics of a good friend? Discuss.

b Read the survey. Does it refer to any characteristics you discussed in Exercise 1a?

What makes a good friend?

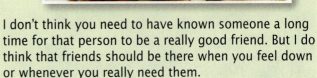

On average each person makes an amazing 363 friends in their life—but only six of them will be true friends! We carried out a global survey to find out what makes a "good friend."

Friends should be there for you all the time, not just when they want to be. They will keep in touch even though you may be far apart. Some of my closest friends live abroad, but it doesn't really make a lot of difference.
Eun Yee, 19, Korea

To me, a good friend is someone you have a lot in common with. You can share your beliefs and passions with them. I'm really lucky since I have three or four friends like that, but I'm still looking for my soulmate.
Haruki, 25, Japan

I think a good friend is somebody you can trust and share secrets with—someone that will never lie to you. If I ever found out that friends of mine had lied to me, I know I couldn't be friends with them anymore.
Emily, 14, Canada

I think that a true friend is someone you can feel completely comfortable with—you don't have to try to be someone you're not. A real friend should accept you for who you are and not try to change you.
Mercedes, 31, Mexico

I don't think you need to have known someone a long time for that person to be a really good friend. But I do think that friends should be there when you feel down or whenever you really need them.
Raquel, 15, Colombia

A good friend is someone who listens to you but, at the same time, doesn't just agree with everything you say. They should definitely tell you if they think you're making a mistake, although that can be hard.
Jason, 23, USA

I think you know someone will be a really good friend as soon as you meet them. You just click right away. Then the most important thing is trust. You have to know they will always look out for you and be totally loyal to you.
Mario, 21, Argentina

For me to call someone a really good friend, we have to see eye to eye on most things. We have a similar sense of humor. I definitely need to feel like we're on the same wavelength.
Fausto, 31, Brazil

2 Read the survey again. Match each idea with a person from the survey.

A good friend:

1. finds the same things funny that you do. _____
2. is similar to you. _____
3. doesn't want you to be different. _____
4. doesn't always say that you are right. _____
5. supports you when you feel miserable or upset. _____
6. stays in contact with you after you move far away. _____
7. is always on your side. _____
8. won't tell other people your secrets. _____

3 **Group Work** Discuss the questions.

1. Which ideas from Exercise 2 do you have?
2. Do you think people look for different things in friends as they get older? If so, why?

Writing

4 **Pair Work** When do you write or get notes or messages? Discuss.

5a Look at the notes and messages on the right. Match each one to its purpose.

    ____ 1. making an apology

    ____ 2. enclosed with something else

    ____ 3. trying to rearrange an appointment

    ____ 4. reminding someone to do something

b Read them again and decide who might have written each one: wife, friend, co-worker, or brother.

c Fill in the missing words in A–C.

d **Pair Work** Message D is a text message. What do the abbreviated words, such as "r" mean? Discuss.

Listening

6a ▶1.02 Listen to three phone messages. What is the purpose of each one?

b Listen again and make notes of the important information. Then write a brief message to each person using your notes.

7 Read these statements and tell other students which ones you agree with and why.
- It's important to hold on to good friends.
- Having at least one very close friend is really important.
- New friends will replace old friends.
- Family is always more important than friends.

8a ▶1.03 Listen to Mark and Zoë talking about friends and friendship. Which of the ideas from Exercise 7 do they have?

b Listen again. Make notes about the people they talk about and how they are significant.

> Angela – Zoë's best friend since childhood

9 **Pair Work** Are your friendships more like Mark's or Zoë's? In what ways? Discuss.

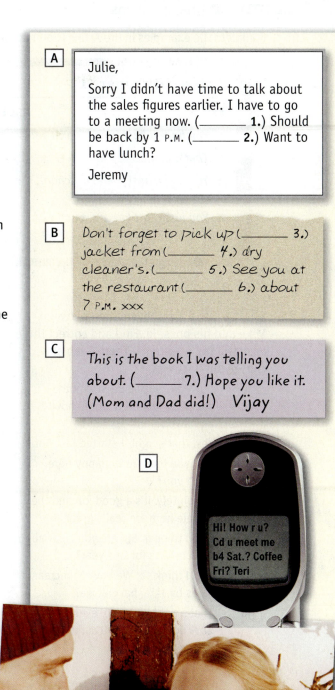

A

Julie,

Sorry I didn't have time to talk about the sales figures earlier. I have to go to a meeting now. (_____ **1.**) Should be back by 1 P.M. (_____ **2.**) Want to have lunch?

Jeremy

B

Don't forget to pick up (_____ **3.**) jacket from (_____ **4.**) dry cleaner's. (_____ **5.**) See you at the restaurant (_____ **6.**) about 7 P.M. xxx

C

This is the book I was telling you about. (_____ **7.**) Hope you like it. (Mom and Dad did!) Vijay

D

Hi! How r u? Cd u meet me b4 Sat.? Coffee Fri? Teri

Grammar | tag questions

10 Complete the examples in the Active Grammar box. Which examples apply to rules a, b, and c?

Active Grammar (1)

Examples	Rules
1. *You have a best friend, don't you?*	a. Negative tag questions are usually put after affirmative sentences and affirmative tags after negative sentences.
2. *That's life, _____ it?*	b. If the main clause has an auxiliary verb, such as *is, can*, etc., it is repeated in the tag question.
3. *You had a best friend in school, _____ you?*	c. If the main clause has no auxiliary, the tag question is a form of the verb *do*.
4. *You just can't keep in touch with everybody, _____ you?*	

See Reference page 127

11a ▶1.04 Read the conversation between Mike and his boss, Jo. Find and correct three incorrect tag questions. Then listen and check your answers.

Jo: So, Mike, you've been with the company for nearly a year now, aren't you?

Mike: Yes, that's right. I started last April.

Jo: And you feel pretty happy here, don't you?

Mike: Absolutely. It's a good job and the people here are really great.

Jo: Good to hear. So, are you clear about your targets for this year?

Mike: Yes, I think so. We have to increase sales by 15%, haven't we?

Jo: That's right. If we do, everyone gets a 20% bonus. That will make *everyone* happy, won't it?

Mike: Definitely.

Jo: Now, let's talk about punctuality. You have trouble getting here on time, haven't you?

Mike: Uh, well, I can explain that . . .

b Circle the best answer to complete the rules in the Active Grammar box. Then use the rules to complete the examples.

Active Grammar (2)

Rules

a. The tag question for *I am* is ~~aren't I~~ / ~~amn't I~~.

b. After negative words like *never, no, hardly*, etc., use a positive / negative tag question.

c. After *nothing* as a subject, use it / they in tag questions.

d. After *nobody, somebody,* etc., use it / they in tag questions.

Examples

1. *I'm too late, _____ I?*

2. *You never go to the theater, _____ you?*

3. *Nothing went wrong today, _____ it?*

4. *Nobody has complained, have _____ ?*

See Reference page 127

---

12 Complete the sentences with tag questions.

1. She's getting pretty tall, _____ ?

2. Nobody seems to like their present, _____ ?

3. You haven't been waiting very long, _____ ?

4. I can't leave the party early, _____ ?

5. You hardly ever go out for lunch, _____ ?

6. Nothing seems to be going right, _____ ?

Express agreement or disagreement

GRAMMAR pronouns using *any/every/no/some*

CAN DO ✓

Listening

1 **Pair Work** Discuss the questions.

1. Do you know any large families?
2. What do you think are the good and bad things about being brought up as part of a large family?
3. How would you feel about working with a member of your family?

2 ▶ 1.05 Listen to part of a radio show. Answer the questions.

1. Why did Larry Boehmer start juggling?
2. How did his children become interested in juggling?
3. Where did the family first juggle for the public?
4. What does Larry believe about the skill of juggling?

3a Read the following expressions. Think about what they mean. Then listen again.

1. to juggle several tasks at once
2. to get your hands on something
3. to put your mind to something
4. a big family man
5. to be only too happy about something

b **Pair Work** Discuss the meaning of each expression above. Then use the expressions to summarize the show.

Grammar | pronouns using *any/every/no/some*

4 Look at the example sentence pairs in the Active Grammar Box. One sentence in each pair is incorrect. Cross it out. Then circle the best answer to complete each rule in the right column.

Active Grammar

Examples

1a. *Not just anybody can learn to juggle.*
1b. *Not just everybody can learn to juggle.*

2a. *No thanks, I don't want something to eat.*
2b. *No thanks, I don't want anything to eat.*

3a. *I've looked anywhere for my keys.*
3b. *I've looked everywhere for my keys.*

4a. *She doesn't have anything to do.*
4b. *She doesn't have nothing to do.*

Rules

a. Anybody / Everybody refers to one person at a time.

b. Use something / anything for amounts in negative statements.

c. Anywhere / Everywhere refers to all possible places.

d. Use anything / nothing in negative sentences.

See Reference page 127

5 Circle the best answer to complete each sentence.

1. I'm going to try and see my boyfriend *every/any* weekend.
2. *Everybody/Anybody* was thrilled to see Naomi.
3. Get me *some/any* soup you can find. It doesn't matter what kind.
4. I can't get rid of this cold. *Nothing/Anything* seems to help.
5. The market had flowers of *every/any* kind.
6. I'd like to go *everywhere/somewhere* hot for my vacation. I need the sun.

Reading

6 **Pair Work** What are the advantages and disadvantages of being born first, middle, or last in a family?

WHO comes first?

1 A child's place in the family birth order may play a role in the type of occupations that will interest him or her as an adult, new research suggests. In two related studies, researchers found that only children—and to a certain extent first-born children—were more interested in intellectual, cognitive pursuits than were later-born children. In contrast, later-born children were more interested in both artistic and outdoor-related careers.

2 These results fit into theories that say our place in family birth order will influence our personality, said Frederick T.L. Leong, co-author of the study and professor of psychology at Ohio State University. "Parents typically place different demands and have different expectations of children depending on their birth order," Leong said.

3 "For example, parents may be extremely protective of only children and worry about their physical safety. That may be why only children are more likely to show interest in academic pursuits rather than physical or outdoor activities. Only children will tend to get more time and attention from their parents than children with siblings. This will often make them feel special, but the downside is that they may suffer occasional pangs of jealousy and loneliness when friends discuss their brothers and sisters and family life."

4 The first-born is an only child until the second child comes along—transforming them from being the center of attention to then sharing the care of parents. Parents also expect them to be responsible and "set an example." The change from being the focus of a family may be quite a shock and so shape the first-born's subsequent outlook on life. Therefore, first-borns may try to get back their parents' attention and approval by achieving success and recognition in their careers. It has been noted that first-borns are significantly more often found as world political leaders than any other birth order position.

5 "As they have more children, parents tend to become more open and relaxed, and that may allow younger children to be more risk-taking," Leong said. "If the first-born or only child wants to be a poet, that may concern parents. But by the fourth child, parents may not mind as much."

6 Being the youngest in the family can sometimes be a stifling and frustrating experience, especially if they're looking to be taken seriously and treated like an adult. The last-born is more likely than the other birth order positions to take up dangerous sports. This may be a sign of the last-born's rebellious streak—a result of being fed up with always being bossed about by everyone else in the family.

7 Middle children, however, have different issues. "Middle child syndrome" can mean feeling sandwiched between two other "more important" people—an older sibling who gets all the rights and is treated like an adult and a younger sibling who gets all the privileges and is treated like a spoiled child. Middle-borns have to learn to get along with older and younger children, and this may contribute to them becoming good negotiators; of all the birth order positions they are most skillful at dealing with authority figures and those holding inferior positions.

8 Leong said the biggest differences in the study were between only children and later-born children. "First-born children are difficult to classify because they start out as only children but later give up that position. It may be that the length of time a first-born child is an only child makes a difference in his or her personality." ■

7 Read the article. Which of the following does it do? Check the answers.

_____ **1.** Says which type of child (first born, middle born, last born, only child) it is best to be.

_____ **2.** Gives advice to parents about dealing with each type of child.

_____ **3.** Describes the possible career consequences according to birth order.

_____ **4.** Advises children how to cope with their position in the family.

8 **Group Work** Which points in the article are true about your family or other families you know? Discuss.

Vocabulary | making adjectives from nouns

9 Complete the charts with the missing information. Use your dictionary if necessary.

Noun	responsibility	art		
Adjective			jealous	lonely

Noun			skill	frustration
Adjective	successful	important		

10 Complete the following sentences with the best words from the chart.

1. Do you realize how _____ these exams are? They'll determine which school you get into.
2. My sister is very _____. She paints and writes poetry.
3. It's so _____ trying to call my bank. I have to wait for hours before a real person will answer the phone.
4. You shouldn't be _____ of Bob. He's not my type!
5. He's lived alone for awhile, but he says he never feels _____.
6. There's a lot of _____ involved in juggling.
7. I wish someone would take _____ for the train crash.
8. His last movie was an incredible _____. Apparently, it won five Oscars.

Speaking

11a ▶1.06 Listen to the conversation. What are the two people talking about?

b Listen again. Check the expressions that you hear in the How To box.

12a **Group Work** Discuss the statements. Try to use expressions from the How To box.

- Parents tend to be stricter with their first-born child.
- Middle children have the worst time.
- The youngest child is usually spoiled.
- An only child tends to be self-sufficient and doesn't need many friends.
- We are attracted to people who are born in the same position within the family.
- Our position in the family affects the kind of career we choose.

b Report your group's discussion to the class using expressions from the How To box.

How To:

Agree and disagree

Expressing agreement	____ I couldn't agree more.
	____ That's probably true.
	____ I think there's some truth in that.
Expressing disagreement	____ I'm not sure if I agree with that.
	____ I don't think that's (completely) true.
	____ I totally disagree.
Reporting agreement/ disagreement	____ We all felt pretty much the same about this question.
	____ There were several different opinions in the group.
	____ One or two people had pretty strong feelings about this.

Speaking

1 **Pair Work** Look at the photos. Describe what you see in each one.

2 **Pair Work** Discuss the questions.

1. Do you have a cell phone? Do you have texting on your phone? How often do you use it?

2. Whom do you usually text? How often do you text each other? What kinds of information do you include in your texts?

3. Do you prefer texting to talking on the phone, chatting online, or using a social networking site? Why?

4. Where (if anywhere) are you not allowed to use your phone?

5. If you could keep only one of these items, which would you keep: a TV, a computer, an MP3 player, a cell phone?

Reading

3 Read the article and circle the topics it refers to.

1. the number of teens who have cell phones

2. the most popular way to communicate among teens

3. teen addiction to texting

4. when texting first began

5. how parents feel about texting

6. things that parents can do to make teens use their cell phones more responsibly

7. the health risks of texting too much

8. the advantages for the family of having cell phones

4 Read the article again. Make brief notes about the topics in Exercise 3 it refers to.

5 **Pair Work** Discuss the questions.

1. Which two facts in the text did you find most interesting? Why?

2. How important do you think cell phones are for young people in your country?

3. How do you think methods of communication will change over the next five years?

Addicted to Texting

Emma Singer is having lunch with a friend. Her phone vibrates by her fork. She calmly picks it up midsentence, reads the message, taps in a response—never missing a beat of the ongoing face-to-face conversation with her friend. Then a few minutes later her friend's phone buzzes. She blushes into the screen, giggles discreetly, and responds. Neither minds the interruptions. These teens are skilled at having multiple conversations at the same time.

Emma admits her dependence on her cell phone. "I can't imagine life without it. I mean, I could live without my computer or my TV. But not my cell phone! How would my friends reach me?" Emma is among the 75% of teens in the US who own cell phones. Texting is the number one way teens communicate with friends today. It is more popular than face-to-face contact, email, IM, and voice calling. According to recent surveys, 50% of American teens send 50 or more messages a day. One in three teens sends more than 100 texts a day. It's no wonder then that 42% can text with their eyes closed!

Why the texting craze? Emma explains, "Texting lets me always be available to my friends. That's so important." With teens today it's the act of staying in touch that matters—not the content of the communication. Teens prefer texting to voice calling because it's private and accessible practically everywhere. "I can respond wherever I am, whatever I'm doing," Emma admits. "With a voice call, my parents or my teacher might hear what I'm saying."

In Japan, teen cell phone use is even higher than in the US: 96% of 16 to 17-year-olds own their own cell phones. Seventeen-year-old Kumiko Azuma is the ultimate texter. She's able to text while studying, talking on another phone, watching TV, doing chores, shopping, exercising, showering—sometimes a combination of several of these. "I've even texted while sleeping!" she admits. Kumiko must

be addicted if her entire existence revolves around this little media tool!

At the root of teen cell phone addictions worldwide are none other than parents. In both the US and Japan, most teens have unlimited phone access that is paid for by parents. In Brazil, 56% of teens ages 15 to 19 pay for their cell phone use out of their own pockets, compared to 27% in the US. If teens are forced to foot the bill and track their usage, they may use their phones more responsibly. Parents could also activate restriction options on phones, limiting who their kids communicate with, when, and how much. One US mother comments, "I just want my daughter to understand that she can't be available to her friends all day every day. It's unhealthy. Some time needs to be set aside for homework or her family. She can't be tapping mindless text messages all day."

In the end, parents and teens should be able to reach a compromise. After all, cell phones offer many benefits: safety, easy contact, and GPS tracking (though teenagers may not be happy that their parents can track where they are at all times). Teens can also get organized on their cell phones with calendars and to-do lists. They can set reminders for assignments and activities. With Internet accessibility on many "smart" phones, the possibilities will soon be endless. Smart phones might eventually replace personal computers. The key now is to help Emma, Kumiko, and teens around the world reap the benefits of cell phones, including texting, yet not become so dependent on them they can't eat a meal uninterrupted or sleep peacefully through the night.

Vocabulary | describing noises

6 **Pair Work** What noises do you typically hear every day? Which ones do you particularly like and dislike?

7a ▶1.07 Listen and match the words in the box to the sounds. Number them in the order you hear them.

> ____ ring ____ scream ____ creak
> ____ shout ____ bark ____ snore
> ____ bang ____ thud ____ crash

b **Pair Work** What typically makes each of these noises? Discuss.

> Phones ring.   And doorbells.

8 ▶1.08 Some of these sounds are from a story. Listen to these sounds and discuss how to link them to tell a story. Use *may, might, could,* etc.

> The crash might be a burglar breaking into a house. Then the dog barks, but maybe the burglar gives him something to eat to keep him quiet. After that . . .

Grammar | modals of speculation

9a ▶1.09 Listen. Match each phone conversation to its subject (a–e) in the Active Grammar box.

b Match each subject (a–e) in the Active Grammar box to its meaning (1–3). Does each subject refer to the present or the future?

10 Complete the second sentence in each pair so it has the same meaning as the first. Use *may, might, could, must,* or *can't* and the verbs in parentheses.

1. I'm sure that Terry is stuck in traffic. Normally he's never late.

   Terry _____ (be) stuck in traffic. Normally he's never late.

2. It's possible that we'll go and visit my brother in Boston.

   We _____ (go) and visit my brother in Boston.

3. It's not possible that Jane wants to go to Guatemala this summer. She hates hot weather.

   Jane _____ (want) to go to Guatemala this summer. She hates hot weather.

4. There's a chance that Susie will come to the party tonight.

   Susie _____ (come) to the party tonight.

5. I have no doubt that there are better ways of solving this problem.

   There _____ (be) better ways of solving this problem.

6. Perhaps Ming will change his mind about lending you his car.

   Ming _____ (change) his mind about lending you his car.

Active Grammar

Subject of conversation	Meaning
____ a. *It **could** be someone talking to his boss.*	____ 1. It is possible.
____ b. *He **might** need help finding his way.*	____ 2. It is not possible.
____ c. *The weather **can't** be very nice.*	____ 3. It is certain.
_1_ d. *He **must** be late.*	
____ e. *They **may** go to the movies later.*	

See Reference page 127

Speaking

11a Choose eight of the following and write them on a separate sheet of paper.

- your father's first name
- the hour of the day you like best
- the name of a pet you have had
- the title of one of your favorite movies
- the name of one of your favorite bands
- the first name of someone you admire
- the place where you were born
- the language you most like the sound of
- the time you got up this morning
- the title of a favorite book
- the place where you spent your best vacation
- the foreign language you speak the best

b **Pair Work** Look at your partner's answers and guess what they mean. Use *might, must, can't,* or *could.*

Portuguese—This could be the language you most like the sound of.   No, it isn't.

Review

1 Match each tag question with its sentence.

    1. Have some cookies,   a. do we?

    2. Everything will be OK,   b. is there?

    3. I'm talking too much,   c. isn't it?

    4. We don't have much time,   d. won't it?

    5. That's the law,   e. aren't I?

    6. There's hardly any bread left,   f. won't you?

2 Some of these sentences have mistakes. Find and correct them.

1. Do you have every idea how I can get to Phoenix?

2. Would you like something else to eat?

3. That dog will eat anything. It's amazing.

4. There isn't nothing else we can do today.

5. FlyFast says that you can go anywhere in North America for under $100!

6. Group tours go somewhere now, so there are no undiscovered places left.

7. About the housework, John washes the dishes and I do everything else.

8. Every student needs to take the test before they can join a class.

9. Anyone said how much they enjoyed the party. It was a great success.

10. Every help you can give with the redecorating would be much appreciated.

3 Circle the best answer to complete each sentence.

1. Your dad *might/can* want some tea. Will you ask him?

2. They *can't/could* win the next election. Nobody trusts them anymore.

3. This cat *may/can't* belong to the people next door. Why don't you go and find out?

4. You *must/could* be David. I've heard a lot about you.

5. We *might/must* need some help this weekend. Will you be free?

6. You realize he *could/can't* be lying. Are you sure he wants to borrow your car to visit his grandmother?

7. She *must/can't* be very ill if she didn't come to school today. She never misses school.

4 Rewrite the sentences so that each one ends with a tag question.

    Ex: *I don't think she can sing very well.*

> She can't sing very well, can she?

1. I think her brother's name is Ivan.

2. I'm pretty sure he never eats meat.

3. Please make yourself comfortable.

4. I think I'm in time for the start of the movie.

5. I don't think anything was taken out of her bag.

6. I don't think anybody told him we were having a party.

Communication |
talk about your family history

A

B

C

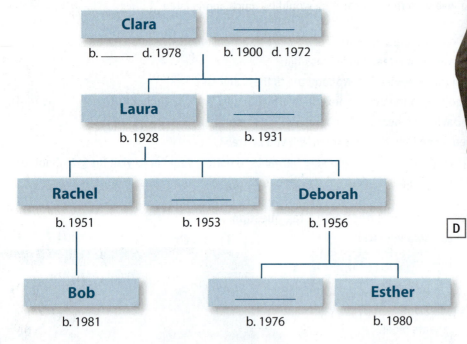

D

5 ▶1.10 Listen to Bob talking to a friend about his family. Who are the people in the pictures?

6 Listen again and complete the family tree below.

Clara	_____
b. _____ d. 1978	b. 1900 d. 1972

Laura	_____
b. 1928	b. 1931

Rachel	_____	Deborah
b. 1951	b. 1953	b. 1956

Bob	_____	Esther
b. 1981	b. 1976	b. 1980

7a Draw a diagram of your family tree, going back to your grandparents or further.

b **Pair Work** Tell a partner about your family. While listening, try to draw each other's family tree.

c Compare what your partner has drawn with your diagram.

d Choose two of the people in your family tree and tell your partner more about them.

UNIT 2
Making a living

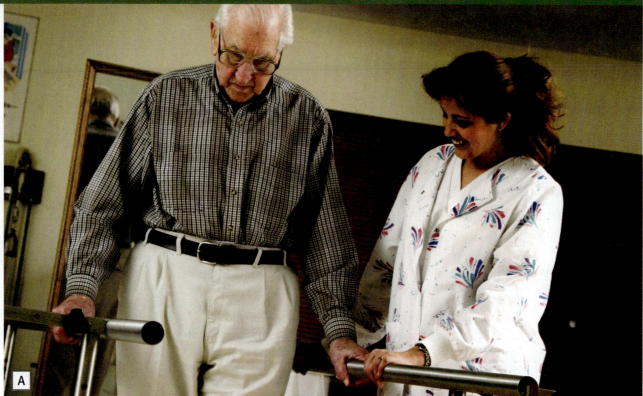

Warm Up

1 **Group Work** Discuss the questions.

　1. Which of the following jobs are NOT in the photos:
　　journalist, civil engineer, social worker, physical therapist, surgeon

　2. Briefly, what do you think each job in the photos involves?

　3. Which of the jobs would you most/least like to do? Why or why not?

2 **Pair Work** Think of a job for each quality in the box.

> stay calm under pressure　　be a people person　　be a good listener　　be a self-starter
> have a "can do" attitude　　have an eye for detail　　bring out the best in other people
> be good with numbers　　be a team player　　be able to meet tight deadlines

3 Which of the phrases in Exercise 2 apply to you? Give details.

Reading

1 **Pair Work** Discuss the questions.

1. What can you see in the pictures?
2. How do you think "work" has changed over the last 1,000 years? In what ways do you think it is the same?

2 Read the article quickly. What does it say about question 2 above?

WORK

the daily grind we just can't do without

Work may sometimes drive us crazy, but when we don't have it, we miss it. We miss it, we want it, and perhaps we even need it. Everyone wants to be valued, and a salary is proof that we matter.

Not any job will do, however. Housework and volunteer work tend to be seen as non-jobs. In our work-centered culture, a "real job" means paid employment. Being paid for a job is better for our self-esteem, too. Of course, we would also prefer work to be useful and interesting, as well, but you don't have to enjoy your job to get psychological benefits from it. According to some experts, completing even unenjoyable tasks at work contributes to our sense of well-being.

The obligation to be in a particular place at a particular time and working as part of a team toward a common goal gives us a sense of structure and purpose that we find difficult to have on our own. For a lot of us, the workplace has also taken over from the community as the place of human contact. For most of us, work often functions as a social club, an information network, and an informal dating agency.

Many of us are even "job addicts" without realizing it. When we can't work for whatever reason, we show signs similar to real addicts who are deprived of their "fix": We become irritable and lethargic. Among newly-retired men, death rates increase significantly in the first six months after leaving the workforce. For most of their lives, their personality, self-esteem, and status have been defined by work; without it, they can lose their appetite for life.

Life wasn't always so driven by employment, however. Work in the pre-industrial age was task-oriented, not time-structured, focusing not on money but on tasks necessary for survival. Whole communities worked together, so there was less division between work and free time. The Industrial Revolution radically changed how people worked. Suddenly, work was no longer structured by seasons, but by the clock. Work was separated from the rest of life, and began to provide money rather than food and goods.

More recently, the revolution in information technology has again changed the nature of work and employment. The workplace itself may become unnecessary. Millions of employees now work from home, keeping in touch via email and phone. Many employers say that working "remotely" improves productivity, as workers are happier and waste less time commuting. There are downsides however, as workers lose touch with the workplace and people there.

We will undoubtedly have to accept that the nature of work has changed and will continue to do so. After all, we were conditioned into accepting the nine-to-five working day, and there is no reason why we can't be conditioned into accepting something else. For example, this article was written at home in the country during bursts of hard work interspersed with periods of inactivity. Perhaps that's the natural work rhythm to which we will return.

3 Read the article again. Mark the statements true (*T*) or false (*F*).

____ 1. Non-paid work is just as good as paid work in terms of increasing self-esteem.

____ 2. Doing tasks you don't enjoy at work is always bad for your mental health.

____ 3. Most people find it difficult to find a purpose to the day without work.

____ 4. The social aspect of work is very important for the majority of people.

____ 5. When people retire, they sometimes feel less happiness than when they worked.

____ 6. One disadvantage of working from home is people feeling isolated.

4 **Group Work** Discuss the questions.

1. In what ways (if any) does your job increase your self-esteem? What things, apart from work, do you think are important for increasing people's self-esteem?

2. Is it common for people to work from home in your area? What do you think the advantages and disadvantages of working from home are? If you don't work from home, would you like to? Why or why not?

Vocabulary | verb phrases about work

5 **Pair Work** Discuss the difference in meaning between the underlined verb phrases in the sentence pairs. Use a dictionary if necessary.

1. a. He was fired after he was caught stealing office equipment.

   b. I'm going to quit my job and go traveling for a year.

2. a. My uncle was very wealthy and retired early at the age of 52.

   b. 2,000 workers were laid off at the car factory last month.

3. a. I like working flextime because I can choose hours that suit me.

   b. She decided not to be a nurse because she didn't want to work the night shift.

4. a. I do volunteer work in a soup kitchen once a week.

   b. She worked part-time in a store while she was studying for her degree.

American English	British English
do volunteer work	do voluntary work

6a Complete the questions with the correct form of the phrases in Exercise 5.

1. Would you like to _____ like reading to the blind?

2. Have you ever _____ to go and do something completely different?

3. Would you ever consider _____ at the age of 45 or 50?

4. For what kinds of reasons can people _____ and have to leave their job?

5. Which do you think is more common in your country: working nine-to-five or _____?

6. Are there any industries in your country which have declined and workers have _____?

b **Pair Work** Choose four of the questions from Exercise 6a to ask and answer with a partner.

Grammar | review of future forms: *will* and *be going to*

7 ▶1.11 Listen to four conversations and answer these questions about Julia, Simon, Maria, and Patrick.

   1. Why does he or she want to change his or her work situation?

   2. Does he or she have any definite plans? What are they?

8 ▶1.12 Complete the examples in the Active Grammar box from memory. Listen and check your answers. Then match the examples with the rules.

Active Grammar

Examples

1. *That's a good idea! I think I _____ to the library now and do it there.*

2. *I've decided I _____ my job and go back to school.*

3. *I _____ them at 8:30 tomorrow morning.*

4. *I think they _____ Sarah the sales manager. She's really good and she's been here forever.*

5. *David _____ assistant manager. I heard him talking to Jim about it.*

Rules

____ a. Use the present continuous to talk about a future arrangement (when details about things like time and place have been decided).

____ b. Use *be going to* to talk about a plan or intention (but no details have been decided).

____ c. Use *be going to* to make predictions based on what you can see or hear now.

____ d. Use *will* to make predictions based on what you know or believe. *Think, hope, believe*, etc. are often used with *will* in this case.

____ e. Use *will* to talk about a decision made at the time of speaking. We often use *I think* with *will* in this case.

See Reference page 128

9 Circle the correct choices to complete the sentences.

   1. We*'ll meet/'re meeting* after work at the café on the corner.

   2. I think she*'s getting/'ll get* the job. She's got the right experience.

   3. I*'ll look for/'m going to look for* a better-paying job.

   4. I*'ll play/'m playing* tennis with a co-worker at 5 P.M.

   5. He's working the night shift, so he*'s being/'ll be* tired tomorrow.

Speaking

10 **Pair Work** Tell your partner about your plans for the future using the How To box. Are any of your plans the same?

> *I've decided to train to be a pilot. When I'm finished with school, I'll probably move to the city.*

How To:

Talk about future plans

Describe plans, intentions, and arrangements	• *I'm planning to go back to school.* • *I decided I'm going to quit my job.* • *I'm meeting them at 10:00 tomorrow.*
Express some uncertainty about future plans	• *I'm thinking about quitting.* • *I'm not sure yet, but I think I'll leave soon.* • *It depends on whether I'm accepted to the program or not.*

Listening

1 ▶ 1.13 Listen to a radio journalist talking about Nek Chand and the Rock Gardens. Which is the best title for the story?

    a. Nearly 50 Years' Work in One Man's Life

    b. 5,000 People Work to Create Unique Gardens

    c. Amazing Rock Gardens Now Closed to Tourists

Nek Chand

Rock Gardens of Chandigarh

2 Listen again and take notes on the following:

    Ex: Chand's appearance: *small, elderly, wrinkled face, gray hair*

    1. His personality

    2. Chand's first job (1958)

    3. Inspiration for his gardens

    4. Reason for his secrecy

    5. Materials used

    6. After 18 years of work . . .

    7. After one year of paid work . . .

    8. Number of visitors per day

    9. How Chand feels about his work

3 **Group Work** Discuss the questions.

    1. Would you like to visit the Rock Gardens of Chandigarh? Why or why not?

    2. How much recycling happens in your area? Do you think it's enough?

    3. Do you consider your lifestyle to be "environmentally friendly"? Why or why not? What could you change?

Grammar | future continuous and future perfect

4 Match the examples in the Active Grammar box with the correct description. Then complete the rules of form.

Active Grammar

Examples

____ 1. *Tomorrow morning, he'll be doing the same thing he's doing today.*

____ 2. *Soon, Chand will have spent half a century working on this garden.*

____ 3. *What will he be doing in five years?*

____ 4. *He won't have finished the garden by the time he retires.*

Description

a. **Future perfect** describes something which will be completed before a definite time in the future.

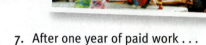

    present   future

b. **Future continuous** describes something in progress at a definite time in the future.

    present   future

Rules of Form

Future perfect: *will/won't + have +* _____

Future continuous: *will/won't + be +* _____

See Reference page 128

5 Complete the sentences with the correct form of the verbs in parentheses.

1. By this time next week, he _____ (finish) his art project.
2. I'm sorry I can't come. I _____ (play) soccer tomorrow afternoon.
3. My boss won't be at work at 5:30 P.M. She _____ (go) home already.
4. Between 10:00 and 12:00 tomorrow, I _____ (have) a meeting so I'll call you after that.
5. I hope you _____ (finish) making dinner by the time I get home.
6. I can't wait! This time next Friday, we _____ (lie) on a beach in California!
7. This article says that by the time you're 50, you _____ (spend) a total of 16.7 years asleep.
8. Don't call between 7:00 and 7:30 because I _____ (have) my piano lesson.

Speaking

6 **Pair Work** Ask and answer these questions.

1. What do you think you will be doing . . .
   a. at 2:00 P.M. this Saturday?
   b. exactly one month from now?
   c. this time next year?
   d. when you're 65?
2. What do you hope you will have done . . .
   a. by this time next week?
   b. by the end of this year?
   c. within the next five years?
   d. by the time you retire?

Vocabulary | after work activities

7a Match each verb in column A with a phrase in column B.

A	B
_h_ 1. spend	a. up with (your email . . .)
____ 2. visit	b. the (bedroom, kitchen, . . .)
____ 3. study	c. a class at night
____ 4. work	d. chat rooms
____ 5. take	e. late at the office
____ 6. keep	f. with friends
____ 7. redecorate	g. for a (law, business, . . .) degree online
____ 8. socialize	h. quality time with (your children, family, . . .)

American English	British English
socialize	*socialise*

b Add more after work activities to the chart above. Compare your ideas with a partner.

8 **Group Work** Discuss the questions.

1. Which of the activities in Exercise 7a do you do most and least often?
2. Do you think you spend your spare time wisely?

Listening and Speaking

9a Look at the life/work balance survey below. What do you think the results of the survey were?

> *I think that less than half the group often works late at the office.*

1. Do you ever work/study late either at the office/school or at home?
2. Have you ever done any volunteer work?
3. Do you take any night classes?
4. Do you usually turn on your computer in the evenings?
5. Do you find it easy to unwind after work or school?
6. How good do you think your work/life balance is?

b ▶1.14 Listen to the results and see if you were right.

10a Write some questions for a survey. First, underline the parts of the questions in Exercise 9a that you can use, for example, *Do you ever . . . ?*

b **Pair Work** Choose which survey to do: 1) the Internet in people's lives or 2) the arts in people's lives. Write six–eight questions for your survey.

c Ask your questions to as many students as you can and make notes of their answers.

11a **Pair Work** Collect the results of your survey and report them to the class. Use the How To box to help you.

How To:	
Report the results of a survey	
Report exact results	• **Nine out of twenty** people stay at work late at least three times a week. • **25% of the group** had done some volunteer work. • **Everyone** said that a good way of relaxing was watching TV. • **Nobody** liked doing this every evening.
Report approximate results	• **Nearly half the** group regularly works late at the office. • **Hardly any of** them thought this was a bad thing. • **Many** people are taking some kind of online course. • **Only a few** people said they turned their computer on every evening. • **The (vast) majority** say they take at least one class at night. • **Only a (small) minority** would like to take more classes at night, though.

b Discuss the results with the class. Were the results of any of the surveys surprising?

Write a cover letter for an application ✓ CAN DO

GRAMMAR *(just) in case*

Reading

1a **Pair Work** Look at the book cover. Where do you think the story is set? What do you think the main character does?

b Read part 1 and see if you were right.

1

Mma Ramotswe had thought that it would not be easy to open a detective agency. People always made the mistake of thinking that starting a business was simple and then found that there were all sorts of hidden problems and unforeseen demands. She had heard of people opening businesses that lasted four or five weeks before they ran out of money and stock, or both. It was always more difficult than you thought it would be.

She went to the lawyer in Pilane, who had arranged for her to get her father's money. He had organized the sale of the cattle, and had got a good price for them. "I have got a lot of money for you," he said. "Your father's herd had grown and grown." She took the check and the sheet of paper that he handed her. It was more than she had imagined possible. But here it was—all that money, made payable to Precious Ramotswe, on presentation to Barclays Bank of Botswana.

"You can buy a house with that," said the lawyer. "And a business." "I am going to buy both of those." The lawyer looked interested. "What sort of business? A store? I can give you advice, you know." "A detective agency." The lawyer looked blank. "There are none for sale. There are none of those." Mma Ramotswe nodded. "I know that. I am going to have to start from scratch."

2 Read part 2 and answer these questions.

1. What equipment and furniture did she get for her office?
2. Who did she hire and how?
3. Were they busy when they first opened? Why do you think this is?

2

There was a lot to do. A builder was called in to replace the damaged plaster and to repair the tin roof and, again with the offer of cash, this was accomplished within a week. Then Mma Ramotswe set to the task of painting, and she had soon completed the outside in ochre and the inside in white. She bought fresh yellow curtains for the windows and in an unusual moment of extravagance, splashed out on a brand new office set of two desks and two chairs. Her friend, Mr. J.L.B. Matekoni, proprietor of Tlokweng Road Speedy Motors brought her an old typewriter which was surplus to his own requirements and which worked quite well, and with that the office was ready to open—once she had a secretary.

This was the easiest part of all. A telephone call to the Botswana College of Secretarial and Office Skills brought an immediate response. They had just the woman, they said. Mma Makutsi was the widow of a teacher and had just passed their general typing and secretarial examinations with an average grade of 97%; she would be ideal—they were certain of it. Mma Ramotswe liked her immediately. She was a thin woman with a rather long face and braided hair in which she had rubbed copious quantities of henna. She wore oval glasses with wide plastic frames, and she had a fixed, but apparently quite sincere smile.

They opened the office on a Monday. Mma Ramotswe sat at her desk and Mma Makutsi sat at hers, behind the typewriter. She looked at Mma Ramotswe and smiled even more broadly. "I am ready for work," she said. "I am ready to start." "Mmm," said Mma Ramotswe. "It's early days yet. We've only just opened. We will have to wait for a client to come."

3 Read part 3 on page 137. How do Mma Makutsi's feelings about the business change?

Grammar | *(just) in case*

4 Read the examples in the Active Grammar box. Circle the correct choices to complete the rules.

Active Grammar

Examples

- *She stayed behind in the office in case the telephone rang.*

- *I called my boss again in case she hadn't got my message.*

- *I'll stay here in case any clients come in.*

- *I might leave early just in case there are problems on the trains.*

- *I always leave plenty of time to get to work just in case.*

Rules

1. Use *in case* to talk about past situations, to explain why somebody did something / how things could have been different.

2. Also use *in case* to talk about future situations, to talk about certainties (things that will definitely happen) / precautions (things we do in order to be ready for a possible future situation).

3. Use *just in case* to add emphasis / politeness.

4. Use *just in case* in the middle / at the end of a sentence to talk about precautions in general (rather than specific situations).

See Reference page 128

5 Write sentences using the cues and *in case*. Change the verb tenses and add words where necessary.

> I always write "to do" lists in case I forget something important.

1. I always write/"to do" lists/forget/something important.
2. I usually leave/more time than I need/get to work/the traffic/be bad.
3. I always take/glass of water to bed/I be thirsty/at night.
4. I usually take/first aid kit on vacation/just.
5. He took/umbrella/just/rain/on the way to the interview.
6. You should write/address/your suitcase/it get lost.
7. I/not go out/last night/just/Daniela/call.
8. They wanted me/enter my email address twice/I make a mistake/the first time.
9. I/give you/phone number/you/get lost.
10. I/buy/extra food/the children/be hungry/after the football game.

Speaking

6a Write four more sentences about your past or future using *(just) in case*. One sentence should be false.

> I'm going to buy a newspaper as soon as I leave the class just in case they run out later.

b **Pair Work** Guess which of your partner's sentences is false.

Writing

7 Read the job ad and the letter applying for the job. Then answer these questions.

1. What relevant experience and qualities does Helen have?

2. What is her goal for the future?

3. Do you think it's a good letter? Why or why not?

Assistant Manager

needed for new pizzeria

We're looking for an Assistant Manager to help run our new pizzeria opening next month. The successful candidate will be enthusiastic, hard-working, and friendly. Previous restaurant management experience a plus.

Send cover letter and resume to:
Mario Ruggiero, 22 Wood Lane,
Chicago, IL 60614

Mario Ruggiero
22 Wood Lane
Chicago, IL 60614

10 Division St.
Chicago, IL 60162

January 9, 2012

Dear Mr. Ruggiero,

1 I am writing to apply for the job of Assistant Manager of your new pizzeria that you advertised in this week's *Sun Times*.

2 As you can see from my enclosed résumé, I have worked as a waitress in a pizza and pasta restaurant for the last nine months, and my previous jobs include working as a server in a small French café. I believe that I have gained valuable experience in the restaurant business and now feel it is time to move into the management side of things. I am hard-working, friendly, and easy to get along with, as well as passionate about working in the restaurant industry.

3 I am particularly interested in this job because I'd like to be involved in setting up a new business. Ultimately, I would like to set up my own restaurant business but need to get more experience first.

4 I can be contacted at (312) 555-6941. I look forward to hearing from you.

Sincerely,

Helen Taylor

Helen Taylor

8a Read the letter again. Match the paragraph to the ideas.

____ a. says how she can be contacted

____ b. describes her experience and why she would be suitable for the job

____ c. includes any extra information you think is important

____ d. says which job she is applying for and where and when she saw it advertised

b Complete the chart with the expressions from the letter.

Informal	Formal
Dear Mario,	1. *Dear Mr. Ruggiero,*
Just a quick note because I'd like the job.	2.
I figure I've got a lot of good experience.	3.
I really want this job.	4.
Call me at (312) 555-6941.	5.
Hope to hear from you soon.	6.
Best wishes,	7.

9 Look at the job ads on page 142. Decide which job to apply for. Then write a letter applying for the job.

Review

1 Circle the correct choices to complete the dialogs.

1. **A:** Why are you turning on the TV?

   B: I*'ll watch/'m going to watch* the game.

2. **A:** What would you like to eat?

   B: I think I*'ll have/'m having* a chicken sandwich.

3. **A:** Wow! Look at those dark clouds!

   B: Yes, I think it*'ll rain/'s going to rain*.

4. **A:** Have you seen John recently?

   B: No, but I*'ll meet/'m meeting* him at 7 P.M.

2 Write the letter of each verb phrase in the box in the correct place in the email.

> **a.** 'll be waiting   **b.** 'll have started   **c.** won't be going
> **d.** 'll have been   **e.** 'll be studying   **f.** ~~'ll have finished~~

Hi Antonella,

I can hardly believe it, but by next Friday afternoon, __*f*__ (**1.**) all my final exams! Until then, I'm completely up to my eyes in studying. I ____ (**2.**) for my exams all weekend and then every spare minute I get next week. I can't wait to get them all out of the way.

I'm really excited though, because I've booked a trip to Mexico as soon as I'm done. In fact, this time next week, I ____ (**3.**) for my flight to Cancún. I'm going with Daniel—we've both been there before and loved it. After this trip, we ____ (**4.**) there four times! Anyway, that's why I'm writing. I just wanted to know if you ____ (**5.**) your job by then. If you haven't, why don't you come with us? I know it's short notice, but it would be great if you could come.

Let me know as soon as you can. Either email me or give me a call anytime. I ____ (**6.**) to bed tonight because I've got so much studying to do. Really hope you can come.

Jackie

3 Complete the sentences using the words in the box. Three of the words cannot be used.

> retirement   deadlines   surgeon   career   detail
> volunteer   pressure   quality   self-starter

1. To be a successful entrepreneur, you have to be a _____.

2. I don't think I'd be a good architect because you need an eye for _____.

3. As a journalist, I'm always having to meet very tight _____.

4. My cousin Isabella is the best heart _____ at that hospital.

5. In my spare time, I do a lot of _____ work with deaf people.

6. My father regrets not spending more _____ time with us when we were children.

Communication | carry out an effective interview

4 **Group Work** How do you feel about interviews? Do you get nervous? Why or why not? Discuss.

5a ▶1.15 Listen to parts of interviews with four different candidates (Karen, John, Leo, and Linda) and answer the questions.

1. Is each interview for a job or for a place in a university program?
2. Do you think each interview is going well? Why or why not?

b ▶1.16 Complete the interviewer's sentences. Then listen and check your answers.

1. Thank you for _____ for the job and coming to the interview today.
2. I'd like to ask you _____ your experience.
3. You say you've worked in an _____ before. Tell me about that.
4. I'm Peter Manning, and I'll be _____ you today.
5. Can I start by asking you about your _____ for applying to the program?
6. _____ do you see yourself in five years?

6a **SPEAKING EXCHANGE** Choose one of the ads on page 138 and prepare to roleplay an interview with a partner. Follow the instructions below.

Interviewees: Prepare for the interview by making notes about:
- any relevant experience and education you have.
- qualities that make you a good person for the program/job.
- your plans for the future.
- any further questions you'd like to ask.

Interviewers: Prepare for the interview by making notes about:
- how to start the interview.
- questions to ask about relevant experience and education.
- questions to ask about personal qualities that make the candidate a good person for the program/job.
- questions to ask about plans for the future.
- how to finish the interview.

b **Pair Work** Roleplay the interview. Change roles. Then prepare and roleplay another interview.

c Would you give your interviewee the job/place in the program? Why or why not? Discuss.

UNIT 3
Lessons from history

A

B

C

D

Warm Up

1 **Group Work** What do you know about the places in the photos? Have you visited any of them? If so, what were they like? Discuss.

2a Three of the underlined adjectives in the questions are wrong. Correct them using the chart below.

1. Do you prefer <u>ancient</u> or modern furniture? Why?
2. Are you interested in wearing <u>fashionable</u> clothes? Why or why not?
3. Does your country have <u>traditional</u> dress? If so, what is it?
4. Do you live in an <u>elderly</u> building?
5. Are there any interesting <u>antique</u> places near where you live?

Places	Buildings	Things	People	Clothes
• ancient • modern	• old/new • modern	• old/new • traditional • modern • antique	• old/young • elderly • traditional (values)	• old-fashioned • trendy • fashionable • traditional

b **Pair Work** Ask and answer the questions with a partner.

3 **Pair Work** Use adjectives from the chart to describe the places in the photos.

Reading

1 **Pair Work** Discuss the questions.

    1. Do you have a favorite hero or heroine from a story or movie? What makes him or her heroic in your opinion?

    2. Do you know who the heroes are in the ancient Greek story of Troy (made into a movie in 2004)?

2a Read about the movie *Troy*. Which characters are mentioned? What are the relationships between them?

DVD WATCH: Troy

In the 8th century BC, the Greek poet Homer wrote about the Trojan War in his epic poem *The Iliad*. In 2004, the tale of the Trojan War was made into an epic movie, *Troy*, starring Brad Pitt and Eric Bana. Like *The Iliad*, the movie is full of passion and the triumphs and tragedies of war.

The movie begins with a party thrown by King Menelaus of Sparta to celebrate a peace treaty made between Sparta and Troy. The two kingdoms had been at war for centuries, and as a result Trojan and Spartan trade had been declining, and some cities had fallen into ruins. Now King Priam of Troy and King Menelaus had agreed on peace terms and were looking forward to a better future.

King Priam had traveled to Sparta with his two sons: Hector, played by Eric Bana, the eldest and heir to the throne, and Paris, a handsome but weak-willed young man. During his stay in Sparta, Paris had fallen in love with Helen, the famously beautiful wife of King Menelaus, and resolved to make her his wife. Helen, who was unhappy with Menelaus, agreed to come with Paris to Troy. While the guests were celebrating, Paris and Helen escaped the party unnoticed. Paris hid Helen aboard one the Trojan ships. Paris waited until the ship had sailed before he told his brother Hector that Helen was on the ship. From that point on, the peace was broken and war between the two kingdoms was inevitable.

When he discovered that Paris had taken Helen, King Menelaus called on his brother Agamemnon, the powerful king of Argos, to help him restore his honor by getting his wife back and destroying Troy. King Agamemnon agreed to help his brother because defeating Troy would increase his wealth and power. Agamemnon put together a huge army from all over Greece.

However, Troy had never been defeated in battle and Hector was a famous warrior and hero. Victory for Agamemnon and Menelaus was not certain. King Agamemnon knew that the key to the war's success was getting the legendary Greek warrior Achilles (played by Brad Pitt) to join his army. Achilles was thought to be the greatest hero alive. Achilles agreed to fight with Agamemnon against Troy; however, he despised Agamemnon's desire for power. Achilles believed that power didn't last long, but glory gained from battle would give him eternal fame. People would remember his name forever.

Troy is exciting and features several strong performances. Eric Bana is brilliant throughout the movie. Despite the performances, some people have criticized the movie for making changes to Homer's story and to the Greek myth it was based on. For example, the famous story of the Trojan Horse, a key scene in *Troy*, never appeared in *The Iliad*, and the party that opens the movie is not part of the original myth. However, others have defended the changes, stating that they made the story easier to follow for modern audiences.

b Read the article again. Mark the statements true (*T*) or false (*F*).

    _____ **1.** The movie *Troy* is mostly about war.

    _____ **2.** The purpose of the party was for King Menelaus to declare victory over King Priam.

    _____ **3.** Paris and Helen left the party without telling anyone.

    _____ **4.** One reason why Agamemnon went to war was to win the city of Troy.

    _____ **5.** Achilles wanted to help Agamemnon to become as powerful as possible.

3 **Group Work** Discuss the questions.

    1. If you've seen the movie, do you agree with the writer's opinions? Why or why not? If you haven't seen it, does the article make you want to see it? Why or why not?

    2. Do you think it matters if a movie is not exactly the same as the book? Why or why not?

Grammar | review of past forms

4a Match the underlined verbs in the Active Grammar box to the past forms. Then complete the rules with the correct past form.

Active Grammar

Examples

- *Trade <u>had been declining</u>* (**1.**) *and some cities <u>had fallen</u>* (**2.**) *into ruins.*
- *While the guests <u>were celebrating</u>* (**3.**), *Paris and Helen <u>escaped</u>* (**4.**) *unnoticed.*

Past forms

_____ **a.** simple past

_____ **b.** past continuous

_____ **c.** past perfect

_____ **d.** past perfect continuous

Rules

1. Use the _____ to talk about completed actions in the past.

2. Use the _____ to talk about completed actions that happened before another action in the past.

3. Use the _____ to talk about actions in progress at a particular time in the past.

4. Use the _____ to talk about actions or situations which continued up to the past moment we are talking about.

See Reference page 129

b Look at paragraphs 1–3 of the article in Exercise 2. Find more examples of past forms.

5 ▶1.17 Circle the correct choices to complete the story of Hannibal. Then listen and check your answers.

Until the 3rd century BC, Carthage *was being/had been* (**1.**) a powerful city which controlled most of the Mediterranean Sea. For the previous few hundred years, the Carthaginians *had been trading/traded* (**2.**) with people in India and the Mediterranean area. There *had been/were* (**3.**) many battles between the Romans and the Carthaginians to try to control the area. Although Carthage *had been taking/had taken* (**4.**) control of many important places, they *weren't managing/hadn't managed* (**5.**) to take Sicily, the island on their doorstep. So, when the Romans won total control of Sicily, Carthage *decided/was deciding* (**6.**) to attack Rome.

The leader of the attack *was/had been* (**7.**) a brilliant young general named Hannibal. He had 40 war elephants, all trained to charge at the enemy. As Hannibal's army *was marching/had been marching* (**8.**) northward toward the Alps, soldiers from Spain and other areas *joined/were joining* (**9.**) them. The icy mountains were difficult to cross, however, and by the time they *reached/were reaching* (**10.**) Italy in 218 BC, many of his soldiers and elephants *had died/had been dying* (**11.**). They famously *won/were winning* (**12.**) three battles, but in the end the Romans were stronger and they took the city of Carthage and won the war.

6a **SPEAKING EXCHANGE** A Students look at page 142 and B Students look at page 140. Use the notes to practice telling your part of the story.

b **Pair Work** Take turns telling the story of Romeo and Juliet together.

Vocabulary | time expressions

7 Look at the underlined expressions in the box. Do they talk about a time before, a time after, a specific time, or actions at the same time?

<u>In</u> 218 BC	<u>In</u> the 8th century BC
<u>After that</u>	<u>Until</u> the 3rd century BC
<u>Since</u> then	<u>During</u> his stay in Sparta
<u>At that time</u>	Eric Bana is brilliant <u>throughout</u> the movie.
<u>From that point on</u>	<u>Previously</u>, the kingdom had been at war.
<u>Up until that point</u>	<u>While</u> the guests were celebrating, Paris and Helen escaped unnoticed.

8 Circle the correct choice to complete each sentence.

1. *While/During* the summer, we traveled around seven European countries.
2. I changed schools when I was 12. *From that point on/Throughout*, I loved school.
3. The Great Fire of London happened *at/in* 1666.
4. She was chatting *throughout/since* the whole class.
5. A movie theater opened in my town last year. *Up until that point/At that time*, the nearest one had been 40 miles away.
6. *While/During* I was waiting for you, I finished my book.

9 **Pair Work** Complete the sentences about you. Then discuss with a partner.

1. Throughout most of last year I _____. Previously, I _____.
2. The best year of my life was _____. At that time, I _____.
3. One of the most important things to happen to me was _____. After that, I _____.

Writing

10 **Pair Work** Discuss the questions.

1. Do you think people such as firefighters, aid workers, or nurses are modern-day heroes? Why?
2. Name people or groups you think are heroic. Give reasons.

11 You are going to write a short story about a hero or heroine. Choose a person and write brief notes on:

- events leading up to the beginning of the story.
- the main events of the story.
- what happens near or at the end of the story.

12a Write your story using your notes. Don't write the name of the hero; just write *he or she*. Use past forms and time expressions.

  b **Pair Work** Read another student's story. Do you know the hero or heroine in his or her story?

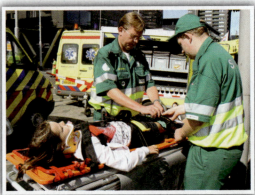

Talk about materials, possessions, and inventions

GRAMMAR articles: *a/an/the/Ø*

Vocabulary | materials

1a Describe the items in the photos using the words in the box.

> porcelain   denim   metal   silk
> plastic   cotton   wool   leather

b ▶1.18 Listen. Which materials from the box are mentioned? What others do you hear?

2 Match the adjectives with their definitions. Then complete each sentence below with the best adjective from the chart.

Adjectives	Describing something that:
1. soft	a. has an even surface
2. stretchy	b. has an uneven surface
3. shiny	c. feels or looks like fur
4. smooth	d. feels uncomfortable; it irritates your skin
5. rough	e. isn't hard or firm, but feels good to touch
6. furry	f. is slightly elastic
7. slippery	g. has a bright surface
8. itchy	h. is wet or difficult to hold or walk on

1. Be careful on the icy path. It's very _____.
2. I really like silk because it feels so _____ on your skin.
3. My new winter boots have _____ insides.
4. I can't wear wool because it makes my skin feel _____.
5. For the interview I wore a suit and my _____ new leather shoes.
6. Wear something _____ to the gym so you can move easily.
7. It was a very uncomfortable trip because the road was so _____.
8. This bed is too _____ for me. I need a mattress that supports my back more.

Speaking

3 **Pair Work** Think of an object you have used today. Ask *Yes/No* questions using the materials or adjectives in Exercises 1 and 2 to guess each other's object.

4 **Group Work** Discuss the questions.

1. Do you have a favorite or least favorite item of clothing? Why do you feel that way?
2. Do you have any allergies to materials?

Listening

5a **Group Work** What things do you associate with modern-day China and ancient China? Discuss.

b ▶ **1.19** Listen to the radio show. Do the speakers mention any of the things you talked about?

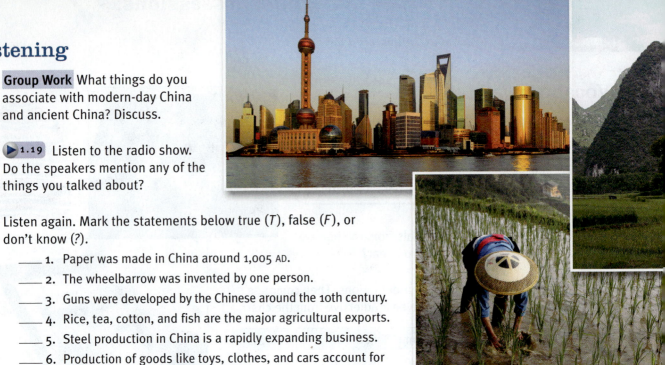

6 Listen again. Mark the statements below true (*T*), false (*F*), or don't know (*?*).

_____ 1. Paper was made in China around 1,005 AD.

_____ 2. The wheelbarrow was invented by one person.

_____ 3. Guns were developed by the Chinese around the 10th century.

_____ 4. Rice, tea, cotton, and fish are the major agricultural exports.

_____ 5. Steel production in China is a rapidly expanding business.

_____ 6. Production of goods like toys, clothes, and cars account for more than 50% of China's economy.

7 **Group Work** Has any of the information from the show made you change your ideas about China? Explain.

Grammar | articles: *a/an/the/Ø*

8 Complete the Active Grammar box with the underlined examples in Audioscript 1.19 on page 151.

Active Grammar

The definite article *the* is used:	Examples	The indefinite article *a/an* is used:	Examples
1. with inventions and species of animals.	• *the gun, the tiger*	8. with jobs.	*a scientist*
2. with national groups (when described as one whole nation).	• _____	9. with singular count nouns (mentioned for the first time or when it doesn't matter which one).	• _____
3. when there is only one of something.	• *the Moon*	**The zero article (Ø) is used:**	
4. with rivers, oceans, and seas.	• *the Yellow River, the Pacific Ocean*	10. with most streets, villages, towns, cities, countries, lakes, and mountains.	• *Main Street, Beijing, _____, Mount Everest.* For countries and groups of islands in the plural use "the"—*the United States, the Himalayas*
5. with superlatives.	• _____		
6. with particular nouns when it is clear what is being referred to.	• _____		
7. with previously mentioned nouns.	• *I have a red umbrella and a black one. I prefer the red one.*	11. with noncount, plural, and abstract nouns used in their general sense.	• _____, *umbrellas*

See Reference page 129

9 Complete these sentences using *the, a, an,* or the zero article (∅).

1. _____ giant panda mostly lives in _____ bamboo forests high in the mountains.

2. _____ Yangtze River is 6,380 kilometers long. It is the third longest river in _____ world.

3. _____ China covers _____ area of almost six million square kilometers and is _____ most populous country on Earth.

4. I have three Chinese silk dresses: _____ red one and two black ones. I think I'll wear _____ red one for my party.

5. _____ umbrella was invented around 450 AD to protect _____ people from sun and rain.

6. Zong Zi is _____ dish made of _____ rice and bamboo leaves and is traditionally eaten during the Dragon festival.

Speaking

10 **Pair Work** Tell your partner about one of these topics. Use *a, an, the,* or the zero article (∅).

- a country or city you like
- a job you'd like
- a species of animal you're interested in

> *I like the Philippines because the weather is great and the people are fun to talk to.*

11a Look at the inventions in the box and decide which three you think are the most important. Make brief notes about your reasons.

paper	the wheel	the television	the telephone	the Internet
the car	gunpowder	the computer	the light bulb	

b ▶1.20 Listen to the conversation. Which invention do the people choose?

c **Group Work** Try to agree on the three most important inventions. Use the language in the How To box to help you.

How To:

Communicate interactively

Asking for someone's general opinion	• *What do you think?* • *What about you?* • *What else do you think is important?*
Asking for someone's specific opinion	• *Do you agree that . . . ?* • *How do you feel about . . . ?*

Give a presentation about a place

GRAMMAR adjectives and adverbs: position

Reading

1 **Group Work** In what ways do you think things nowadays are the same as or different from 20 years ago? Think about food, clothes, music, etc. Discuss.

2 Read the excerpt from a newspaper article below. Does the writer mention anything you talked about?

The Good Old Days

Can we escape the uniformity of globalization? Is every city in the world doomed to be the same? And why does it feel like English is dominating other languages? Mark Wright reports on international travel today and longs for the good old days.

I travel often for my job. One month I'm in Asia, another in Latin America, sometimes Europe. But it almost doesn't matter where I go anymore. I see the same Starbucks at the airport in Tokyo, Lima, and Munich as I do back home in New York. My company always puts me up in a practically identical Hilton no matter where I travel. Even on TV you can't escape the same popular American shows like *House* or *24*.

Each city I travel to, I am annoyed by retail and restaurant chains like McDonalds polluting the authentic feel of the city.

I hear the same ringtones no matter where I go. Everyone carries the same iPhones, listens to the same music. Why do we strive for uniformity? I miss the days when I discovered new cultures and different ways of life when traveling abroad. I also miss communicating in foreign languages. Now when I use my broken Spanish or try some Japanese phrases, people generally answer me in English. International travel was a whole other experience 20 years ago.

3 **SPEAKING EXCHANGE** Divide into two groups: A Students and B Students.

A Students: Read the letter on page 139 and answer the questions below.

1. Does the writer mostly agree or disagree with Mark Wright?
2. What does she mean by "a more international view"?
3. What is the main point she makes about food?

B Students: Read the letter on page 140 and answer the questions below.

1. Does the writer mostly agree or disagree with Mark Wright?
2. What does he mean by "our world today is richer"?
3. What is the main point he makes about food?

4 **Pair Work** Work in pairs of one A Student and one B Student.

1. Tell your partner about your letter using your answers from Exercise 3.

> *The writer of the letter I read disagrees strongly with Mark Wright. The writer says that . . .*

2. In what ways are the opinions in the two letters the same or different? Which letter is the closest to your point of view?

5 **Group Work** Do you think the old days really were "the good old days"? Why? Discuss.

Grammar | adjectives and adverbs: position

6 Look at the underlined adverbs and adverbial phrases in the letters on pages 139 and 140. Write them in the correct place in the Active Grammar box.

Active Grammar

Adjectives

Adjectives are used to describe nouns.

Position of adjectives: usually directly before the noun

Adverbs

Adverbs (and adverbial phrases) are used to modify verbs, adjectives, and other adverbs.

Position of adverbs: varies

Adverbs at the beginning of a sentence

1. Connecting adverbs (which join a clause to what came before): *Nevertheless, Then*, _____, etc.

2. Time adverbs (if the adverb is not the main focus of the message): *Tomorrow, Last year*, _____, etc.

Adverbs in the middle of a sentence (before the main verb)

3. Adverbs of certainty and completeness: *probably, nearly*, _____, etc.

4. Adverbs of indefinite frequency: *often, sometimes*, _____, etc.

5. Adverbs of comment: *stupidly, ignorantly*, _____, etc.

6. Some adverbs of manner (if the adverb is not the main focus of the message): *quickly, rudely*, _____, etc.

Adverbs at the end of a sentence

7. Adverbs of manner (also see 6 above): *slowly*, _____, etc.

8. Adverbs of place: *upstairs, in the corner*, _____, etc.

9. Adverbs of time (also see 2 above): *this morning, a while ago*, _____, etc.

See Reference page 129

7 Write the words in parentheses in the correct place in the sentences. Two different positions may be possible.

1. I want to try the local food when I'm in Thailand. (definitely)
2. I work in a really modern building. (on the 19th floor)
3. I went on a tour of six capital cities in Europe. (last month)
4. My grandmother has been on an airplane in her life. (never)
5. The new building is designed to be both attractive and practical. (expertly)

8 Fill in the blanks with the correct choice to complete the questions. Then ask and answer the questions with a partner.

1. complete/completely
   a. Do you usually finish a book _____ before starting a new one?
   b. How do you feel about working when your desk is a _____ mess?

2. definite/definitely
   a. Is there anything you _____ want to do this weekend?
   b. Have you got any _____ plans for your next vacation?

3. late/lately
   a. Are you the kind of person who is often _____ for things?
   b. Have you bought any new DVDs _____?

Vocabulary | verb phrases with *take*

9 Match the underlined verb phrases with their definitions on the right.

____ 1. Is English <u>taking over</u> the world?

____ 2. Thousands of people <u>took part in</u> a demonstration to save the old town hall.

____ 3. Tourism in my city began to <u>take off</u> about ten years ago.

____ 4. I found it hard to <u>take in</u> what the tourist guide was saying.

____ 5. He's always very calm and <u>takes</u> everything <u>in stride</u>.

____ 6. The Italian people I met were really friendly. I <u>took to</u> them immediately.

a. to start to increase/improve

b. to start to like someone or something

c. to understand what you see, read, or hear

d. to take control of or take responsibility for something

e. to do something together with other people

f. to cope calmly with things without making a fuss

10 Complete the sentences with the correct form of the underlined phrases in Exercise 9.

1. I didn't _____ the piano at first, but now I love it.

2. I decided not to _____ the race because I hurt my ankle.

3. He's quite old now, so his son is going to _____ the business.

4. She hadn't done very well before, but her career _____ when she joined this company.

5. It was hard to _____ all the details because she was talking so fast.

6. He _____ your criticism _____ and didn't get upset.

11 **Group Work** Discuss the questions.

1. When was the last time you took part in a race or a competition?

2. Are you the type of person who usually takes things in stride?

3. Was there a point when you felt your English really started to take off? If so, when and why?

Speaking

12a Give a short presentation about a place you know. First, make notes about the following:

- main events in its history
- main tourist attractions
- any difficulties or problems the place has
- any recent changes
- likely future situation/ changes/problems

b **Pair Work** Practice giving your presentation to your partner. Then listen to your partner's presentation, and give some advice on how to improve it.

Review

1   Fill in the blanks with the correct form of the verbs in parentheses.

   1. I _____ (work) on the report for five days when she told me it _____ (not/be) necessary.

   2. What _____ (you/do) when I called? It _____ (be) very noisy.

   3. It wasn't until I _____ (get) home that I realized my wallet _____ (steal).

   4. I was embarrassed because she _____ (arrive) before I _____ (wrap) her birthday present.

   5. _____ (you/learn) the guitar for a long time before you joined a band?

   6. I can remember exactly what I _____ (do) at midnight last New Year's Eve.

2   Fill in the blanks with *a*, *an*, *the*, or the zero article (∅).

   1. She lives on _____ Oak Road. It's not far from _____ post office.

   2. People say that _____ British are reserved.

   3. Don't forget your _____ sunscreen. _____ sun is very strong _____ today.

   4. Leisure time is decreasing for most _____ people in _____ United States.

   5. We stayed at _____ very nice hotel in _____ Barcelona.

   6. That was one of _____ best books I've read in a long time.

   7. I think that maybe I'd like to be _____ architect when I grow up.

3   Circle the correct choice to complete each sentence.

   1. The new shopping center is *enormous/enormously*.

   2. I couldn't believe it. The test was *incredible/incredibly* easy.

   3. I can't go out until I've *complete/completely* finished my homework.

   4. I thought dinner would be cheap but it was *surprising/surprisingly* expensive.

   5. I'm absolutely *certain/certainly* that you got the answer right.

4   Fill in the blanks to complete the sentences with the correct adjective or adverb.

   1. bad/badly

     a. I hurt myself pretty _____ when I fell.

     b. The pollution is very _____ in this part of town.

   2. careful/carefully

     a. Don't worry. He's a very _____ driver.

     b. You really need to listen more _____ .

   3. perfect/perfectly

     a. Your English pronunciation is absolutely _____ .

     b. Haruko speaks English _____ .

5   One word is wrong in each sentence. Find and correct it.

   1. I don't usually wear wool because I find it too shiny.

   2. I've decided to take part of a writing competition.

   3. I've been working in a café while the summer.

   4. There's too much information to take off at once.

   5. I broke my leg last year. Since that, I haven't gone jogging.

Communication | talk about lessons learned from the past

6 **Group Work** Discuss the questions.

1. What was your most or least favorite subject in school? Why?
2. Which do you think are the three most important subjects to study in school? Why?
3. Are there any subjects you had to stop studying before you wanted to? Why?
4. Are there any subjects you wish you'd studied harder? Why?

7a ▶ 1.21 Listen to two friends, Kevin and Debbie, and answer these questions.

1. How did Kevin feel about Spanish when he was in school?
2. What is he studying now? Why?
3. What is one of the biggest lessons that Kevin has learned?

b Think about your school days and complete the sentences below to make them true for you.

1. Now that I'm older and wiser, I realize . . . _____
2. One of the biggest lessons I've learned in life is . . . _____

c **Pair Work** Compare and discuss your sentences.

42

UNIT 4
Taking risks

Warm Up

1 Describe how the people in each photo might be "taking a risk."

2 Circle the underlined choice in each sentence that is NOT possible.
   1. Moving abroad without a job can be a _risk/gamble/hazard_.
   2. You'll never get another _luck/opportunity/chance_ like this to travel.
   3. We need this contract. There are a lot of jobs at _stake/risk/gamble_.
   4. My one real _ambition/dream/belief_ is to go to the North Pole.
   5. If we don't go back now, there's a _big/substantial/vast_ risk that we'll get caught in a storm.

3 **Group Work** Discuss the questions.
   1. When is the last time you (or someone you know) took a big risk?
   2. How did you (or he or she) feel before, during, and afterward?
   3. Would you (or he or she) do something like that again? Why?

Reading

1 **Group Work** Do you like to spend a lot of time on your own? Why or why not? Do you prefer working in a group or on your own? Why? Discuss.

2 Read the article and check the topics that are mentioned.

_____ 1. Zac's parents' opposition

_____ 2. His attitude about his boat

_____ 3. His boat's facilities

_____ 4. Dangers he encountered

_____ 5. Descriptions of places

_____ 6. His future plans

Seventeen-year-old sailor realizes dream

On July 16, 2009, when Zac Sunderland sailed back into Marina del Rey Harbor in Los Angeles, California, he was welcomed as the youngest person to ever sail solo around the world. Zac, who was 17 years of age at the time, spent 13 months and two days alone at sea.

This was not the first time Zac had spent long periods at sea. _____ **(1.)** As a child, his family sailed to Australia, New Zealand, the UK, and Mexico. In Mexico, his father, shipwright and yachtsman Laurence Sunderland, bought a 16 meter (51 feet) Aleutian sailboat that he and young Zac fixed up to make suitable for family life. The Sunderland family then spent three years on the boat cruising around California's Channel Islands, the Baja peninsula, and mainland Mexico. His time sailing and an encounter with a book about a trip around the world gave him his dream: to sail solo around the world, and Zac was convinced he would achieve it if he really focused on it.

When he turned 16, Zac began to train himself both mentally and physically by racing, navigating, and repairing yachts. _____ **(2.)** Finally, he was able to purchase a 12 meter (36 feet) yacht that he and his father prepared for the solo voyage. He christened the yacht *The Intrepid*. He chose the name because he felt that in order to make the journey, he needed a boat that was "resolutely fearless, dauntless, brave, courageous, and bold" to carry him around the world.

His voyage would be even harder because Zac planned to continue his education on the boat. Before setting sail, Zac reported that he had all his school books with him and that he would send his assignments by email home to his mother for grading. _____ **(3.)** If his mother helped him study, he was sure he would do well. He departed from Marina del Rey on June 14, 2008 to make his way around the globe.

He initially planned to make about 30 stops along his journey, beginning with Micronesia. _____ **(4.)** He changed course and set sail for Oahu, Hawaii where he could stock up on provisions and do some surfing.

Although he was the only person aboard his boat, Zac was not completely alone. In addition to having the best safety and communication equipment with him in case something went wrong, he also stayed in touch with family, friends, and the world at large through his blog. Zac documented his experiences with a video camera. At times he felt scared: "If I live to see this thing through, everything will go well," he said to a video camera he used to record his personal diary during the journey.

Before returning to California, Zac's eventual route contained 20 stops, which included places such as The Marshall Islands, Australia, Mauritius, South Africa, Panama, and Mexico. _____ **(5.)** One of the high points of his journey was when he met the President of the Marshall Islands, Litokwa Tomeing, who personally welcomed him to the island of Majuro. Low points included being chased by pirates off the coast of Indonesia, and having his boat badly damaged in a huge storm at sea. However, he said the biggest obstacle to overcome had been sleep deprivation, and the hardest part of the journey may have been in the days just after launching 13 months before. But he was never discouraged enough to quit.

You will not find his name among a list of World Record holders, though. In a somewhat controversial move, the World Sailing Speed Record Council (WSSRC), the world sailing authority, refused to grant him the record as the youngest sailor to circumnavigate the globe solo. The WSSRC stated that although Zac Sunderland had sailed more than 28,000 miles, he had not sailed along an approved route. If he had only sailed around Cape Horn, his route would have been approved and he would have received the record. Zac is not disheartened. What are his plans now? To finish high school and to compile his writings and videos into a documentary. For Zac, it looks like smooth sailing ahead.

3 Each of these sentences is missing from the article. Read the article again and decide where each sentence belongs.

    a. His experiences along the way were both good and bad.

    b. He saved his money from sailing jobs and solicited sponsors to help him pay for his trip.

    c. However, his plans soon changed after he had some minor problems with the boat, and he realized he didn't have enough provisions to make the trip.

    d. The Sunderland children have been home-schooled by their mother for years.

    e. His first home was a 17-meter (56 feet) Tradewind sailboat where he grew up learning the skills that he would eventually use as a solo sailor.

4 **Group Work** How would you feel about making a similar trip? What and whom would you miss the most? Discuss.

Grammar | conditionals with *if*

5 Read the Active Grammar Box. Then match each rule to its example.

Active Grammar

Examples	Rules
_____ 1. *If his mother helped him study, he was sure he would do well.*	a. **Real conditional:** Use *If* + present tense, + *will* to talk about future possibility.
_____ 2. *If he had sailed around Cape Horn, his route would have been approved.*	b. **Present unreal conditional:** Use *If* + past tense, + *would* + verb to talk about present or future unreal or imagined situations or to give advice.
_____ 3. *If I live to see this thing through, everything will go well.*	c. **Past unreal conditional:** Use *If* + past perfect, + *would have* + past participle to talk about unreal or imagined situations in the past.
_____ 4. *If I were you, I'd get my own TV show.*	

See Reference page 130

6 Correct the mistake in each sentence.

             Would
    Ex: ~~Do~~ *you call me if anything goes wrong?*

    1. What you have done if a nearby boat hadn't picked up your distress call?

    2. I had stop taking so many risks if I were you.

    3. What you like to do if you had some free time and money?

    4. If you'll see John, can you ask him if he's going sailing with us?

Speaking

7 **Pair Work** Think about major decisions you have made in the past. Imagine you had made a different decision. Explain to another student what might have happened if you'd done things differently.

> If I hadn't had children in my 20s, I would have traveled more. I've always wanted to go to Brazil and . . .

Writing

8 Read these excerpts from Zac's blog. What is the main thing he writes about in each post?

June 26, 2008

Rough night last night. The motion of the boat and slapping of the genoa made it hard to sleep. There are the most incredible stars out here. I have never seen anything like it. There are thousands of stars in a black, black sky. There is a hazy, cloud-like thing up there too. Not sure if it is the Milky Way? Awesome!

December 10, 2008

I altered course so I would get as far upwind from the squall as I could. But bashing into 25 knots makes it 30 knots so I had a pretty wild ride for about an hour. At its closest point I had lightning about a mile away while going through a squall. At 3-something this morning I was able to get back on course and go back to sleep. Over the night I passed about ten ships.

July 20, 2009

It has been a pretty crazy time since I've been back with tons of press and interviews keeping me really busy. It has been great to sleep in my bed, hang with my family and also been having an awesome time seeing my old friends.

9 **Pair Work** There are many different ways of keeping a blog. What do you notice about the style of Zac's blog?

10a Which of the following reasons do you think are the most typical for writing a blog?
- as a personal record of experiences
- as a way of thinking things through
- as a way of communicating with someone else
- as an emotional outlet
- your own idea

b Now read the blog entry on page 141 and answer these questions:
1. What reasons are given to explain why some people write blogs?
2. How do these reasons compare with your ideas?

11 Write a 100-word journal or blog entry. First, decide what you would like to write about. Then use the following ideas to help you.
- what you did last night or last weekend
- how you are feeling
- something important that has happened recently
- something else

Vocabulary | outdoor activities

1a Match each icon to a word or phrase in the box.

____ camping	____ mountain climbing
____ kayaking	____ whitewater rafting
____ rappelling	____ rock climbing

A.

D.

B.

E.

C.

F.

b Pair Work Discuss the questions.

1. What do you know about these sports?

2. Which have you tried? Which would you like to try?

2 Look at the words and phrases in the box. Which outdoor sport do they go with? Write the letter of the icon. Some words can describe more than one sport.

____ rope	____ paddle	____ handhold	____ pitch a tent
____ rapids	____ summit	____ foothold	____ sleeping bag
____ waves	____ hang on	____ harness	____ take in the view

Listening

3 ▶1.22 Listen to people talking about outdoor adventures they experienced. Write the name of the sport each person is talking about.

1. _____
2. _____
3. _____
4. _____
5. _____
6. _____

Reading

4 Read the article quickly and answer these questions. What is Outward Bound? What are a few ways that people benefit from it?

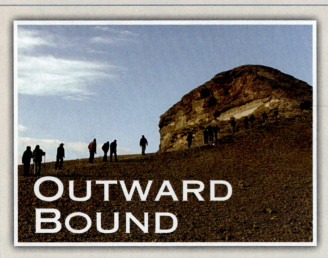

OUTWARD BOUND

Imagine a mountain before you. It is so mighty and powerful that you feel insignificant in comparison. Climbing it is daunting. It feels impossible–almost. But maybe, just maybe, you have what it takes to climb it. It won't be easy, of course, but something inside you is telling you that you *think* you can do it. Imagine the reward—not only the breathtaking view, but more importantly, the reward of pushing yourself to your limits and beyond and succeeding!

The outdoor education program Outward Bound creates leaders based on the philosophy that risk and uncertainty are essential for personal growth. People of all ages and walks of life are challenged to achieve more than they ever thought possible as they navigate waves in kayaks, rappel down mountains, or spend nights on their own in the wilderness. With 40 schools around the world, over 200,000 participants each year benefit from this extraordinary program.

Sun Yun Chen attended Outward Bound Hong Kong after finishing college. "I couldn't find a job, and I was so depressed. I had to do something different," she explains. "During the course I was encouraged to take risks, make mistakes, and learn from them. What better life lessons?" The turning point for Sun Yun was a demanding rock climb. "The struggle helped me realize that I didn't have to follow a specific path in my life," Sun Yun shares. "I thought I was supposed to get a job like all my friends. Instead, I'm continuing my studies in graduate school."

At Outward Bound Canada, Albert Henderson acquired life-changing leadership skills. "The freezing rain blew in our faces, but we continued to climb," he recalls. "The raging river flipped our raft over and over, but our team didn't give up. I faced the impossible, challenged my mind and my body, and realized how much more I have to give." Albert successfully transferred his experience to the corporate world, where he soon earned a significant promotion.

So, what does it take to do Outward Bound? You don't have to be in perfect shape, but you do have to prepare yourself physically and mentally for the experience. Here are a few suggestions:

- You must prepare yourself to live without the comforts of home. Participants are supposed to leave their cell phones, electronic devices, personal items, and even deodorant behind.

- You should start an exercise routine. This should include doing aerobic exercise, lifting weights to build strength, and stretching for flexibility.

- You should decrease intake of caffeine and alcohol, and you must quit smoking.

If you can't quite envision yourself summiting a mountain, or spending the night in a rainstorm, or parting with your iPhone for a couple of weeks, then perhaps Outward Bound *is* indeed for you. After all, it's when you intentionally try something you're not sure you can do, that you are taking a risk, pushing yourself to your limit, and potentially discovering the best that you could possibly be.

5 Read the article again. Mark the statements below true (*T*) or false (*F*).

_____ 1. The greatest reward for climbing a mountain is the view.

_____ 2. Sun Yun was depressed because she had to do something different.

_____ 3. Sun Yun realized that she didn't have to do what her friends did.

_____ 4. Albert did mountain climbing and rafting on Outward Bound.

_____ 5. You don't need to exercise before starting Outward Bound.

_____ 6. Outward Bound is for experienced outdoorspeople only.

6 **Group Work** When was a time that you challenged yourself to do something scary or new? What did you learn from the experience? Discuss.

Grammar | modals of obligation

7 Match the present examples (1–5) in the Active Grammar box with their meanings (a–e). Then complete the past examples (6–10) to express the meaning in the past.

Active Grammar

Present examples	**Meanings**	**Past examples**
____ 1. *You should start an exercise routine.*	a. It's not necessary for you to do it.	6. *We should _____ _____ an exercise routine.*
____ 2. *You must stop at a red light.*	b. It is expected.	7. *We _____ _____ quit smoking.*
____ 3. *You have to quit smoking.*	c. The obligation comes from how the speaker feels.	8. *We _____ prepare ourselves mentally.*
____ 4. *You don't have to be in perfect shape.*	d. It's extremely important.	9. *We _____ _____ be in perfect shape.*
____ 5. *You're supposed to leave your cell phone behind.*	e. The obligation comes from outside, such as a law.	10. *We _____ _____ leave our cell phones behind.*

See Reference page 130

8 Decide if there are any differences in meaning between each pair of sentences. Explain what they are.

1. a. I must stop smoking.
   b. I have to stop smoking.

2. a. You don't have to wear a tie.
   b. You shouldn't wear a tie.

3. a. You should tell her how you feel.
   b. You ought to tell her how you feel.

4. a. You didn't have to wait for me.
   b. You didn't need to wait for me.

> **American English**
> *I really should lose weight.*
> **British English**
> *I really must lose weight.*

9a The words in the box are missing from the description. Note where each one should go.

> should had (x2) to
> supposed didn't

b ▶1.23 Now listen and check your answers.

Speaking

10 **Pair Work** Tell another student one thing you:

- should have done by now.
- must do this week.
- had to do as a child.
- didn't have to do as a child.
- were supposed to do recently (but didn't).

> One of the best things we did on vacation was to go whitewater rafting. At first I was pretty nervous, especially when they told us we to sign something which said we wouldn't hold the company responsible if we got injured or died! Anyway, before we started off, the guy in charge of our raft told us we had to wear life jackets. I was surprised that we have to wear any kind of helmet. We were also to wear sneakers but I'd forgotten mine so I had wear my sandals. Once we got going though I calmed down and the whole thing was fantastic. There were eight of us in the raft and there really were a lot of rapids. It was kind of like being on a roller coaster. At one point, I almost fell in. The one thing I'm sorry about is that I didn't get any photos. I have taken my camera but I was afraid I would drop it in the water.

Compare and contrast photos CAN DO ✓

GRAMMAR emphasis

Listening

1a Look at the photo from the movie *Million Dollar Baby*. What do you know about it?

b ▶ 1.24 Listen to this conversation about the movie and answer the questions.

1. Did both people like the movie?
2. What is one important theme of the movie?
3. In what way does the Clint Eastwood character not take a risk in the movie?
4. What connection is suggested between the young woman boxer and Clint Eastwood's daughter?

Million Dollar Baby

Grammar | emphasis

2 Match the examples in the Active Grammar box with the ways of emphasizing.

Active Grammar

Examples	Ways to add emphasis
___ 1. *I do like Clint Eastwood.*	a. Use repetition.
___ 2. *It was much, much better than that.*	b. Add an emphasizing word like *so, such, really, just*, etc.
___ 3. *There are so many different themes running through the movie.*	c. Use the structure: *It is/was . . . which/that . . .*
___ 4. *It's the best movie that I've seen in a long time.*	d. Add an appropriate form of *do*.

See Reference page 130

---

3 Match the beginning of each sentence with its end. Add *do, does,* or *did* for emphasis. Change the form of the verbs where necessary.

Ex: *She does know the movie starts at 7:30 P.M.*

_c_ 1. She knows	a. for being so late.
___ 2. I sent	b. some help with her homework.
___ 3. They like	c. the movie starts at 7:30 P.M.
___ 4. He apologized	d. you a message this morning.
___ 5. She needs	e. oysters.
___ 6. I understand	f. how you are feeling.

4 Rewrite the sentences below to add emphasis to the underlined words and phrases.

1. She had always wanted <u>this job</u>.
2. I went and saw my doctor <u>yesterday</u>.
3. She really doesn't like the <u>words</u> to their new song.
4. He wants to study <u>sociology or psychology</u> at college.

> It was the job that she had always wanted.

Speaking

5 **Pair Work** Choose one of the following topics. Make a few notes about what you want to say, and decide which points you want to emphasize.

- a physical or financial risk you have taken
- a place that you love
- an actor or musician you really like who has taken risks
- a person who is important to you

Vocabulary | phrasal verbs with *out*

6 Match the underlined phrasal verbs in these sentences to their meanings.

_____ 1. Something happened that we never really <u>find out</u> about.

_____ 2. She <u>turns out</u> to be a very good boxer.

_____ 3. We've <u>run out</u> of milk. Will you go next door and ask Tilda for some?

_____ 4. Could you <u>pass out</u> one worksheet to each student, please?

_____ 5. It took them several hours to <u>put out</u> the fire at the hotel.

_____ 6. There's been a mistake with the bill, but they said they'll <u>sort it out</u> as soon as possible.

_____ 7. I thought we had a buyer, but he <u>backed out</u> of the deal at the last minute.

_____ 8. What does this say? I can't <u>make out</u> his handwriting.

a. give to each person

b. become, happen in a particular way

c. extinguish, stop a fire or cigarette from burning

d. put something in order, correct a mistake

e. use all of something so there is none left

f. discover

g. change your mind, not do something you had agreed to do

h. understand, make sense of

7a Complete each question with the correct form of a verb from Exercise 6.

1. Have you ever had to _____ a fire? What happened?

2. When you want to _____ a piece of information, what do you normally do?

3. Have you ever been in a car that has _____ of gas? What happened?

4. Have you ever met someone who _____ to be very different from what you imagined they were like at first? In what way were they different?

5. Have you ever _____ of something you promised to do? Why? What happened as a result?

6. In general, is it easy or difficult for people to _____ what you're really thinking? Why do you think that's true?

b In pairs, ask and answer the questions.

Listening and Speaking

8   ▶1.25   Listen to someone comparing and contrasting the two photos. How would she feel about being in each situation?

9a   Complete these sentences from Audioscript 1.25 in Exercise 8 on page 152.

1. They're _____ ironing.
2. In the first picture, I _____ _____ a man ironing some _____ of white shirt . . .
3. I can't _____ _____ he got there . . .
4. The second picture is of a _____ more ordinary situation.
5. His wife _____ be out at work.
6. The guy in the first picture _____ more relaxed than the man in the second picture, _____ though it must be very dangerous.

b   Listen again and check your ideas.

10   **SPEAKING EXCHANGE** Work in pairs. A Students look at the two photos on page 137. B Students look at the photos on page 138. Show your partner your two photos. Then compare and contrast them using the language in the How To box.

How To:

Compare and contrast

Use comparing words or phrases	*also, as well as, both*
Use contrasting words or phrases	*on the other hand, but, however, whereas, while*
Speculate about the situation	*His wife might/may/ could/must be at work.*
	He doesn't seem/appear to be enjoying himself much.
Give your own reaction	*I wouldn't like to be in either situation!*
	It makes me want to quit my job and go traveling.

Review

1 Match the beginning of each sentence with its end.

____ 1. If the check arrives today,	a. I would be extremely angry.
____ 2. If I had more time,	b. I wouldn't have gone hiking in the mountains.
____ 3. If I had heard the weather forecast,	c. I'll buy something expensive like a new car.
____ 4. If I exercised more,	d. I would like to take a pottery class.
____ 5. If anyone spoke to me like that,	e. I would probably start losing weight.
____ 6. If I hadn't fallen in the race,	f. I'm sure I would have won it.
____ 7. If I come to the party,	g. I'll pay my rent.
____ 8. If I get my bonus,	h. will you get them a present from both of us?

2 Rewrite the first sentence using the words in parentheses so that the meaning stays the same.

> **Ex:** **There was no need for you to wait for me. (You/have)**
> *You didn't have to wait for me.*

1. The rules say I have to take some ID. (I/supposed)

_____

2. It wasn't necessary for me to get up early this morning. (I/need)

_____

3. It's necessary for us to be in our seats at the theater by 7:30 P.M. (We/got)

_____

4. It wasn't a good idea to forget Janine's birthday. (You/should)

_____

5. Were you obliged to do military service when you were 18? (Did/have)

_____

3 Use the cues and the correct form of the verbs to write sentences.

1. What will we do if/taxi/not come/time?

_____

2. If I/you/I/go/long vacation.

_____

3. What/you do if/you/offer/better job?

_____

4. I/not rent/car/if I/known how expensive/it/going to be.

_____

5. If she/study/hard/between now and exams/probably pass.

_____

4 Unscramble each of the words in *italics* below.

1. Most children have a *aremd* of what they want to be when they grow up. _____

2. Starting a new business was a *emaglb*, but after a few years it was a big success. _____

3. You must check the safety *srensha* before going rappelling. _____

4. Did you ever *stro* out why the budget numbers were off? _____

5. The view from the *imtums* was worth the climb. _____

6. Can you believe that skinny guy *udernt* out to be such a great climber? _____

Communication | exchange information on familiar matters

5 **SPEAKING EXCHANGE** Read the rules on page 140 of the Speaking Exchange and then play the game.

Looking back

Warm Up

1 When do you think each photo was taken: the 1940s, 1950s, 1960s, or 1980s? What details make you think this? Discuss.

2a Match the sentences to the photos.

_____ 1. I get <u>nostalgic</u> when I see old photos with men in hats.

_____ 2. Do you <u>remember</u> family TV nights? I have such fond <u>memories</u> of those times.

_____ 3. So, <u>remind</u> me, which punk band were you in back then?

_____ 4. My mother is pretty <u>forgetful</u> these days, but she likes to <u>reminisce</u> about her days as a hippie.

b **Pair Work** Decide if the underlined words above are verbs, adjectives, or nouns. Explain their meanings. Write sentences that are true for you using the underlined words from Exercise 2a above.

3 **Group Work** What is the most memorable evening or day you have had in the last year? What made it special? Discuss.

Reading

1 <mark>Group Work</mark> What do you know about the movie *The Pursuit of Happyness*? Discuss.

2 Read the article and answer these questions.
   1. Who is Chris Gardner?
   2. What is the main idea of Gardner's speeches? How is his life story an example of that idea?
   3. What was Gardner's life like before he achieved his dream?

3 Read the article again and decide where the sentences belong.
   a. Gardner struggled to provide for them, never wavering in his pursuit of a better life.
   b. Gardner's success didn't stop there, however.
   c. He says to find something that you can't wait to get to when you wake up in the morning.
   d. He tells him to protect his dreams, and if he wants something, to just go get it.

4 <mark>Group Work</mark> What is something you're passionate about? What are you doing to pursue it? Discuss.

How to Find Happiness

The Pursuit of Happyness starring Will Smith

What is happiness? Do we ever actually achieve it? Or is it just something we pursue all our lives? Listen to one of Chris Gardner's motivational speeches, and he will not only tell you that it is possible to attain happiness—he will also show you how.

Gardner's primary message is to do something you are passionate about. ＿＿ (**1.**) Gardner's "something" was becoming a stockbroker. Being poor and having little education, the odds were stacked against him. But this was his chance at happiness and he would not give up. In his motivational speeches, Gardner recounts the obstacles he overcame in his own life—poverty, homelessness, the challenges of being a single father—and leaves his audiences excited about the prospect of creating their own destinies.

This inspiring story has been the basis for both a book and a 2006 movie starring Will Smith. Both stories show what Gardner's life used to be like before his remarkable success. In the early 1980s, he found himself suddenly single with custody of his young son, Christopher. The father and son duo faced many hardships. Even when given the opportunity to work as an intern at a prestigious finance firm, there was a twist. The internship was unpaid. But Gardner didn't give up. After numerous additional setbacks, Gardner became homeless. He used to ride the trains all night with his young son, or stay in subway stations or parks. When things got tough they would hide away in public bathrooms. Later they would sleep in a homeless shelter. Little Christopher got

used to this lifestyle, at least having one constant in his life: his dedicated father. ＿＿ (**2.**)

In one memorable scene in the movie, Gardner passionately tells his son (played by Will Smith's real-life son, Jaden) to never let anyone tell him he can't do something. ＿＿ (**3.**) Gardner lived by these words. In the end, he achieved his dream of becoming a stockbroker, beating out 19 other competitors for the full-time position. After years of struggle, he wasn't used to this sudden feeling of relief and security.

＿＿ (**4.**) He went on to start his own multi-million dollar brokerage firm and become the successful author and speaker he is today. More recently, he has also collaborated with the shelter that once housed him and his son to build low-income homes and create jobs for the homeless. Through his work, more and more people are inspired each day to pursue their own happiness in life.

Grammar | past routines: *used to/would/get used to*

5 Match examples in the Active Grammar box with their meanings.

Active Grammar

Examples

_____ 1. He **used to** sleep in a shelter.

_____ 2. He **is getting used to** sleeping in a shelter.

_____ 3. He **is used to** sleeping in a shelter.

_____ 4. He **would** sleep in a shelter.

Meanings

a. He is familiar with sleeping in a shelter. It is not strange or difficult for him.

b. Sleeping in a shelter is becoming less difficult for him.

c. Sleeping in a shelter was part of his typical day and behavior.

d. In the past, he regularly slept in a shelter, but now he doesn't.

See Reference page 131

6a Circle the correct choices to complete the sentences.

1. I *didn't use/wasn't used* to like jazz very much.
2. I'm getting used to *work/working* from home.
3. I'm *used/used to* living on my own.
4. My family *would/were used to* always go to the same place for their summer vacation.
5. He *would/used to* have a beard.
6. We can't *get/getting* used to the noise.

b **Pair Work** Explain to another student what each sentence means.

> *When the speaker was younger she didn't really like jazz, but now she does.*

7 There is one word missing from each of these sentences. Decide what it is and add it.

1. We used to our new diet. We've only been vegetarians for a few weeks.
2. I can't used to my new boss. She's not very friendly.
3. You use to be so close to your brother when you were children?
4. We slowly getting used to living in the country, but sometimes it feels isolated.
5. I used play a lot of soccer in school.

Speaking

8 **Pair Work** Discuss the questions.

1. Name two or three things you used to enjoy doing when you were younger but no longer do. Why did you stop doing them?
2. Describe one or two big changes in your life, such as moving or getting married. What were the most difficult things to get used to?

Vocabulary | describing appearance

9 Write the words and phrases from the box in the chart. Write the chart on a separate sheet of paper.

straight	wavy	muscular	a bit overweight	round
elegant	slim	wrinkled	clean-shaven	spiky
stocky	dyed	tanned	going bald	
scruffy	curly	chubby	good-looking	

Hair	Face	Build	General
straight			

10 Read these descriptions. Correct the mistake in each one.

1. He's got short, black hairs and a small mustache.
2. I like having a wrinkles face. I think it gives me character.
3. She has spiked blond hair and blue eyes. You can't miss her.
4. Simon's changed in the last few years. He's going balding now.
5. His hair used to be very curled when he was a baby.

11 **Group Work** Choose one of the categories below and describe a famous person to your group. See how quickly they can guess the person.

| pop star | politician | athlete | TV star | actor |

> *He used to be one of the most famous politicians in the world. He has gray hair now, but he's not going bald at all. He has a great smile and very bright blue eyes. His wife is also a well-known politician.*

Writing

12 Read this excerpt from an email. Then look at the pictures on the right. Decide which person is being described.

> It's really nice of you to meet me at the airport even though we've never met. Jo's told me so much about you that I already feel like I know you. Anyway, just so you know who to look for when I get through customs: I'm about 5 feet 7 with short, spiky, black hair. I guess some people would call me stocky. I prefer to think of myself as muscular. I don't know what I'll be wearing; that depends on the weather.

13a **Pair Work** Describe the other three people in as much detail as you can.

b Now imagine you have met one of the other people at a party. Write a brief email to a friend telling them what he or she looks like.

Talk about memories

GRAMMAR expressing degrees of ability

Listening

1 Look at the photo and read the sentences. Check the sentences that describe the photo. Correct the others to make them true.

_____ 1. They're playing in front of a house.

_____ 2. The woman is looking a little anxious.

_____ 3. The woman is wearing boots and a heavy jacket.

_____ 4. It's probably early summer.

_____ 5. The child looks as if he's having a bad time.

_____ 6. The child is only a few months old.

_____ 7. The woman is probably in her late 40s.

2 ▶1.26 Listen to the conversation between Scott and his friend Cara and answer these questions.

1. What is the relationship of the woman in the photo to the child?

2. What kind of child does Scott say he was?

3 Listen again. Write appropriate questions for these answers.

Ex: *Vermont—Where did Scott grow up?*

1. Just one floor. _____

2. Because she went back to teaching. _____

3. Until he was almost seven. _____

4. A lot of fun. _____

5. Eight months. _____

6. Four. _____

Speaking

4 **Pair Work** Describe a vacation photo and explain how it makes you feel. Either refer to one of your favorite photos or choose one of these photos. Explain where it was taken, who the people are, and why it is one of your favorite photos.

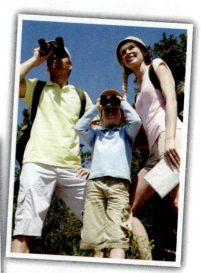

Grammar | expressing degrees of ability

5a Complete the example sentences and rules with *can, could, able, manage(d),* or *succeed(ed).*

Active Grammar

Examples

1. _____ you read the writing on that sign at the end of the road?

2. *Will you be* _____ *to come to Sam's birthday dinner on Sunday?*

3. *I was* _____ *to walk by ten months.*

4. *I* _____ *play simple tunes on the piano by the age of four.*

5. *Did you* _____ *to find the photos you were looking for?*

6. *We* _____ *in finding the perfect present for my sister.*

Rules

a. Use _____ to talk about present or "general" ability.

b. Use *will be* _____ to talk about future ability.

c. Use _____ or *was/were* _____ to talk about past or "general" ability.

d. Use *was/were* _____, _____ *to,* or _____ *in* to talk about ability on a particular occasion.

See Reference page 131

b **Pair Work** Decide which of the sentences have approximately the same meaning.

1. She can ski.
2. She could ski really well as a child.
3. She's able to ski very well.
4. She knows how to ski.
5. She's pretty good at skiing.
6. She's terrible at skiing.
7. She's not very good at skiing.
8. She was great at skiing as a child.

6 Fill in the blanks with the correct form of the words in parentheses and a verb from the box.

> drive   meet   clean   spend   beat   swim

1. You _____ (can) the night here if you want. The spare room's free.

2. I _____ (could not) until I was almost 30. I just never got around to taking the test.

3. I'd like to _____ (able), but I have problems holding my breath under water.

4. I was surprised that Chris _____ (able) Steve at tennis. Steve is a very good player.

5. The sales reps have _____ (succeed) all their targets this month, and so everyone will get a bonus.

6. Fortunately, we _____ (manage) up the house after the party before our parents got home.

7 ▶1.27 Listen to Cara describing things that she and her brother did growing up. Make notes about Cara and her brother.

Cara	Her brother
	could ride a bike on his own at five

Listening

8a ▶ **1.28** Listen to Scott talking about the photo below. Check the topics he mentions.

____ 1. the people   ____ 3. the animals

____ 2. the place   ____ 4. the weather

b Listen again and then read the summary below. Find three mistakes.

> Both of the photos show Scott as a child. This photo shows him with his parents and two friends of theirs. They are staying at their friends' hotel in Boston. Scott enjoyed staying there because there was a lot to do, whereas he got bored in the summer when he just stayed at home. There were dogs at the hotel, which he liked. They were very friendly, similar to his cat at home. In general, he had a good time and liked going on vacation there.

Speaking

9 **Group Work** Describe one or two of your earliest memories of childhood. Is there anything you could do well as a child but you can't do so well now? If so, what is it? Discuss.

CAN DO ✓

Vocabulary | describing feelings

1 ▶1.29 Listen to these people. Which of the words in the box best describes each person? Write the correct number.

> _____ suspicious _____ uneasy _____ curious _____ annoyed
> _____ optimistic _____ shocked _____ relieved

2 Fill in the blanks with words from Exercise 1.

1. She's very _____ that the police have dropped all the charges against her.

2. Sam's _____ about selling his house soon. He's had a few offers already.

3. My sister's _____ with me because I borrowed her favorite jacket without asking her.

4. Environmental groups are _____ that the government is serious about dealing with climate change.

5. The fact that he didn't want to answer the police officer's questions made them _____.

6. Julie's mother was very _____ when they told her they were going to get married in June. They've only been together since November.

3 **Pair Work** Choose three of the feelings from Exercise 1. Tell a partner about the last time you had each of them.

Reading

4a Look at the cover of the book *The Memory Box* and discuss with other students what you think it might be about.

b Read the excerpt. Who are Susannah, Charlotte, and Catherine?

5a Read the excerpt again and answer these questions.

1. "Susannah was apparently perfect, as the dead so often become." (lines 1–2) What do you think this means?

2. How did Catherine feel about what people said about her mother?

3. "The existence of the memory box may have troubled my father from the beginning." (lines 9–10) Why do you think this might have been?

4. Why do you think Catherine didn't want to think about her real mother as she was growing up?

5. How do you think Catherine felt when she first came across the memory box?

b Find examples in the excerpt of five of the feelings referred to in Exercise 1. Explain who has the feelings and what causes them.

6 **Group Work** Discuss the questions.

1. What do you think Susannah might have left in the memory box for Catherine?

2. What do you think the point of the memory box was?

3. How would you feel about making or being given a memory box?

*S*usannah was apparently perfect, as the dead so often
become. She was, it seemed, perfectly beautiful, perfectly
good, and perfectly happy during her comparatively short
life. They said she met life with open arms, ever positive
5 and optimistic. I do not believe a word of this. How, after
all, could she be happy, knowing she was likely to die soon,
when she was a mere thirty-one years old and I, her baby,
was hardly six months old?

I have a feeling that the existence of the memory box may
10 have troubled my father from the beginning. He didn't give
it to me until my twenty-first birthday even though it had
been in our house all that time. Charlotte knew about it, of
course, but neither she nor my father could bring themselves
to mention it. I think they were both afraid of its significance.
15 Also, I was a highly imaginative child and they simply didn't
know how to introduce this memory box into my life.

Now, however, their nervousness makes me curious.
What exactly were they afraid of? Did they think I might
be shocked, and if so why? At any rate, both of them
20 were visibly on edge, almost guilty, when finally on the
morning of my twenty-first birthday they told me about
it. It was clear they were relieved when I showed little
interest in it. I said I didn't want to open it, or even see it.

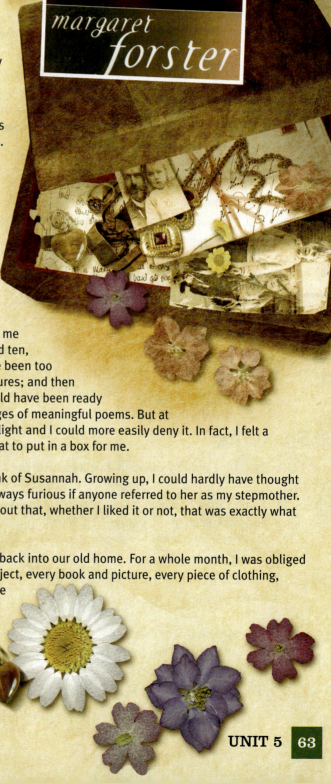

This was a lie, and yet not a lie. The box did, in fact, make me
25 curious even if I found I wanted to suppress the feeling. Aged ten,
I don't think I would have been able to. I'm sure I would have been too
excited at the thought that it might contain all sorts of treasures; and then
around fifteen I'd have found it irresistibly romantic and would have been ready
to weep on discovering dried roses pressed between the pages of meaningful poems. But at
30 twenty-one I was very self-centered; my curiosity was only slight and I could more easily deny it. In fact, I felt a
kind of nausea, at the notion of a dying woman choosing what to put in a box for me.

Nevertheless, there was no doubt that it forced me to think of Susannah. Growing up, I could hardly have thought
of her less, wanting Charlotte to be my only mother. I was always furious if anyone referred to her as my stepmother.
However, Charlotte herself would try to calm me by pointing out that, whether I liked it or not, that was exactly what
35 she was.

After Charlotte died, the hardest thing I had to do was go back into our old home. For a whole month, I was obliged
to go there day after day until every bit of furniture, every object, every book and picture, every piece of clothing,
every last curtain and cushion was sorted out and ready to be
collected by all manner of people. This was, of course, how
40 I found the box, even though I very nearly missed it. My
attention might not have been caught if it had not
been for an odd-looking pink label attached to the
parcel. On the label, written in ink which had faded
but which you could still read, was my own name—
45 *"For my darling Catherine Hope, in the future."*

Grammar | connectives for contrast: *although/however/nevertheless*

7 Look at the pairs of sentences in the Active Grammar box. In each pair, one sentence is correct and one is not. Cross out the incorrect sentence. Explain your decision.

> ### Active Grammar
>
> 1. a. *He didn't give it to me until my 21st birthday.* **Although** *it had been in our house all that time.*
>
>   b. *He didn't give it to me until my 21st birthday,* **although** *it had been in our house all that time.*
>
> 2. a. **However** *I was always furious if anyone referred to Charlotte as my stepmother, she would always point out that that was exactly what she was.*
>
>   b. *I was always furious if anyone referred to Charlotte as my stepmother.* **However,** *she would always point out that that was exactly what she was.*
>
> 3. a. *The idea of a dying woman putting things in a special box for me was very strange.* **Nevertheless,** *it forced me to think about her.*
>
>   b. *The idea of a dying woman putting things in a special box for me was very strange* **nevertheless** *it forced me to think about her.*

See Reference page 131

8 Circle the correct choice to complete each sentence.

1. She bought the shoes *although/nevertheless* they were too expensive.
2. The jacket was cheap. *Although/However*, it wasn't the color she wanted.
3. It is true that Mr. Billingham left the store without paying for the camera. *Nevertheless/Although*, he has been under a lot of stress.
4. They decided to get a dog, *however/although* they didn't have a yard.

9 **Pair Work** Complete each of the sentences below in a logical way. Then compare with a partner.

1. The food in the restaurant was extremely good. *However, . . .*
2. I realize that you have worked for this company for many years. *Nevertheless, . . .*
3. We decided to buy the house, *although . . .*

Speaking

10a ▶ 1.30 Listen to someone talking about *The Memory Box*. What did they think of it?

b Think about a book you have read or movie that you have seen or remember well. Make notes about the following:

- the basic plot
- things you particularly liked about it
- any criticisms you had of it

c Now tell other students about a book or movie you remember. Refer to the plot, things you liked, and any criticisms. Use the expressions from Exercise 9 where appropriate.

Review

1 Complete the text with *used to* or *get used to* and the correct form of a verb from the box.

> have   finish   not be able to   teach   be

I recently went back to Seoul where I _____ (**1.**) English as a foreign language in the early 1980s. A lot had changed. The area where I lived _____ (**2.**) very quiet but it's much busier now. There are more modern buildings and bigger roads. I remember when I first arrived that it took a while to _____ (**3.**) read most of the store signs, as they were in Korean. Now a lot of them are in English, too. Every evening we _____ (**4.**) our classes at 9:30 P.M. and then all go out to a nearby club which had a great disco. I looked for the club, but sadly it had gone. Seoul is a marvelous place and I really missed it when I came back home. It took me a while to _____ (**5.**) a very different lifestyle.

2 Rewrite the pairs of sentences with correct punctuation, using the words in parentheses.

1. I managed to get a few hours' sleep. The party upstairs was very noisy. (however)
2. I would say that Charlotte is my best friend. I've only known her for a few months. (although)
3. She seems to be in love with him. He is very unreliable. (nevertheless)
4. Sandra is a very good student. She will need to work a bit harder if she wants to pass her exams. (however).
5. I had all the necessary qualifications. I didn't get the job. (although)

3 Use the words in parentheses to complete the second sentence of each pair. Both sentences in the pair should have the same meaning.

> **Ex:** She is able to play the piano very well. (can)
>
> *She can play the piano very well.*

1. Will it be possible to finish the presentation by Friday? (able)
   Do you think you _____ finish the presentation by Friday?
2. They finally succeeded in getting the car out of the mud. (manage)
   They finally _____ to get the car out of the mud.
3. He failed to persuade his mother to buy a him an iPad. (able)
   He _____ to persuade his mother to buy a him an iPad.
4. She couldn't get his camera to work. (succeed)
   She _____ in getting his camera to work.
5. Were you able to speak to Brian before he went back? (manage)
   _____ to speak to Brian before he went back?

4 Complete the sentences with one of the words or phrases from the unit vocabulary section on page 131.

1. We were all very _____ when she arrived home safely at midnight.
2. What's happened to your beard? I've never seen you _____ before.
3. Jim has become pretty _____ since he started going to the gym—he's short but strong.
4. He said the investment was a sure thing, but I'm a little _____ that it's so easy to get rich.

MAKE YOUR HISTORY!

Imagine someone—a child, a future archaeologist, or even an alien being—discovering your time capsule in 100 years, 1,000 years, or 1,000,000 years from now.

Consider the sensation that it will cause: "Ancient artifacts from the 21st century found in buried time capsule!" These future people will study your chosen objects from the past—a crumbling newspaper, a coin, a birthday photo, a piece of technology—and they will learn a little bit more about us.

Leave your mark on the future.

Be a part of history.

Bury a time capsule.

TimeLine Inc.

5 Look at the picture and ad. What are the people putting in the ground and why?

6 ▶ 1.31 Listen to someone talking about what she put in a time capsule in 1977. Make a note of five general pieces of advice she gives to other people who want to prepare a time capsule.

7 **Group Work** Choose five things to put in your time capsule. Use the examples below or other ideas. Give reasons to justify each of your ideas.

> *I think we should include a globe so that they know how the world is divided.*

> *In my opinion, we should put in a typical piece of clothing like jeans so that they know how we dress.*

> *What about putting in a newspaper so that they know the important things that are happening in the world today?*

UNIT **6**
Exploring the world

A

B

C

D

Warm Up

1 **Pair Work** What can you see in the photos? Which of the places would you most like to explore? Why? Discuss.

2 Complete the expressions with the words in the box. What do you think they mean?

> wandering   bug   territory   culture   solo

1. I was a little worried about going into *uncharted* _____!
2. I went as a _____ *traveler*, on my own.
3. I spent a month _____ *around* the town.
4. I was *bitten by the travel* _____ and wanted to explore a lot of other places.
5. The first two months were difficult and I experienced real _____ *shock*.

3 **Pair Work** Why do you think people are bitten by the travel bug? Has it ever happened to you? Discuss.

Write an informal email

GRAMMAR present perfect vs. present perfect continuous

CAN DO ✓

Bitten by the jungle bug!

Sand flies, sweat bees, 80-meter (260 foot) high trees . . . Horrible for most of us, but all in a day's work for Charlotte Uhlenbroek. She moves as elegantly through the lounge of the Savoy Hotel as she does through the Amazon jungle. But while she loves the adventure, she is also glad to be back in civilization, at least for the moment.

She's just finished filming a TV series called *Jungle*—a grueling 19-week job that involved her exploring the dense jungles of the Congo, the Amazon, and Borneo. She says that it was fascinating but daunting as well. So what was her most challenging experience? "Definitely climbing an 80-meter (260 foot) high tree in Borneo, when I'm petrified of heights! I had to keep going up and up, when a voice inside me was saying, 'Down! Down!' I kept thinking the ropes were going to break and send me plummeting down below."

And "down below" was where the bugs were—clinging, stinging, sucking beasts. In the Amazon rainforest, she was plagued by sand flies. "I've had some horrible bug bites, but these really are the itchiest bites I've ever had. At one stage, I counted 70 bites on one arm," she says. "Just as annoying were the sweat bees in the Congo. They try to drink the sweat on your face and even the tears from your eyes. The most disgusting thing, though, was trying to pull the slimy leeches off your skin. The more I pulled, the more they stretched and the tighter their jaws clung to my leg. I kept shouting, 'Get them off!' and the film crew kept saying, 'Just a minute . . . this makes a really good shot!'"

Charlotte's journey into the heart of the world's most significant rainforests was an inspiring experience. "The rainforest really is like a city. Each tree is like a city block with hundreds of residents. If you knock it down, you cause just as much disruption and damage as if those residents were human. The jungle is extraordinary because although it only covers about six percent of the world, it contains over 50% of all known animal and plant species, plus a lot more that are unknown, too."

What has she been enjoying since her return to civilization? "I've been taking lots of nice, long showers," she says. "In the Congo I was always worried about using up all our water supplies. And I find that when I've been in hot, uncomfortable conditions for a while, the things I look forward to more than anything else are being with my family and enjoying my favorite meal."

Reading

1 **Pair Work** Charlotte Uhlenbroek spent over four months in the jungle. Read the article about her. Then discuss these questions.

    1. Which things did she find difficult in the jungle?

    2. Which things does she most like to do when she's back in civilization?

2 Read the article again. Mark the statements below true (*T*), false (*F*), or don't know (*?*).

    ____ 1. Charlotte looks and feels out of place in the Savoy Hotel.

    ____ 2. She had to climb tall trees without the use of ropes.

    ____ 3. She cried because she couldn't stand the sweat bees on her face.

    ____ 4. The film crew helped her to get the leeches off her leg.

    ____ 5. The water she used in the Congo was usually dirty.

    ____ 6. When she gets home, she loves doing the cooking for her family.

3 **Group Work** Would you like to go on a jungle expedition? Why or why not? Discuss.

Grammar | present perfect vs. present perfect continuous

4 Match each example with a rule in the Active Grammar box. Then circle the correct choice to complete the usage explanations.

Active Grammar

Examples

____ 1. *She's just finished filming a TV series called Jungle (and is glad to be back in civilization).*

____ 2. *I've had some horrible bites but these really are the itchiest bites I've ever had.*

____ 3. *I've been in jungles for a total of 19 weeks, and I'm going home today.*

____ 4. *What has she been enjoying since her return to civilization? "I've been taking lots of nice, long showers."*

Rules

a. Use the **present perfect** to talk about an action or experience in the past when the time is not important or not known.

b. Use the **present perfect** to describe an action that started in the past and continues in the present, when you're focusing on the finished action (or on the number of times the action has been completed up to the time of speaking).

c. Use the **present perfect continuous** when you're focusing on the activity itself. *For* or *since* are often used to talk about the duration of the activity.

d. Use the **present perfect** to describe an action that happened in the past but has the result in the present. *Just*, *yet*, or *already* are often used in this case.

Usage: *just, already, yet*

- *Just* means a long / short time ago. It usually comes between *has* and *have* and the past participle.

- *Already* shows that something happened later / sooner than expected. It usually comes between *has/have* and the past participle or at the end of the sentence.

- *Yet* shows that the speaker expected something to happen after / before now. It is used at the end of negatives and questions.

See Reference page 132

5 Correct the mistake in each sentence.

1. I've been visiting friends in Italy three times this year.
2. What you been doing since I last spoke to you?
3. Have you yet seen that movie, *Sahara*?
4. He just has spoken to the tour guide about it.
5. Have you been knowing each other long?

6 Complete the sentences by using the words in parentheses. Use the present perfect, present perfect continuous, or simple past.

1. _____ (you/go/ever) to the jungle?
2. _____ (you/decide) where to go for your next vacation?
3. How long _____ (you/study) English?
4. What do you want to do today that _____ (you/not do/yet)?
5. Where _____ (you/go) for your last vacation?
6. Where _____ (you/live) for the last year?

American English	British English
I just came	*I've just come*

7 **Pair Work** Ask and answer the questions in Exercise 6.

Vocabulary | adjective pairs ending in *-ed/-ing*

8a **Pair Work** Find these adjectives in the article on page 68. Discuss what you think they mean. Use the sentences around the word to help you.

1. fascinating (paragraph 2)
2. daunting (paragraph 2)
3. challenging (paragraph 2)
4. petrified (paragraph 2)
5. annoying (paragraph 3)
6. disgusting (paragraph 3)
7. inspiring (paragraph 4)
8. worried (paragraph 5)

b Look at the words in the article again and circle the correct choices to complete these rules.

1. Use adjectives ending in *-ed/-ing* to describe someone's feelings.
2. Use adjectives ending in *-ed/-ing* to describe a situation.

9a Complete the dialogs with the best adjectives from Exercise 8a. Use the *-ed* or *-ing* form as needed.

1. **A:** Do you like camping?
   B: I hate it! I went once and I was _____ (1.) because I kept hearing animals. I even found pitching my tent pretty _____ (2.).

2. **A:** Are you scared of flying?
   B: Not really. I went up in a small airplane. I was a little _____ (3.) at first because it was pretty bumpy. But in the end I found the whole experience really _____ (4.).

3. **A:** How do you feel about eating food you've never tried before?
   B: Well, the other day, a friend of mine got me to try snails. I was _____ (5.) with him because he didn't tell me what they were. Well, when I found out, I was nearly sick to my stomach! They were really _____ (6.)!

4. **A:** How would you feel about a job that involved working with animals?
   B: Actually, I've just spent the summer holidays working at a monkey sanctuary, and I loved it. Monkeys are _____ (7.) when you get to know them. Catching them to give them medicine was pretty _____ (8.), but it was all very rewarding.

b ▶1.32 Listen and check your answers.

c **Group Work** Ask and answer the questions in Exercise 9a. Use the adjectives from Exercise 8a.

Writing

10a Read the email and the Useful Phrases box on page 143. Do the exercises.

b Choose a situation from Exercise 9a and write an email to a friend telling him or her about your experience. Use Mary's email and the paragraph plan to help you.

- **Paragraph 1:** Explain where you are and why and how you feel.
- **Paragraph 2:** Describe what you've been doing.
- **Paragraph 3:** Say how you feel about finishing.

Ask and answer questions about unusual places

GRAMMAR direct and indirect questions

Reading

1a **Group Work** Look at the photo of Bhutan and discuss the questions.

    1. What do you think life is like there?

    2. Why do you think few tourists go to this country?

b Read the article below quickly and check your ideas.

2 **Pair Work** Read the article again. Then summarize the article's main points about: **a)** important beliefs of Bhutanese people, **b)** nature in Bhutan, and **c)** tourism in Bhutan.

3 **Pair Work** Would you like to visit Bhutan? Why or why not? Do you think Bhutanese people would experience culture shock if they visited your country? In what ways? Discuss.

Vocabulary | weather

4 ▶1·33 Listen and decide which of these questions each of the three people are talking about:

    a. What's the weather like in your country?

    b. What's your favorite type of weather?

5a Look at Audioscript 1.33 on page 153 and write the underlined words in the correct place in the chart below.

Cold	cool
Warm or hot	
Rain	pours
Windy	
Sky	clear
Weather in general	

b **Pair Work** Explain the differences in meaning between the words in each column in the chart. Use a dictionary if necessary.

6 ▶1·34 Listen to people talking about the weather. Write the word from Exercise 5a that best describes the weather in each place.

    1. _____   5. _____

    2. _____   6. _____

    3. _____   7. _____

    4. _____   8. _____

7 **Group Work** How would you describe the weather in your area or country? Discuss.

BHUTAN is a country of about 750,000 people in the eastern Himalayas. Visitors may be surprised how much culture, tradition, and nature are all flourishing in this very private country. The Bhutanese people believe that all forms of life, human and nonhuman, are precious and sacred. Because of this attitude, they live in harmony with nature and their environment remains pristine, with an astonishing variety of animals, birds, and plants. The people live in harmony with each other too, with no discrimination of any kind.

In order to safeguard this rich natural environment and peaceful culture, Bhutan has adopted a cautious and controlled approach to tourism. In 2003, there were fewer than 6,000 tourists, and this number is not expected to increase greatly. No independent travelers are permitted in Bhutan; all tourists must go on a pre-planned, prepaid, guided, package tour. However, if you make the effort and manage to get a visa and arrange a trip, you will certainly have a life-changing experience in this magical kingdom.

Listening

8a **Pair Work** If you were going on vacation to Bhutan, what kinds of things would you like to know about in advance? Discuss.

b ▶1.35 Listen to a question and answer session with an expert on traveling to Bhutan. In what order do they talk about the things below?

___ a. special events/festivals   ___ d. food

___ b. the ideal time of year to visit   ___ e. what to take

___ c. what to do there   ___ f. organized trips

c Listen again and complete the notes below.

TRIP TO BHUTAN

WHEN TO GO:

Spring and fall are the best seasons to go.

Don't go in winter because _____ (1.).

Don't go in summer because _____ (2.).

ACTIVITIES:

Trekking is fantastic – amazing views and a lot of different _____ (3.).

CLOTHES:

Don't forget to take: rain gear and good _____ (4.).

Also, for the sun: a hat and _____ (5.).

Don't bring _____ (6.) or _____ (7.) for trekking (it's all provided).

FOOD:

One of the main ingredients used is _____ (8.).

FESTIVALS:

The main reason for festivals is for people to _____ (9.).

FLAGS:

The Bhutanese believe that wind blowing through them _____ (10.).

9 **Group Work** Would you like to go on the organized trekking trips described in the listening? Why or why not? Have you been to any festivals or celebrations in your country or abroad which you particularly enjoyed? Discuss. Give details.

Grammar | direct and indirect questions

10 Complete the questions in the Active Grammar box. Use Audioscript 1.35 on page 154 to help you.

Active Grammar

Direct questions

There are two main types of direct questions:

- *Yes/No* questions   _____ (1.) *to carry all our own equipment?*

                     _____ (2.) *provide a guide?*

- *Wh-* questions   *What activities* _____ (3.)?

                     When _____ (4.) *the best time to go?*

Subject questions

Subject questions are used when the question word (Ex: *who*) refers to the subject of the sentence. When a *wh-* word replaces the subject in a question, do not use the auxiliary verb.

Who _____ (5.) *with the trekking group?*

Indirect questions

Use indirect questions when you want to be polite, such as when you don't know someone. There are different ways of starting indirect questions.

Use the word order of positive statements. Use *if* or *whether* for indirect *Yes/No* questions.

Can you tell me what _____ (6.)?

Could I ask you what _____ (7.) *like?*

Do you know _____ (8.) *any interesting festivals at that time?*

I'd like to know _____ (9.) *to take anything special.*

See Reference page 132

11 Use the cues to change the questions into indirect questions.

1. Where are you living at the moment? (Can you tell me . . .)
2. Has he ever been trekking before? (Do you know . . .)
3. Who gave you those lovely flowers? (Can I ask you . . .)
4. What time will you be here tomorrow? (Can you tell me . . .)
5. Are you taking a vacation soon? (Do you know . . .)
6. When was this company started? (I'd like to know . . .)

Speaking

12a **SPEAKING EXCHANGE** Find out about two other types of vacation. In groups, write questions using the situations below to help you.
A Students: Write questions about camel trips in Egypt.
B Students: Write questions about bird watching in Mexico.

b A Students: Read the text about bird watching in Mexico on page 139.
B Students: Read the text about camel trips in Egypt on page 137.

c **Pair Work** Take turns asking and answering questions.

13 **Group Work** Which vacation would you rather go on: bird watching in Mexico, camel riding in Egypt, or trekking in Bhutan? Why? Discuss.

Vocabulary | verb phrases about moving or traveling

1   **Pair Work** Match the underlined verb phrases with their definitions below. Use a dictionary if necessary.

_____ 1. My parents are Brazilian, but they <u>emigrated</u> to the US.

_____ 2. My brother has <u>lived abroad</u> for ten years, so I don't see him much.

_____ 3. My sister <u>left home</u> when she was 18 and went to college in New York.

_____ 4. I spent a lot of vacations just <u>roaming around</u> the countryside, exploring.

_____ 5. After weeks of planning, we finally <u>set off</u> on our around-the-world trip.

_____ 6. We all cried when we went to <u>see her off</u> at the airport.

_____ 7. I'<u>m off</u> to the mall. Is there anything you need?

a. to live in a foreign country

b. to leave your country and go to live in another country

c. to walk or travel, with no definite purpose

d. when you are ready to go or you're going to go somewhere very soon

e. to leave at the start of a trip (especially an important, exciting, or difficult journey)

f. when a young person leaves his or her parents' house and goes to live somewhere else

g. to go to an airport, train station, etc., to say goodbye to someone who is leaving

2   Complete the questions with the correct form of a phrase from Exercise 1.

1. At what age do young people in your country typically _____?

2. Do you like people to come and _____ (you) at the airport?

3. What time did you _____ when you last went on vacation?

4. Which country would you move to if you _____?

5. What would you miss if you _____?

6. Where _____ (you) to after class today?

7. When was the last time you went to a new place and just _____ without any clear direction?

3   **Pair Work** You are going to ask your partner the questions from Exercise 2. First predict what you think his or her answers will be. Then ask the questions. How many did you get right?

Reading

4 **Group Work** What are some reasons people move to a new country? Discuss.

5 Read the article and match each paragraph with the most appropriate summary below. Two of the summary sentences cannot be used.

___ **a.** The appeal of many places is the price of property, better wages, and good weather.

___ **b.** For most people who emigrate, it's the best thing they've ever done.

___ **c.** Many people find that the grass is not always as green as they had hoped.

___ **d.** There is a trend in recent times for increasing numbers of people to emigrate.

___ **e.** Some people go abroad for about three years in order to make money and save enough to go back home with.

___ **f.** Although emigrating can be hard, it can also provide people with greater job satisfaction.

On the Move!

1 **Every day, thousands of people are on the move, and either temporarily or permanently, setting up homes abroad. Their move may be job-related or perhaps they think the grass is greener somewhere else. Whatever their reasons, it's clear that more and more people are stepping into the unknown and leaving their own country. But where do they go and why? And do they live happily ever after?**

2 Typically, a lot of people move abroad because of their jobs. In some cases, their company is moving them overseas, but many people make their own decision to move, believing they will have <u>more successful careers</u> abroad. Paul Derwin is a scientist who used to be based at a prestigious London university. He was dissatisfied, however, with the level of funding and recognition he was getting and decided to explore the possibilities that California had to offer. "Emigration is incredibly difficult, emotionally as well as practically," he says. "But after ten years in California, I've got a <u>far nicer</u> life than before. I have a fantastic job and the recognition I wanted. People take my work much <u>more seriously</u> here. It would be difficult to give that up now."

3 The <u>most popular</u> reason for emigrating, however, is the desire for a <u>better</u> quality of life. Destinations that place a greater value on leisure and have a more laid-back lifestyle are the most popular. People also look for places that will give them a <u>sunnier</u> climate and generally <u>hotter</u> weather. <u>Cheaper</u> property is another reason given for moving abroad. The cost of living in Canada, for example, is <u>much lower than</u> in the US, and often salaries are often about the same. Sue Riddell, a 30-year-old nurse, wants to emigrate to Australia with a group of friends. "We're fed up with the conditions we work and live in," she says. "I traveled to Australia after college and I loved it—the beaches, the fresh air, the sense of space. If I can, I'm going. And I don't know if I'll come back."

4 Despite the fact that so many people move abroad, most of them go back home after only about three years. Often living overseas is <u>not as attractive as</u> it seems at first. Generally, people emigrate because they think life is going to be better. They get certain feelings on vacation, and they romanticize about what it would be like to live there. They tend to focus on the <u>best</u> aspects of living there and think it will be like this all the time, when that is often not the case. Making enough money and getting work can be more difficult abroad than at home, and people tend to find they miss family, friends, and things they took for granted back home.

6 **Group Work** Discuss the questions.

1. What type of person do you think you need to be to emigrate or study abroad?

> *I think you need to be an independent person.*

2. Have you ever lived abroad? If so, where did you go and what was it like? What did you miss? If not, would you ever consider doing so? Why or why not? Where would you like to go?

3. Is it common for people to emigrate from your country? If so, where do they go and what are their reasons? Do you think they find what they are looking for?

Grammar | making comparisons

7 Complete the rules in the Active Grammar box. Use the underlined words in the reading on page 75 to help you.

Active Grammar

1. The comparative and superlative of one-syllable adjectives (**Ex:** *cheap*) and adverbs (**Ex:** *fast*) are generally made by _____.

Exceptions:

- Adjectives that end in a vowel plus a consonant (**Ex:** *hot*). These comparatives and superlatives are made by _____.

- Adjectives that end in *-e* (**Ex:** *nice*). These comparatives and superlatives are made by _____.

2. The comparative and superlative of two- and three-syllable adjectives (**Ex:** *popular*) and adverbs (**Ex:** *carefully*) are generally made by _____.

Exception:

- Two-syllable adjectives ending in *-y* (**Ex:** *sunny*). These comparatives and superlatives are made by _____.

3. (*Not*) *as . . . as* can also be used to make comparisons.

- Use (*not*) *as . . . as* to compare things that are _____ (**Ex:** *Often living overseas is not as attractive as it first seems*).

- Use *as . . . as* to compare things that are _____ (**Ex:** *The lifestyle in New Zealand is as laid-back as in Australia*).

4. Some adjectives and adverbs have irregular forms.

- good/well → better → _____
- bad/badly → _____ → the worst
- much → more → most
- little → less → least
- far → further → furthest

5. *Very* cannot be used to modify comparatives, but:

- *a bit*, *a little*, and *slightly* can be used to show _____ differences.

- *far*, *much*, and *a lot* can be used to show _____ differences.

See Reference page 132

8 Complete the second sentence so that it means the same as the first. Use the words in parentheses.

> **Ex:** *Spain is sunnier than the UK.*
> *The UK* _isn't as sunny as_ (isn't) *Spain.*

1. I'd prefer to live somewhere drier than this.
   I'd prefer to live somewhere that _____ (wet) this.

2. I'm a bit more adventurous now than I was ten years ago.
   Ten years ago I was _____ (slightly) I am now.

3. At home my life was a lot more complicated than it is abroad.
   My life abroad is _____ (much) than it was at home.

4. I don't think I planned my time on vacation carefully enough.
   I think I should've planned my time on vacation _____ (carefully).

5. My lifestyle in Canada now is not better or worse than it was in the US.
   My lifestyle here in Canada is _____ (as) it was in the US.

Speaking

9 Write six sentences about yourself using comparatives and superlatives as well as the ideas in Exercise 8 to help you. Write four true sentences and two false sentences.
Then read your sentences to another student. He or she will guess which two are false.

I'm more adventurous than I used to be.

Review

1 Circle the correct choices to complete the sentences.

1. I*'ve written/'ve been writing* emails all morning.
2. I*'ve seen/saw* a really awful movie yesterday.
3. My brother is in Shanghai. He's been there *for/since* a week.
4. She's very well traveled. She's *been/gone* to more than 20 countries.
5. Billy's the nicest person I've *ever/already* met.
6. I live in an apartment in Boston. I*'ve lived/lived* here for three years.
7. He's *worked/been working* in the yard for hours, and he's exhausted.
8. Would you like some coffee? I've *yet/just* made some.

2 Use the cues to write indirect questions for the underlined answers.

1. **A:** Would _____?
   (you/finish your homework)

   B: I'll definitely finish it by 12:00.

2. **A:** I'd _____?
   (can buy/theater tickets here)

   B: Yes, you can.

3. **A:** Can _____?
   (this store)

   B: It closes at 5:30.

4. **A:** Can _____?
   (the most interesting country/you ever visit)

   B: I'm not sure—either Japan or Russia.

3 Circle the correct choices to complete the sentences.

1. My suitcase is *much/more* heavier than yours.
2. Tania got the *worse/worst* test results in the whole class.
3. The exam wasn't as difficult *than/as* I'd expected.
4. You're the *most/more* helpful person I know.
5. People are far more *friendly/friendlier* here than in my country.
6. This one is *a/the* little more expensive than that one.
7. Which actor is the *better/best*: Brad Pitt or Leonardo DiCaprio?

4 One word is wrong in each sentence. Find the word and correct it.

1. We'll need an alarm clock because we're putting off very early in the morning.
2. I experienced country shock at first and found it hard to get used to living in a new place.
3. It was lovely having so many people to see me away at the station.
4. I'm glad I visited Japan as an independence traveler. You meet so many people that way.
5. I was petrifying the first time I tried to use the local language, but everything turned out fine.
6. Once you've been bitten by the tourist bug, you never want to come home.
7. We spent the day roaming on the park.
8. I'm at to Sue's house for the day.

Communication | exchange detailed information

5 **Pair Work** Which of the vacations in the photos appeals to you most? Why? What is the best vacation you've ever been on? Why? Discuss.

6 Do the quiz below with as many different students as possible. Make notes.

7a **SPEAKING EXCHANGE** Look at the notes you made about other students and read the descriptions on page 139. Which one do you think you are most like? Which one do you think each person you questioned is most like?

b Which students do you think would be the best and worst traveling companions for you? Why?

Who's your **ideal traveling** companion?

Are you an intrepid adventurer who loves sleeping under the stars, or someone who prefers a home away from home and all of life's luxuries? Who is your ideal traveling companion? And who would be a traveling companion for you?

Do the quiz and find out.

1 What would your ideal summer vacation be?
package vacation/beach/pool   independent travel
alone/with friends   camping   exploring jungle/desert, etc.
sports/activities (skiing, scuba diving, etc.)

2 What would you definitely pack in your suitcase?
romantic "easy-reading" novels   serious novels
magazines   guidebooks   study/work books
first aid kit   sunscreen   sleeping bag   penknife

3 How would you spend your ideal evening on vacation?
in the hotel restaurant   in your tent
in local restaurants trying different food
in various nightclubs

4 How long do you like your vacations to be?
not more than a week   two weeks
at least three or four weeks   open-ended

5 What do you dread most about your vacation?
missing favorite TV shows   missing friends/family
being bored   spiders/mosquitoes, etc.
toilets that don't work properly
being on a beach with only people of my nationality
not being able to speak the language   getting robbed

6 What are you most likely to bring home?
cheap perfume   a lot of photos
souvenirs from the airport   a tropical disease
a fantastic suntan   arts and crafts made by the locals

UNIT 7
Indulging yourself

A

B

C

D

Warm Up

1 **Pair Work** Discuss the questions.

1. What can you see in each photo? How do they represent self-indulgence?

2. In what other ways might people's lifestyles be described as "excessive" or self-indulgent?

2 **Pair Work** Discuss the meaning of the underlined words. Then ask and answer the questions.

1. Do you think spending $300 on a haircut is <u>excessive</u>?

2. When was the last time you bought something really <u>extravagant</u>?

3. If you could take one <u>luxury</u> to a desert island, what would it be?

4. Do you ever order <u>extra-large</u> portions in restaurants?

5. Do you think you were <u>spoiled</u> as a child? Why or why not?

6. When was the last time you bought something you thought was <u>overpriced</u>?

7. Do you think the idea of having a self-cleaning house in the near future is <u>far-fetched</u>?

8. Do you know anyone who would go on a <u>spending spree</u> to cheer him or herself up?

LESSON 1
Describe how to prepare and cook a dish CAN DO ✓
GRAMMAR count and noncount nouns

Reading

1 How does the photo below make you feel? Do you eat a lot of fast food? Why or why not? Discuss.

2a Read the article quickly. According to the filmmaker, what is the main message of the movie?

b Read the article again, and explain what each phrase means in context.
1. "the reality was a nightmare" (line 3)
2. "just how unhealthy it turned out to be" (lines 35–36)
3. "recommended stopping the experiment" (lines 45–46)
4. "an obligation to give their consumers information" (lines 63–64)
5. "his sense of humor and upbeat style" (line 81)
6. "have a relationship with each other" (lines 92–93)

3 **Group Work** Have you seen this movie? Would you like to see it? Why or why not? Discuss.

SUPER SIZE ME

Three trips to McDonald's a day might be every little boy's dream. But the reality was a nightmare for Morgan Spurlock, whose movie *Super Size Me*
5 **documents his one-month existence on fast food and its disastrous consequences. So, if it was so awful, why did he do it? And does it work as a movie?**

10 The premise of the movie is that Spurlock promises to eat three McDonald's meals a day, every day, for a month. He must only eat food from McDonald's, and every time an employee asks if he would
15 like to "super size" the meal, he must agree. "Super sizing" refers to the fact that with this type of meal you get a considerably larger portion of everything. Instead of the normal burger, fries, and
20 a drink, you get an extra-large burger, extra-large fries, and an extra-large drink for only a very small price increase.

Spurlock admitted that the whole experiment ignored any sensible eating
25 plan. He knew that by eating three McDonald's meals a day, he would be consuming more calories, fat, salt, and sugar per meal than he needed. Before he started, three doctors certified
30 that Spurlock was 183 cm tall (6 feet), weighed about 84 kg (184 lbs), and was in good health. Although both Spurlock and his doctors knew this diet was unhealthy, none of them were quite
35 prepared for just how unhealthy it turned out to be. The changes in his body were horrifying. In the first week, he put on 4.5 kg (9.9 lbs) in weight, and by the end of the 30 days he had gained nearly
40 14.5 kg (32 lbs), bringing his total weight to a massive 98 kg (216 lbs).

Weight gain was only one of the negative effects, however. When all three doctors saw the severe damage to his
45 liver, they all recommended stopping the experiment after 20 days. Spurlock continued to follow the diet, however, because he wanted to show people what this kind of diet can do to you. And you
50 begin to realize that the movie could be a picture of your own life: in 30 days you get to see what could happen to you over 20 or 30 years of overconsumption. You're on a path to heart disease, liver
55 failure, high blood pressure, diabetes, depression, and more.

"I think we need to take responsibility for ourselves," says Spurlock. "There also has to be some
60 responsibility on the part of the fast food companies. McDonald's alone feeds 46 million people every day. They have an obligation to give their consumers information about exactly what they're
65 eating." Spurlock also focuses on the advertising and marketing of fast food products, especially to children. McDonald's markets to children through Happy Meals (a children's meal in a box
70 including a free toy) and playgrounds in the restaurants. "The playgrounds aren't there just for kids to come and play," he says. "You're only allowed into the playground when you've bought a burger
75 or some fries or a Coke."

It's the humor above all that makes this movie work. Even toward the end of the month, when he admitted to feeling lethargic, depressed, and smelly,
80 the audience remains entertained by his sense of humor and upbeat style. Spurlock says that he hopes that the movie is entertaining, but he also hopes that it encourages people to take better
85 care of themselves. He says, "I'd love people to walk out of the movie and say, 'Next time I'm not going to super size. Maybe I'm not going to go there at all. I'm going to sit down and eat dinner
90 with my kids, with the TV off, so that we can eat healthy food, talk about what we're eating, and have a relationship with each other.'" Judging by critics and audiences alike, the movie certainly does
95 seem to be food for thought.

Grammar | count and noncount nouns

4a Look at the underlined words in the examples in the Active Grammar box. Is each one count or noncount?

Active Grammar

Examples

1. *He ate three McDonald's meals a day, every day, for a month.*

2. *He must only eat food from McDonald's.*

3. *I'll have sausage, beans, and a black coffee, please.*

4. *If I drink coffee in the evenings, I don't sleep well.*

Nouns

furniture	travel	meal	diet
chocolate	chicken	salt	trip
weather	burger	cake	hair
equipment	advice	food	iron
information	coffee	meat	fruit
business	sugar	news	
luggage	bread	paper	

See Reference page 133

b Divide the nouns in the Active Grammar box into three groups: count, noncount, and those that can be both. For the words that can be both, discuss what the difference in meaning is.

> *You can say "a coffee" when you're talking about a cup of coffee.*
> *You can say "some coffee" when you're not saying how much.*

Count	Noncount	Both

American English	British English
Use singular verb forms with collective nouns: the team/the government is	*Use plural verb forms with collective nouns: the team/the government are*

5 Circle the best choice to complete each sentence.

1. You haven't eaten very *much/many* fries.
2. I only have *a little/a few* sugar in my coffee nowadays.
3. There is too *much/many* traffic downtown.
4. She gave me *a little/a piece* of paper with her address on it.
5. He gave me *some/a piece* really good advice.
6. I've got *lots/many* of bags to carry. Can you help me?
7. I'll just have one *slice/piece* of pizza, please.
8. There were only *a little/a few* stores still open.

6a Correct the mistakes in the questions.

1. Have you given anyone a good advice recently?
2. How often do you watch a news on TV?
3. How many fruits do you usually eat every day?
4. Do you like a very hot weather?
5. Do you ever use the Internet to get an information?
6. When did you last buy some new furnitures?

b **Pair Work** Ask and answer the questions in Exercise 6a with a partner.

Vocabulary | food and cooking

7a Put these words into the correct place in the word map.

beef	an oven	a wooden spoon
salty	to bake	to scramble
sour	to boil	a frying pan
spicy	to grill	cabbage
bitter	a stove	to roast
sweet	a plate	a peach
to fry	parsley	a sauce pan

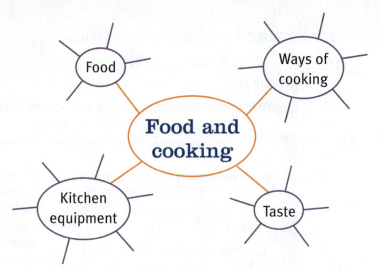

b **Pair Work** What is the difference between:

1. a range/an oven?
2. a vegetable/a vegetarian?
3. a plate/a dish?
4. rare/raw?
5. to stir/to beat?
6. to slice/to chop/to grate?

c Add at least two more words to each group of words in the word map.

8 Circle the correct choices to complete the sentences.

1. Sushi is a Japanese dish made with _raw/rare_ fish.
2. First, you _slice/chop_ the onion into small squares.
3. I don't eat many cookies. I find them too _sweet/sour_.
4. Fill a large saucepan with water and _bake/boil_ the pasta for ten minutes.
5. Macaroni and cheese is my favorite _dish/plate_.
6. On Thanksgiving, it's traditional to _bake/roast_ a turkey in the oven.
7. _Beat/Stir_ the sauce every five minutes.
8. What vegetable would you like—_cabbage/parsley_ or broccoli?

Speaking

9 ▶2.02 Listen to someone talking about a traditional Thanksgiving dinner. Do you think you would enjoy this meal?

10 **Group Work** Choose one of the things in the list below. Talk about how it is prepared and cooked.

1. your favorite dish
2. the last meal you made for guests
3. a traditional dish from your country
4. a dish you loved as a child
5. a dish you eat when you're feeling depressed
6. a dish you can't stand

Write a formal letter of complaint CAN DO ✔

GRAMMAR passive forms

Listening

1 **Group Work** What can you see in the photos? How do you think they are connected? Discuss.

2 ▶2.03 Listen and check your ideas.

3 Listen again and answer the questions.

1. Which items were mentioned in the report?
2. How much did each item sell for? Which was the most expensive, and why was it so valuable?
3. How much did the sellers originally pay for each item?
4. If you had the money, would you bid on any of these items? Why or why not? Discuss.
5. Have you ever visited eBay or a traditional auction? What do you think of these ways of buying and selling things? Discuss.

Vocabulary | verb phrases about money

4 **Pair Work** What is the difference in meaning between the underlined verb phrases in each pair of sentences? Discuss.

1. a. Lots of people <u>bid on</u> the chewing gum on eBay.
   b. That bag is very expensive. Why don't you try and <u>haggle for</u> it?
2. a. These boots were only $30. I think I <u>got a bargain</u>.
   b. I'd like to buy this T-shirt but it's slightly damaged. Could I <u>get a discount</u>?
3. a. You can <u>get a refund</u> within 28 days if you are not completely satisfied.
   b. <u>Get a receipt</u> just in case you want to take the CDs back.
4. a. I'd love to get a new camera, but I <u>can't afford</u> it at the moment.
   b. It'll cost $10 to take a taxi—it's <u>not worth</u> it. Let's walk instead.

5 Rewrite the sentences using the correct form of the phrases in Exercise 4.

1. One man offered to pay $5,000 for a chair at an auction.
2. Ten CDs for only $50—that's really cheap!
3. I asked if I could pay less, but the sales clerk said no.
4. I'd like to buy a motorcycle, but I don't have enough money.
5. The rent on that tiny house is much too expensive.
6. Don't forget to keep the paper they give you when you buy something.
7. This cell phone broke after only a week. I want my money back.
8. The merchants at the street market expect you to negotiate a lower price.

Grammar | passive forms

6 Look at the rules and examples in the Active Grammar box and answer these questions.

1. Which of the underlined verbs are active and which are passive?

2. For each pair of sentences, what is the reason for using the passive (not the active)?

Active Grammar

Examples

1. a. *The bikini was bought for $61,000.*

   b. *Someone bought the bikini for $61,000.*

2. a. *The bikini was bought by Robert Earl, the co-founder of Planet Hollywood.*

   b. *Robert Earl, the co-founder of Planet Hollywood, bought the bikini.*

Rules

- Use the passive when you want:

   a. to talk about actions, events, and processes when who or what causes the action, event, or process is unknown or unimportant. This is often the case in writing (or more formal speech).

   b. to put new information or longer expressions later in the sentence.

- **Form:** verb *to be* + past participle

See Reference page 133

7 Complete the email with the appropriate active or passive form of the verbs in parentheses.

Hi John,

Just a quick message to tell you about an auction I was ___taken___ (1. take) to in the city last week. I _____ (2. persuade) to go by some friends of mine, and although I wasn't very interested at first, I ended up having a great time. When we first got there, we _____ (3. give) a list of all the items in the auction, and then we _____ (4. have) some time to look at everything. Most of it was rock-and-roll memorabilia and there were some old records and things. I was a little nervous about bidding for things at first, but soon got into it.

Anyway, to cut a long story short, I _____ (5. buy) a large jukebox. It's really fantastic—and a real bargain, I think. It _____ (6. deliver) next week. But can I ask you a huge favor? You see, they said it _____ (7. could/not/send) more than 100 miles, so I _____ (8. give) them your address in the city. I hope that's OK! I _____ (9. arrange) for my uncle to pick it up from your place very soon, I promise. Then he'll look after it until I'm in the city again in the summer. Don't worry, when it arrives, you _____ (10. ask) to sign something but you won't have to pay anything. All the payment _____ (11. arranged) already.

I'll call soon to let you know the exact time of delivery.

All the best,

Gary

Speaking

8 **Group Work** Discuss what you would do in each situation and why.

1. You ordered your meal 40 minutes ago and you are still waiting.

2. Your brand new washing machine just broke down and some soapy clothes are stuck inside it.

3. You have just arrived at your vacation hotel. The hotel brochure claimed there was a swimming pool, but it hasn't been finished.

4. You realize that you bought four DVDs in a store yesterday, but you were charged for five.

9 **Pair Work** Roleplay one of the situations in Exercise 8. Use the language in the How To box to help you.

How To:

Complain in a store, restaurant, hotel, etc.

Customer asks to speak to someone	*I'd like to speak to the manager, please.* *Could I speak to Customer Service, please?*
Manager/ Assistant asks what problem is	*Can I help you?* *Can I be of any assistance?* *What seems to be the problem?*
Customer says what problem is	*My washing machine has stopped completely and there's a load of soapy clothes stuck inside.* *We've been waiting for our food for over an hour.*
Manager/ Assistant apologizes and offers a solution	*Oh, I'm very sorry about that, ma'am.* *I apologize for the inconvenience.* *We'll provide a replacement free of charge.* *Would you like a refund?*

Writing

10 Read the letter and the Useful Phrases box on page 144. Do the exercises.

11 Choose one of the situations in Exercise 8 or one of your own ideas and write a formal letter of complaint. Use the paragraph plan to help you.

Paragraph 1: State briefly what you're complaining about.

Paragraph 2: Give details about your complaint.

Paragraph 3: Give further details about your complaint (if necessary).

Paragraph 4: Say what you would like them to do.

CAN DO ✓

Reading

1 **Pair Work** Discuss the questions.

1. Do you have any pets? Did you use to have any pets when you were a child? If so, which ones? If not, why not?

2. What do you think are the main reasons people keep pets? Do you think it is a good idea for children to have pets? Why or why not?

3. What can you see in the photos?

2 Read the article quickly. Which of the things in the photos are mentioned?

3a Read the first paragraph again. Mark the statements below true (*T*), false (*F*), or don't know (*?*).

_____ 1. British owners spend €4 billion on their pets every year.

_____ 2. One quarter of owners buy their pets presents.

_____ 3. More pets than before have psychological problems.

_____ 4. Some owners have a problem knowing what to buy for their pets.

b Read the rest of the article. Which pets are mentioned? What do their owners do for them, and why?

4 **Group Work** Do you think pets should be treated like members of the family? In general, what is the attitude toward pets in your country? Discuss.

Pet heaven?

In some parts of Europe and the US, many pet owners see their cat or dog as a member of the family. In the UK, owners spend an amazing €4 billion (about $5,640,000,000) annually on keeping their pets in shape, healthy, and entertained. In one survey, it was found that up to 40 percent of owners said they bought gifts for their pets, including Christmas and birthday presents. Owners happily pamper their pets with increasingly lavish lifestyles, including toys, furniture, accessories, and "gourmet" food. There are also pet psychologists for those with problems, pet passports for those who want to travel, and a whole range of services on offer. There are hundreds of retail outlets offering owners a vast array of products. But many pets have everything they could ever ask for. The question for many owners now is: What do you give to the pet that has everything? We asked some owners what their pet got for his or her last birthday . . .

Sylvia and Brad Phillips and their cat Princess: The Phillips family, from California, acquired Princess three years ago when some friends emigrated. "We didn't really know much about cats then, and at first we didn't know how it would work out," says Sylvia. "But right from the start, she just made our family complete and the kids adore her. They're always finding new things to buy for her. She probably is spoiled but it's fun." Last year, they got her a present they were really excited about: a custom-made outfit that cost about $150. "She doesn't really wear it because it seems to irritate her, but we took some great photos!" says Sylvia.

Claudette and Pierre Leroi and their dog Mignon: Claudette and Pierre live in Paris with their Yorkshire terrier, Mignon. Because Mignon is a longhaired dog, Claudette says that it's necessary to take her to the hairdresser regularly. "I take her to the beauty parlor once a week to have her hair done. I don't think it's a luxury really." Mignon has it washed and brushed and sometimes cut and even curled. On special occasions, like her last birthday, for example, Mignon had the hair on the top of her head pulled back and tied as a ponytail, while the rest of her hair was cut short. "She looked so cute—like a little Barbie doll," says Claudette. She gets the dog anesthetized to do these things so that she stands still for long enough, but Claudette thinks it's worth it.

So has all this pet indulgence gone too far? Or is it simply spoiling a valued member of the family?

Grammar | causative forms: *have/get (something) done*

5a Complete the examples in the Active Grammar box using *had*, *have*, and *gets*. Then complete the rule of form with the correct part of speech.

b In the examples, is this structure used to talk about: **a)** doing something ourselves or **b)** arranging for something to be done by somebody else?

Active Grammar

Examples

- *I take her to the beauty parlor to _____ (1.) her hair done.*

- *On her last birthday, Mignon _____ (2.) the hair on the top of her head pulled back and tied as a ponytail.*

- *She _____ (3.) the dog anesthetized so that she stands still at the hairdresser.*

Form: *have* (or *get*) + object + _____ (4.)

Rules

We can use the causative:

- with *have* or *get*, to talk about things that happen to us.

  *I **had** my bag stolen on my way home from work.*

  *She **got** her fingers caught in the car door.*

- with *get* only (not *have*), to mean "finish doing something."

  *As soon as I **get** this essay written, I'll take the dog out.*

See Reference page 133

6 Find the mistakes in six of the sentences and correct them.

1. I've never had my car clean.
2. I've had my house broken into several times.
3. I never my house have decorated—I do it myself.
4. I haven't had my eyes testing in years.
5. I've got a lot of things to get doing by this weekend.
6. I have dry-cleaned some of my clothes every month.
7. I really need to have my hair cut soon.
8. I'd like to get my photo took by a professional photographer.

Speaking

7 **Pair Work** Discuss.

1. Change the sentences in Exercise 6 so they are true for you. Tell another student.

> *It's true I haven't had my eyes tested in years. I think I should have it done soon because my eyes hurt when I use a computer.*

2. What things do you have done regularly? Why? What things can you have done in your neighborhood?

> *I have my hair colored once a month! I know it's extravagant, but I hate doing it myself.*

Vocabulary | animal idioms

8a **Pair Work** With a partner, divide the animals in the box below into six groups.

Ex: *eagle, duck = birds*

dog	~~duck~~	spider	bear
fly	cat	whale	~~eagle~~
bat	fish	horse	bull

b Add at least three more words to each group.

9a ▶2.04 Label the parts of the animals in the pictures using the words in the box. Then listen and check your answers.

fur	paws	wings	feathers
fins	horns	hooves	whiskers
tail	claws	beak	talons

b **Pair Work** Describe an animal using the words in the box. Your partner will guess which animal it is.

> *This animal's body is covered in furry hair. It has four paws, and it wags its tail when it's happy.*

10 ▶2.05 Complete the expressions in *italics* by writing the name of one animal in each blank. Then listen and check your answers.

1. I didn't just hear about Kim's party from someone else—she told me herself. It was *straight from the _____'s mouth.*

2. I've got to tell John the bad news, but I feel really bad about it. I'll just have to *take the _____ by the horns* and do it.

3. I need glasses for most things nowadays. *I'm as blind as a _____* without them!

11a Match the expressions in Exercise 10 with their definitions below.

____ **a.** to have very bad eyesight

____ **b.** first hand information from the original source

____ **c.** to confidently deal with a difficult or dangerous situation

b **Group Work** Choose two of the expressions and tell other students about a person or situation using them.

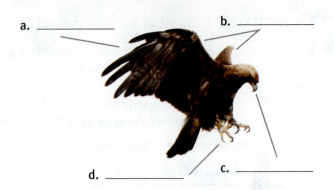

a. _____   b. _____

c. _____

d. _____

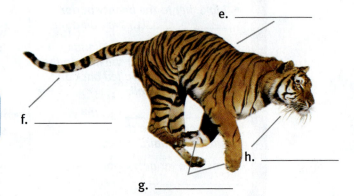

e. _____

f. _____

g. _____   h. _____

i. _____

j. _____

k. _____

Review

1 Circle the correct choices to complete the sentences.

1. Could you give me *an/some* information about train times, please?
2. I've got two large pieces of *luggage/luggages*.
3. How *many/much* furniture do you have in your living room?
4. The news *is/are* always so depressing.
5. He's been doing *a/some* research into global warming.
6. There were only *few/a few* people there when I arrived.
7. I'd like *a/some* piece of toast with jam and an orange juice, please.
8. Can I give you *an/some* advice about studying for your exam?

2 Complete each sentence with the correct tense of a verb from the box. Use the passive form.

> fix   catch   employ   deliver   open   send   charge   include

1. Service _____ in the bill so you don't need to leave a tip.
2. I _____ some flowers yesterday but I don't know who they're from.
3. The goods that you ordered _____ next Friday.
4. My car broke down last week. It _____ right now.
5. Don't use the medicine if the bottle _____ already.
6. It's unlikely that the robbers _____ .
7. I was annoyed because we _____ for a dessert we didn't order.
8. She was fired after she _____ by that company for over 15 years.

3 Look at part of Tilly's schedule and imagine that today is Tuesday and it's 1:30 P.M. Write sentences about what she *had done*, *is having done*, and *will have done*.

> She had her living room
> decorated yesterday.

1. _____
2. _____
3. _____
4. _____
5. _____
6. _____
7. _____
8. _____

Monday

10:30 A.M. Decorator (living room)
Pick car up from garage (change tires)
Delivery of new stove (after 5 P.M.)

Tuesday

Haircut (& highlights) 9:15 A.M.
Carpet installers (living room)—between 1
and 2 P.M.
Take watch to repair shop—don't forget!

Wednesday

Eye exam (optician on Main Street) 10:00 A.M.
Window washer (A.M.)
Don't forget to take coat to dry cleaners

Communication | use persuasive language to get satisfaction from a service provider

4a **Pair Work** Complete the word maps for each of the places in the photos. Include as many words as you can which are related to each place.

b Compare your words with other students.

5a Which of the sentences would you expect to hear in a restaurant, a shoe store, or a hair salon?

<u> shoe store </u> ____ 1. I'd like to try these on, please.

_____ ____ 2. I'll have the grilled tuna, please.

_____ ____ 3. Just a cut and blow-dry?

_____ ____ 4. I have a black in size 38, but not in 39.

_____ ____ 5. Rare, please.

_____ ____ 6. I'd also like to have some highlights done.

_____ ____ 7. A bottle of mineral water—sparkling, please.

_____ ____ 8. Oh, they look really nice on you. How do they feel?

_____ ____ 9. I'd like to make an appointment.

_____ <u>1</u> 10. Yes, we have a reservation for two for Morrison.

waiter

restaurant

knife

clothes store/ shoe store

fitting room

b ▶2.06 Listen to three conversations and number the sentences in Exercise 5a in the order you hear them.

hair salon

scissors

6a Look at the chart and make notes about some more things that people complain about in the three places.

Restaurant	Shoe or clothes store	Hair salon
undercooked food *slow service*	*dirty shoes* *missing buttons*	*hair cut too short* *hair dyed wrong color*

b **Pair Work** Choose a place from the chart and decide on one or two things to complain about. Roleplay the situation. Then change situations and roles.

UNIT 8
Aiming for success

A

B

C

D

Warm Up

1 **Pair Work** Describe the photos. What do you think the people had to do to achieve their success?

2 ▶2.07 Complete the sentences with the correct form of the words and phrases from the box. Then listen and check your answers.

> go under   best-seller   have had their day   give up   up to snuff   give it a try

1. If the business continues to lose money, it will probably _____ and have to close.
2. His book's been an instant _____. Everybody's talking about it.
3. Just because you failed this exam doesn't mean you should _____. You can always retake it in October.
4. I think these reality TV shows _____. No one watches them anymore.
5. I'm afraid your work really isn't _____. You'll just have to redo it.
6. I'm not sure that pushing the car will help start it, but you can _____.

3 **Pair Work** Tell another student about the last time you felt you achieved something special.

Reading

1 Discuss the questions.

1. Is leadership a natural-born talent or a learned skill?
2. What qualities does a successful leader need?
3. In what situations do people need to work together as a group?
4. Does every group need a leader? Why or why not?

2 Read the article quickly and match the questions above with the correct paragraphs. Write the number in the box.

3 Read the article again. Mark the statements below true (*T*), false (*F*), or don't know (*?*).

____ 1. Being able to work in a group is one of the most important life skills.

____ 2. Groups of people doing social activities generally don't need leaders.

____ 3. Members of leaderless groups often stop attending.

____ 4. Antonio Carluccio thinks he is a natural-born leader.

____ 5. Good leaders are often slightly afraid of their role.

____ 6. Good leaders should do more work than the other group members.

Are YOU a successful leader?

Our company specializes in training you to be a successful leader for whatever situation you're in.

A

Almost nothing we do in this world is done in isolation. At work or at play, you'll find yourself in groups, working with other people: your team at work, a meeting with co-workers, your family, a vacation with friends, a group of students working together, a day out hiking in the mountains, a group of neighbors wanting to make changes. It is now recognized that being able to work successfully with other people is one of the major keys to success, partly because we need to do it so often.

B

In almost every situation where you're in a group, you will need a skilled leader. All groups need leaders, and all successful groups have good leaders. Groups without leaders or with weak leaders almost always break down. Members of a leaderless group often begin to feel dissatisfied and frustrated. Time is wasted and the tasks are not achieved. There are often arguments and tension between people, as there is nobody to keep the goals clear. Some personalities dominate and others disappear. Often group members begin not to come to meetings in order to avoid more disharmony.

C

Some people are natural leaders. The celebrity chef Antonio Carluccio says, "True leaders are born and you can spot them in kitchens. They're people who combine toughness, fairness, and humor." Although a lot of people agree that there are some natural-born leaders, most people now recognize that leadership can also be taught. Our professional and experienced staff can train almost anyone how to be a successful leader. Good leaders don't make people do things in a bossy, controlling way. You can learn how to involve everyone, encouraging the whole group to work toward a common goal.

D

Our training courses use activities and techniques to develop a range of qualities that are necessary to be a good leader. Self-confidence is vital to overcoming your own fears about being a leader. Successful leaders also need to be calm and intelligent. They need to be able to work out good strategies and make sound judgments under pressure. Finally, and probably most importantly, good leaders need to be sensitive, sociable, and be able to get along with a wide range of people. Good leadership is essentially the ability to influence others, and good leaders allow all members of the group to contribute.

Grammar | stating preferences: *It's time/I'd rather/I'd better*

4 ▶2.08 Listen to the work appraisal session and decide which sentence best summarizes the main points.

    1. He's doing well in his role of team leader but would like some more training.

    2. He's interested in becoming a team leader but would like some training first.

5a ▶2.09 Complete the examples from the listening in the Active Grammar box. Then listen and check your answers.

Active Grammar

Examples

1. *I think I _____ you did the first course.*

2. *I feel that _____ I moved up.*

3. *I _____ not wait for two months.*

4. *I _____ get your name on the list right away.*

Rules

a. **Form:** *It's time* + subject + _____

   Meaning: to talk about when you should have done something already or at least started it

b. **Form:** subject + *would rather* + object + _____ (+ *than . . .*)

   Meaning: to talk about what you'd prefer someone else to do

c. **Form:** subject + *would rather* + _____ (+ *than . . .*)

   Meaning: to talk about what you'd prefer to do

d. **Form:** subject + *had better* + _____

   Meaning: to talk about something when it is advisable to do it (in the present or future)

See Reference page 134

b Complete the rules in the Active Grammar box by writing *past tense* or *verb*.

6 ▶2.10 Complete the excerpt from the dialog. Use *it's time, I'd rather,* or *I'd better* and the correct form of the verb in parentheses. Then listen and check your answers.

Anna: Hi, Will. How did your appraisal go?

Will: It went well, thanks. My boss thinks _____ (**1.** take) more responsibility and maybe even became a team leader.

Anna: Oh, that's good.

Will: Yeah. I was thinking of looking for a new job, but now I think _____ (**2.** stay) here.

Anna: I'd love it if you were our team leader. _____ (**3.** have) you in charge than someone we don't know.

Will: Thanks. Listen, I've got a meeting in five minutes. _____ (**4.** go). See you later.

Speaking

7 **Pair Work** Write three sentences about you starting with *It's time . . .* Then compare with a partner.

> *It's time I changed jobs.*

Vocabulary | describing personality

8 **Group Work** Work in two groups. Find the meanings and pronunciation of the adjectives in your group below. Then explain them to the other group.

> **Group A:** outgoing   open   proactive   opinionated   single-minded

> **Group B:** easygoing   selfish   witty   manipulative   headstrong

9 ▶ **2.11** Listen to people describing different people they know. Which adjective from Exercise 8 describes each person?

10 **Pair Work** Tell your partner about three people you know who you can describe using some of the adjectives in Exercise 8.

> *My sister is a very headstrong person. She really wanted to travel around the world on her own. Everyone tried to persuade her not to because it was dangerous, but she decided to do it anyway and . . .*

11 Match the expressions in the box with the correct picture. In pairs, say what you think each expression means.

> _____ be really high maintenance   _____ be a party animal   _____ be a complete doormat
> _____ be the center of attention   _____ be down-to-earth

12 **Group Work** Talk about yourself and the different sides of your personality. First think about how you behave in different situations. Use the situations from the box and your own ideas.

> leading a discussion at work or school
> making a complaint in a store or restaurant
> talking about yourself in a job interview
> being in a crowd of people at a party
> cooking for a small group of friends
>
> giving a presentation at work
> performing on stage
> playing a team sport (**Ex:** football)
> organizing a group of children

Report and describe what people say CAN DO ✓

GRAMMAR reported speech

Vocabulary | gradable and nongradable adjectives

1 Match each photo with the most appropriate feeling in the box. What do you think is happening or has happened in each case?

> ____ totally single-minded
> ____ completely ecstatic
> ____ absolutely devastated

2a Read the examples in the chart below. Then complete the rules with the missing words.

Examples
Gradable (common) adjectives
*He missed a very **important** goal.*
*He is a really **big** success.*
Nongradable (intense) adjectives
*He missed a completely **vital** goal.*
*He is feeling totally **distraught**.*

Rules
Gradable (common) adjectives:
• Use common intensifiers such as _____ or _____ to make these adjectives stronger.
Nongradable (intense) adjectives:
• These adjectives are already strong, so use special intensifiers such as _____ or _____ to make these stronger.

b Match the adjectives on the left to those with similar meanings on the right.

____ 1. happy   a. starving

____ 2. upset   b. ecstatic

____ 3. hungry   c. exhausted

____ 4. tired   d. devastated

c Circle the correct intensifier to complete each sentence.

1. She must be *very/totally* ecstatic about her success.

2. A *completely/really* big sports stadium just opened near here.

3. She was *absolutely/very* filthy after playing soccer all afternoon.

4. I love running. I'd be *totally/very* devastated if I had to give it up.

3 **Pair Work** Think of a true story about you that relates to one of the phrases in the box in Exercise 1. Tell your partner what happened.

> *I couldn't believe it when I won the prize for best actor. I was completely ecstatic!*

Grammar | reported speech

4a ▶ 2.12 Listen and complete the sentences and questions with the missing words.

1. _____ to be the best player on the field.
2. _____ the race easily.
3. _____ to practice _____ .

4. _____ succeed if you're confident.
5. Why _____ so negative?
6. _____ help _____?

b Compare the reported speech in the Active Grammar box with the direct speech above. Find examples of the changes and write them on the lines.

Active Grammar

Examples

- *Andy Cole said (that) he wanted to be the best player onto the field.*

- *She said (that) she had won the race easily.*

- *He told me (that) he wasn't going to practice that day.*

- *I told him (that) he could succeed if he was confident.*

- *I asked him why he was feeling so negative.*

- *She asked me if I would help her the next day.*

1. Tense changes
   Ex: go → went: _want → wanted_

2. Modal verb changes
   Ex: can → could: _____

3. Subject pronoun changes
   Ex: I → he: _____

4. Object pronoun changes
   Ex: me → him: _____

5. Time reference changes
   Ex: now → then: _____

6. Word order changes
   Ex: were they going → they were going: _____

Rules

a. *That* can be used after both *say* and *tell*, but it isn't necessary.

b. Don't use an object after *say*.

c. An object must be used after *tell*.

d. A question word is used when reporting *Wh-* questions.

e. *If* is used when reporting *Yes/No* questions.

f. The rule that changes the tense or modal verb back is sometimes ignored. This can happen if the situation is still true, or for dramatic effect when telling a story.

See Reference page 134

---

5 Read the rules in the Active Grammar box and correct these sentences.

1. She told that she couldn't come to practice this evening.
2. She said him she had taken up basketball the previous January.
3. I asked her she wanted to come over and watch the game.

6a Check that you understand the meanings of the underlined verbs in the sentences below.

1. Nobody needed to <u>remind</u> him to focus on the goal.
2. She <u>admitted</u> feeling totally out of control.
3. He <u>explained</u> that he wanted to compete in the Olympics.
4. I <u>promise</u> to go swimming at least three times a week.
5. I <u>suggested</u> talking to a sports psychologist.
6. They <u>decided</u> to buy tickets for the football game.
7. My coach <u>warned</u> me that the training would be very hard.

b Write the underlined verbs from Exercise 6a in the correct place in the chart.

Verbs	Constructions
say,	verb + (*that*)
tell,	verb + object + (*that*)
ask,	verb + object + infinitive
	verb + infinitive
	verb + gerund

7 Report these statements, starting with the words in parentheses.

1. "I broke the window yesterday when I kicked a ball through it by mistake." (He admitted . . .)
2. "Why don't we try the new Italian restaurant when we go out on Friday?" (He suggested . . .)
3. "I think I'll stay in tonight because I'm completely exhausted." (She decided . . .)
4. "I'm going to buy my girlfriend some flowers." (He told . . .)
5. "Are you going to get movie tickets in advance, or are you going to just show up?" (She asked . . .)
6. "You really shouldn't be late for your interview this afternoon." (She warned . . .)
7. "Please all bring your homework to me by 9:00 on Monday morning." (The teacher reminded . . .)
8. "I'll pay you back all the money I owe you by tomorrow." (He promised . . .)

Speaking

8 **Pair Work** Tell your partner about one of the following. Use reported speech.

1. three things that you've seen or heard in the news in the last week
2. three things that three different people have said to you in the last 24 hours

9a Look at the photos. Discuss what you think is happening in each one.

b Think about someone who has helped you to succeed in something. Make notes using the questions below to help you.

1. What were you trying to do? And when?
2. Who helped you?
3. What did he or she suggest that really helped?
4. What did you learn from this person?
5. How did you feel when you succeeded?

10 **Group Work** Tell other students about the person who helped you succeed.

Reading

1   **Group Work** Look at the photo and discuss the questions.

    1. How old is the child in the photo? Is he old enough to be in school? Why?

    2. At what age did you start going to school? Did you study or learn anything at home before that?

    3. Do you remember your childhood as a stressful time?

2   Read the article. Compare your answers in Exercise 1 to Maddie's life.

Getting into Preschool— Hardly Easy!

1   Madison Evans was listening to Mozart and Beethoven while still in the womb to enhance her intelligence and creativity. She was hardly born when her parents hooked her up with the Baby
5   Einstein DVD program. The colors, music, and shapes all stimulated her brain. At ten months she started an early reading program. It is no surprise then that at the ripe old age of 2, hardly out of diapers, she is going through a rigorous school application process
10 comparable to high school seniors trying to get into college. Madison, known to most as Maddie, lives in New York City, and she is trying to get into preschool.

Maddie's parents are preparing applications to ten schools. Today she is at her sixth interview, and she
15 knows the drill. Unlike the little boy before them, she didn't have a tantrum when the director asked him to come into the classroom with her. And unlike three interviews ago she didn't cling to her mom, making an immediate negative impression. Today she bravely took
20 the woman's hand and marched into the classroom for her interview. Now Maddie's parents anxiously wait behind closed doors, hoping their little girl makes a good impression. They've been working so hard on this application process. They can hardly wait to reap the
25 rewards. She has to get in somewhere, right?

Why is it so hard to get into a preschool in large US cities like New York, Boston, or Washington DC? More families are choosing to live in large cities rather than move to the suburbs. The result is more children,
30 fewer spots in schools, and parents willing to spend a lot of money to secure one of those spots. There is also pressure for kids to attend the best high schools to get into the best colleges, and getting into the best high schools in turn means getting into the best elementary
35 schools, and so on—all the way down to preschool.

But in reality, there is hardly any guarantee. After a long year which was hard both on her and her parents, Maddie got into two very good preschools. But who's to say that Maddie really has a greater chance of getting
40 into Harvard in 16 years? She may very well crack under the fierce competition of her private school. She might drop out of high school and not even make it to college. But don't let Maddie's parents hear this. They would be totally devastated—and understandably so.
45 After all, they are just trying give their child what they think is best.

3 Find these words and phrases in the article. Write a short definition for each one.

1. in the womb (line 2)
2. ripe old age (line 8)
3. rigorous (line 9)
4. knows the drill (line 15)
5. have a tantrum (line 16)
6. cling (line 18)
7. reap the rewards (lines 24–25)
8. in turn (line 34)

4 **Group Work** What are the advantages and disadvantages of pushing children to study and learn at such a young age? Discuss.

Grammar | adjectives and adverbs: *hard* and *hardly*

5 Look at the examples in the Active Grammar box. Decide if the words in bold are adjectives or adverbs. Explain the meaning of each one in other words (not using *hardly*).

> ### Active Grammar
>
> **Examples**
>
> 1. *Studying every weekend for my exams was **hard** work.*
> 2. *The children are encouraged to work **hard** for their exams.*
> 3. *At the age of 2, she is **hardly** out of diapers.*
> 4. *I'm very tired this morning. I **hardly** slept last night.*
> 5. *I have **hardly** any money. I must go to the bank.*
> 6. *She **hardly** ever comes to visit us. Just once or twice a year.*
>
> *Hardly* means almost not or very little. It is often used with *any*(thing/one/where, etc.) and *ever*. It is not used with negative words (~~I hardly never eat chocolate~~).

See Reference page 134

6 Complete the sentences with *hardly* and the correct form of a verb from the box.

> know   say   believe   walk   change   have

1. I'm very busy these days. I _____ any time to go to the gym.
2. Are you OK? You _____ a word during dinner.
3. Doesn't Tom look amazing? He's _____ at all since we were in college.
4. I don't understand why that woman from the office was so friendly. I _____ her.
5. Her leg is hurting her a lot. She says she can _____ at the moment.
6. I was shocked when she told me he had left. I could _____ it.

Speaking

7 **Pair Work** Complete the sentences so they are true for you. Then compare your answers in pairs.

1. The last time I studied hard . . . _____
2. At school/work, I hardly ever . . . _____
3. Recently, I've hardly been to any . . . _____

8 Read the questions below and make notes of your answers.

1. What are the three most important things that help children to do well at school?
2. Which three subjects should children spend the most time studying at school?
3. What are the most important qualities of a good teacher?
4. What are the three most important things that help people to do well at work?
5. Which three job skills should people be trained in?
6. What are the most important qualities of a good manager?

9a **Group Work** Ask other students the questions in Exercise 8 and note their responses. Use the How To box to help you answer.

How To:	
Give your opinion	
Give your opinion	*I believe small class sizes are crucial . . .*
	As far as I'm concerned, math is the most important subject . . .
Justify your opinion	*. . . because the teacher can spend more time with each child.*
	. . . for several reasons; first, you need math for a lot of things in everyday life . . .
	If a teacher is approachable, then children will feel free to ask questions.

b Report the main findings to the class.

Writing

10 Read the report and the Useful Phrases on page 145. Do the exercises.

11 **Group Work** Discuss with other students which words or phrases in the report might be useful in other similar reports.

12 Write a 120–140 word report on one of the topics in Exercise 8. Divide the report into separate paragraphs.

Review

1 Correct the mistakes in the sentences.

1. I'd better went to the stores before they close.
2. Had you rather I didn't say anything to your boss?
3. I'd rather not working this weekend, if at all possible.
4. Would you better take a raincoat in case it rains?
5. What's that smell? I think it's time you get the cake out of the oven.
6. I'd rather took just carry-on luggage on the plane than a large suitcase.

2 Write sentences in the past using the cues.

Ex: Zoë/say/can't remember/where/leave/keys

Zoë said she couldn't remember where she had left the keys.

1. Tony/ask/I like/play/tennis/this weekend

_____

2. They/tell/best time/visit Egypt/be/in January or February

_____

3. Helen/say/not know/what time/firework display/start

_____

4. He/ask/me when/I want/go/see/the play

_____

5. My boss/tell/I have to/make/presentation/at sales conference/in March

_____

6. The newspaper/say/one/our athletes/win/a big race

_____

3 Circle the correct choices to complete the sentences.

1. She promised *to do/doing* all her homework before she went out to see her friend.
2. Can you explain *me/to me* exactly how this gadget works?
3. They decided *to sell/selling* their house and move to the country.
4. My doctor suggested *taking/to take* a week off work.
5. Will you remind me *to go/going* to the post office this afternoon?
6. He admitted *being/be* wrong about the train schedule.
7. They warned *us/to us* that the weather conditions would make walking into the mountains very dangerous.

4 Complete the sentences with *hard* or *hardly*.

1. I'm going to work _____ on my math homework from now until the end of the year.
2. We _____ have any time to see friends at the moment. Life is just too busy!
3. I could _____ believe it when she said they were going to get married!
4. If you look _____, you can just see Michael on the other side of the parking lot.
5. _____ anyone came to opening night of the restaurant. It was very disappointing.
6. It will be a long, _____ climb to the top of the mountain.

Communication | give and seek personal views and opinions

5   Discuss the questions.

   1.   What can you see in the picture above?
   2.   How often do you listen to the radio?
   3.   What different kinds of radio programs do you know?

6a   ▶ 2.13   Listen to the excerpt from a radio call-in show. What is the reason for each person's call?

b   Listen again and decide what advice you would give each caller and why.

7   Do you ever listen to this kind of radio program? Why or why not? Who do you usually go to for advice about problems? Discuss.

8a   **Group Work** Decide on some interesting problems for a radio call-in show.

b   **Pair Work** Roleplay calling a radio program and asking for advice. Then change the situation and change roles.

Crime solvers

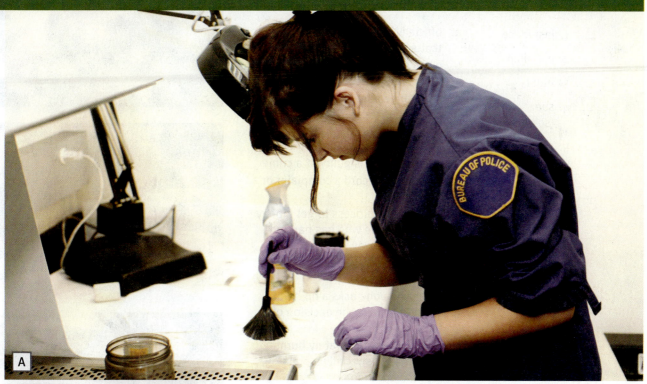

A

B

C

D

Warm Up

1a How are the photos connected to the topic of crime?

b Think of words and expressions connected with crime and the law. Write them in the chart.

Court	Crime	Criminal	Evidence	Punishment
			fingerprints	*community service*

2 Explain these newspaper headlines. Use a dictionary if necessary.

1. **Cyber Crime Up by 50%**

2. **Overcrowded Prisons Slammed in New Report**

3. **Chaos in Fraud Case after Witness Intimidation**

4. Suspended Sentence for Teacher in Road Rage Incident

3 Do you think crime is increasing or decreasing where you live?

Vocabulary | insurance and court cases

1 Match the words and phrases to their definitions.

_____ 1. insurance

_____ 2. premium

_____ 3. fraud

_____ 4. sue (someone)

_____ 5. an appeal

_____ 6. arson

_____ 7. convict (someone of)

_____ 8. sentence (someone to)

_____ 9. file (a lawsuit)

a. officially decide in a court of law that someone is guilty of a crime

b. when someone deceives people to get money

c. an arrangement to pay a company money and it pays the costs if you are sick, have a car accident, etc.

d. give a legal punishment to someone who is guilty of a crime

e. to officially record a complaint or a law case

f. start a legal process to get money from someone who has harmed you in some way

g. an amount of money that you pay for insurance

h. when someone asks a higher court to change the decision of a lower court

i. the crime of deliberately burning something, especially a building, for insurance money

2 Complete the sentences with the correct form of the words and phrases from Exercise 1.

1. She plans to _____ the hospital after they gave her the wrong operation.

2. Bart was _____ to three years in prison for his part in the robbery.

3. We lost the case this time, but there's going to be _____. We will never give up.

4. My health insurance _____ has gone up again. They say it's because of rising medical costs.

5. My neighbor was _____ of shoplifting, but luckily he doesn't have to go to prison.

6. Does this _____ policy cover things that are stolen from me while I'm on vacation?

7. They don't think the fire was an accident. They think it was _____.

8. He's been arrested and charged with _____. Apparently, he pretended that an expensive painting had been stolen to get the insurance money.

9. Ted's wife has _____ for divorce. I hope he has a good lawyer.

3 **Group Work** Discuss the questions.

1. Imagine you buy coffee in a fast food restaurant. Then you spill the hot coffee and are badly burned. Should you sue the fast food company? Why or why not?

2. Do you know of any famous cases of fraud? If so, what happened?

3. What different things do people insure? Have you ever heard about anyone insuring something strange?

Listening

4 ▶ **2.14** Listen to a story about a crime involving cigars. What was the crime? Why do the people find it funny?

5 Listen again. Put these sentences in the order in which they happen in the story.

_____ a. The lawyer is arrested.

_____ b. The insurance company refuses to pay.

_____ c. He makes a claim against the insurance company.

_____ d. The lawyer is sentenced to jail.

_____ e. He smokes the cigars.

_____ f. The insurance company pays the lawyer.

_____ g. He insures the cigars against fire.

_____ h. The lawyer sues the insurance company.

_____ i. A lawyer buys some rare cigars.

Grammar | dependent clauses: sequencing

6 Look at the examples in the Active Grammar box. Then circle the correct part of speech to complete each rule.

Active Grammar

Examples	Rules
• *Having cashed the check, the lawyer was arrested.* • *After cashing the check, the lawyer was arrested.*	Use the following two forms to describe the order of events in a story.

(Clause 1)		(Clause 2)
a. *Having +* present participle / past participle,		simple past
b. *After +* present participle / past participle,		simple past

See Reference page 135

7 Complete each sentence with the correct form of a verb from the box.

> stay   promise   go   win

1. Having _____ to the bank a number of times, the robbers knew just how to rob it.
2. After _____ to pick his friend up from the police station, Terry completely forgot.
3. Having _____ her lawsuit, she decided to go out and celebrate.
4. After _____ at the office until midnight, she decided to give herself the next day off.

8 **Pair Work** Tell a partner about three things that happened to you last week and what you did after each one.

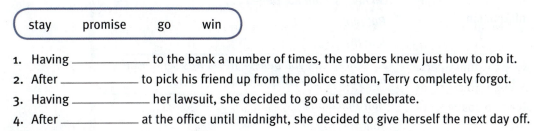

> *After doing my English homework, I collapsed on the sofa and fell asleep.*

Speaking

9 **SPEAKING EXCHANGE** Work in two groups: A Students and B Students. A Students look at the pictures for Story 1 below. B Students look at the pictures for Story 2 on page 142. Work with a partner from your group. Use the pictures to figure out your story.

Story 1

10 Check your ideas by reading the story.
(Story 1 is on page 138. Story 2 is on page 141.)

11a Use the expressions in the How To box to prepare to tell your story.

How To:	
Tell a funny story	
Introduce the story	***Did you hear the story about*** the man who stole a parrot?
	Have you heard the one about the robber who fell asleep?
Introduce important information	*So here's what happened . . .*
	But that's not all . . .
	And then . . .
Keep the funny part until the very end	*. . . and so can you believe it? He was sentenced to 24 months in jail and a $24,000 fine.*
Reacting to the story	*How ridiculous!*
	You're kidding!
	Unbelievable!
	No way!

b **Pair Work** Show your partner your pictures and tell your story. Use the How To box to react to your partner's story.

Grammar | past modals of deduction: *must/might/can't have*

1 Look at the photos. What do you think is happening?

2 ▶ 2.15 Listen to the conversation. What do the people say is happening in the photos?

3 Use the examples in the Active Grammar box to complete the rules.

Active Grammar

Examples

1. He **must have set up** some kind of security camera.

2. He **might have done it** before.

3. He **can't have realized** he was being caught on tape.

Rules

a. Use _____ _____ + past participle to say that you think something is possible in the past.

b. Use _____ _____ + past participle to say that you think something is not possible in the past.

c. Use _____ _____ + past participle to say that you are certain about something in the past.

See Reference page 135

4 ▶ 2.16 Complete the sentences using *must have*, *might have*, or *can't have*, and the correct form of a verb from the box. Then listen and check your answers.

> go   forgot   drop   tell   finish   be   leave   spend

1. We don't know who took the money. There were a lot of people in the office during the day and it _____ any of them.

2. I wonder why Pete didn't turn up to do his community service. He _____ about it. I reminded him yesterday.

3. I'm not sure where Jo is. She _____ over to Sally's. They're working on a school project together.

4. How did you know about the surprise party? Someone _____ you!

5. You _____ your whole paycheck already. You only got paid yesterday!

6. I _____ my keys at home. I remember feeling them in my jacket pocket when I got on the bus.

7. She _____ her homework yet. She only started it a few minutes ago.

8. I lost one of my gloves. I _____ it on the way to work.

5 ▶ 2.17 Listen to the news program. How did the police find the photos from Exercise 1?

Vocabulary | compound adjectives

6 Combine a word from column A with a word from column B to make a compound adjective. Check in a dictionary, if necessary.

A	B
_e_ 1. single-	a. minute
___ 2. one-	b. aged
___ 3. middle-	c. time
___ 4. left-	d. called
___ 5. home-	e. minded
___ 6. last-	f. made
___ 7. part-	g. new
___ 8. so-	h. consuming
___ 9. time-	i. way
___ 10. brand-	j. handed

7 Complete the sentences with the compound adjectives from Exercise 6.

1. Apparently, she said that the computer and TV that were stolen were _____, when in fact they were several years old.

2. They arrested a _____ man for joy-riding last night. It's surprising because joy-riders are usually in their teens.

3. In his interview for inspector, he came across as very _____, which is exactly what we want. We need someone who will get things done.

4. He said he just wanted a _____ ticket, which made me a little suspicious.

5. I'm doing some volunteer work with young offenders. I really like it, but it's pretty _____. It's taking up most of my weekends these days.

6. It was a _____ decision to go to Mexico, but I'm really glad we did. After all the hassle of the court case we needed a break.

7. The fact that the thief was _____ was a key clue that helped the police catch him. They found some specially designed scissors in his apartment.

8. The _____ expert for the defense was very vague in his answers. I'm not sure he really was an expert.

9. I'm starting work as a _____ police officer in January. It's Monday and Friday mornings, which is perfect for me.

10. You must try a piece of this _____ chocolate cake. A prisoner made it in the cooking class.

8 **Group Work** Discuss the questions.

1. Do you consider yourself to be a single-minded person? Why or why not?

2. When do you think someone is middle-aged?

3. Are you a "last-minute" kind of person? If so, give some examples.

4. Do you think homemade cooking is always the best?

5. Have you ever had a part-time job? If so, what was it? Did you enjoy it?

6. What things in your life are particularly time-consuming?

Reading

9 **Pair Work** How many different ways can you think of to steal one million dollars? Discuss.

10 Read the article and briefly summarize how D.B. Cooper managed to steal the equivalent of over one million dollars in today's money.

D.B. COOPER

At 2 P.M. on November 24, 1971, a middle-aged man of average height, dressed in a dark suit, white shirt, dark glasses, and a black tie, handed a $20 bill to a clerk at the Portland airport, asked for a one-way ticket, and then boarded Flight 305 for Seattle. Identifying himself as Dan Cooper, he carried only a briefcase. Just before take-off, he handed the flight attendant a note. Watching her put the note in her pocket, he said quietly, "Miss, you'd better look at that note. I have a bomb." The message demanded $200,000 (about $1,100,000 in today's money) and four parachutes—by 5 P.M. To remove any final doubts, Cooper opened his briefcase and showed the flight attendant sticks of dynamite, attached to wire and a battery. As the plane circled over Seattle, the pilot, William Rataczak, quickly learned he was not dealing with an amateur. This man was totally single-minded. With the confidence of an army commander, Cooper told Rataczak that after the money and parachutes had been delivered, he wanted him to head south from Seattle, fly no higher than 10,000 feet, and leave the rear door open.

The plane landed in Seattle and by 7 P.M., it had refueled and the parachutes and money were on board. The plane took off again a few minutes after 7:30 P.M. Then Cooper carefully collected all his handwritten notes and strapped the money bag to his body using cords he cut from one of the parachutes.

At 8:12 P.M., "we felt a little bump and the air pressure changed," Rataczak said. And that was the last fix on D.B. Cooper. The Air Force had sent up two F-106 fighter planes to chase the Boeing 727 and try to keep Cooper's parachute in sight but they were too fast and had to keep making giant S-curves in the sky. For the next few weeks, hundreds of federal agents, helped by Army troops, searched around the area under where Cooper jumped.

A small submarine also searched nearby Lake Merwin. But they found nothing. In fact, there was no concrete evidence of any kind until February 1980, when an Oklahoma boy, having a picnic with his family on the shore of the Columbia River, came across a waterlogged bag containing 294 moldy $20 bills. The serial numbers matched those on the notes given to D.B. Cooper. This find got the FBI's attention. Helicopters flew over the area, squads of agents dug up the shore, searching for more money, Cooper's body, or his parachute, but again—nothing.

D.B. Cooper entered the history books as an authentic American legend. "There's a good reason for this," says Larry Goldfine, a Seattle lawyer who was sitting on Flight 305 that day. "It was the first airplane hijacking for money, and then the hijacker disappeared without a trace. No one was hurt and it all happened right under the noses of the FBI." Most people think Cooper got away with it. The Cooper of the legend has the coolness of a Steve McQueen or Clint Eastwood. In the end, no one has ever figured out just who he was—or is. In his enduring anonymity, he has inspired three books, a play, a movie, a song, and thousands of D.B. Cooper bars and restaurants. Perhaps the ultimate tribute is the annual "D.B. Cooper Days" festival in the tiny Washington town over which Cooper was thought to have parachuted. There's a D.B. Cooper look-alike contest (lots of forty-ish men in dark suits and dark glasses), and half-a-dozen skydivers make a jump.

11 Read the article again. What do these numbers refer to?

    a. 2   **b.** 20   **c.** 305   **d.** 200,000   **e.** 10,000   **f.** 294

12 Find three examples of compound adjectives in the article.

13 **Group Work** Discuss the questions.

    1. What do you think of what D.B. Cooper did?

    2. How do you think he got away with it?

    3. Do you understand why some people admire what he did?

    4. Do you know any stories about famous criminals from your country?

Reading

1a   **Pair Work**   What do you know about Sherlock Holmes? Was he a real person? Why and when was he famous? Discuss.

b   Now read the article and check your ideas.

The Real *Sherlock Holmes*

Was Sherlock Holmes a real person? Not exactly, but Dr. Joseph Bell, the man who inspired the character of Sherlock Holmes, shared many qualities with the famous detective. Arthur Conan Doyle, the writer and creator of Holmes, met Dr. Bell in 1877 at the University of Edinburgh Medical School. Conan Doyle was studying to be a doctor and Bell was one of his professors.

Bell was 39 years old when Conan Doyle first attended one of his lectures. He is said to have walked with great energy. His nose and chin were angular and his eyes twinkled with intelligent humor. Bell, who was a brilliant doctor, liked writing poetry, playing sports, and bird-watching.

By the end of Conan Doyle's second year, Bell had selected him to serve as his assistant. Being at work with Bell, where he had plenty of opportunity to observe, only increased Conan Doyle's admiration for the great doctor. Among other things, he was able to witness Dr. Bell's remarkable ability to quickly deduce a great deal about the patient.

Dr. Bell observed the way a person moved. The walk of a sailor, who had spent many years at sea, varied greatly from that of a soldier. If he identified a person as a sailor, he would look for any tattoos that might assist him in knowing where the person's travels had taken him. He trained himself to listen for small differences in his patients' accents to help him identify where they were from. Bell studied the hands of his patients, because calluses or other marks could help him determine their occupation.

Conan Doyle published the first Holmes story in 1887. His innovation in creating a character that would appear over and over in a series of self-contained stories meant that Holmes's popularity grew with each installment. Soon the character was so beloved that people refused to believe he wasn't a real person; letters addressed to "Sherlock Holmes, Consulting Detective" arrived daily at Baker Street and Scotland Yard, each begging him to take on a real case.

2   Read the article again and complete the information on the right.

3   **Group Work**   Discuss the questions.

1. What new information have you learned about Sherlock Holmes?

2. Do you think you are observant like Dr. Bell? Would you be a good witness in a crime situation?

3. Would you ever be interested in being a detective? Why or why not?

The Real Sherlock Holmes

Person who Sherlock Holmes was based on: _____ (1.)

Relationship to Conan Doyle: _____ (2.)

Where/When met Conan Doyle: _____ (3.), _____ (4.)

Dr. Bell's hobbies: poetry, _____ (5.), _____ (6.)

Things Dr. Bell observed about patients: the way they moved, _____ (7.), their accents, _____ (8.)

Date first Holmes story published: _____ (9.)

Letters for Sherlock Holmes sent to: _____ (10.)

Grammar | relative clauses

4 Read the information in the Active Grammar box. Decide which examples contain defining relative clauses and which contain nondefining relative clauses.

Active Grammar

Defining relative clauses

- The underlined part of the sentence is essential to the meaning of the sentence.

- Commas are not used to separate the clauses.

- *Who* can be replaced by *that*.

Nondefining relative clauses

- The underlined part of the sentence gives us extra information. This clause can be removed without affecting the central meaning of the sentence.

- Use commas at the beginning and end of these clauses unless they end the sentence.

- *Who* and *which* cannot be replaced by *that*.

Examples

1. *Dr. Joseph Bell was the man who inspired the character of Sherlock Holmes.*

2. *Bell, who was a brilliant doctor, liked writing poetry, playing sports, and bird-watching.*

3. *Bell was 39 years old when Conan Doyle first attended one of his lectures.*

4. *Being at work with Bell, where he had plenty of opportunity to observe, only increased Conan Doyle's admiration for the great doctor.*

5. *Conan Doyle, whose Sherlock Holmes novels were enormously popular, died in 1930.*

See Reference page 135

5 Combine these pairs of sentences to make one sentence.

Ex: The police still haven't found the man. He stole my bag.

> The police still haven't found the man who stole my bag.

1. John's been my best friend for years. He's helping me start a new business.
2. My current house needs redecorating. I've been in it for a couple of years.
3. Tara's going to Australia for the winter. Her parents moved there last year.
4. My neighbor gave me his old computer. I've always liked him.
5. The family down the street is thinking of moving. Their dog barks constantly.
6. Tina's car is for sale. She's had it for years.

6 Complete the sentences in a way that makes sense.

1. Where are the jeans that . . . ?
2. That's the pop star who . . .
3. She's the little girl whose . . .
4. I'd like to find a place where . . .
5. I think that's the couple whose . . .
6. We went to a store where . . .
7. Wasn't it your father who . . . ?
8. She bought the cell phone that . . .

Speaking

7 **Pair Work** Tell another student three interesting things about you. Begin like this:

1. X is the place where . . .
2. Y is the person who . . .
3. Z was the time when . . .

> *Libya is the place where I was born. My mother was an English teacher there.*

Listening

8 ▶ **2.18** Listen to an interview with an ordinary American whose name is Sherlock Holmes. Answer these questions.

    1. Why do you think he has this name?

    2. What do you think are the possible consequences of having a name like this?

9 Listen again and explain the significance of the following things in the interview:

    1. the name "Holmes"
       Ex: *This is what the American Sherlock Holmes likes to be called.*

    2. the original Conan Doyle stories

    3. a favorite literary figure

    4. the question "Where's Dr. Watson?"

    5. TV magicians

    6. the mother of an old family friend

    7. $7,000

    8. his flashlight and magnifying glass

10 **Group Work** Discuss the questions.

    1. How do you feel about your name? Does it mean something?

    2. Were you named after someone in your family or someone famous? If so, who and why?

    3. What reasons do people have for changing their names? Do you know anyone who has changed his or her name? If so, why did he or she do it?

Writing

11 Read the article and the Useful Phrases box on page 146. Do the exercises.

12 ▶ **2.19** You are going to write an article about a famous crime.

    1. Listen and take notes on how Nick Leeson broke the Barings investment bank.

    2. Decide on the main points for your article.

    3. Organize your ideas into paragraphs.

    4. Write your article in 100–150 words.

    5. Read your article through. Is it interesting and easy to read? Make any necessary changes.

Review

1 Combine the following pairs of sentences. Use *After* + present participle or *Having* + past participle.

1. She traveled for hours to get to the village. She thought she should stay there for at least a couple of days.

2. He saw his neighbor struggling with a lot of heavy bags. He offered to help her.

3. She took home an injured cat she had found by the side of the road. She felt she had to keep it.

4. He saw a young man take a CD without paying. He told the security guard.

5. He spoke to his father. He told his boss he wanted a raise.

6. They got a long letter from their cousin. They decided to go and see him.

2 Complete the second sentences so that they mean the same as the first. Use *must*, *might*, *can't* and the correct form of the verbs in parentheses.

1. It is possible he stayed late at the office.
   He _____. (stay)

2. There's no chance that I left my gloves in the car.
   I _____. (leave)

3. I'm sure she's shown me her vacation photos at least ten times.
   She _____. (show)

4. It's not possible that she's finished all her homework already.
   She _____. (finish)

5. I have no doubt that they were really pleased to win the game.
   They _____. (be)

6. There's a chance my letter got lost in the mail.
   My letter _____. (got)

3 Add commas to the sentences where necessary.

1. I'm afraid I lost the book that she lent me.

2. I'm going to spend a few days in Miami where I first met Rachel.

3. These are the apples that I picked from the tree in my yard.

4. The young man who I spoke to gave me a refund.

5. We decided to stay at the Regina Hotel which some friends had recommended to us.

6. Tim whose job involves a lot of traveling has offered to let us stay in his house for a few weeks.

4 Correct the mistakes in the sentences.

1. Steve works for a small company makes kitchen equipment.

2. I think the name of the movie what I'd like to see is *Collateral*.

3. Did you hear exactly that he said?

4. The demonstration, had been going on for several days, is finally over.

5. Isn't that the place where you grew up?

6. My sister, that speaks Spanish and English fluently, wants to be an interpreter.

Communication | speculate on the reasons for a problem

5a Try and solve the lateral thinking problems. Read each one and find the meaning of any new vocabulary.

b **Pair Work** Discuss ideas you have to explain each problem.

1 A police officer was sitting on his motorcycle at a red traffic light when two teenagers in a sports car drove by him at 50 mph. He did not chase them or try to apprehend them. **Why not?**

2 A man was driving alone in his car when he went off the road at a high speed. He crashed through a fence and went down a steep slope before the car plunged into a fast-flowing river. As the car slowly settled in the river, the man realized that his arm was broken, and that he could not release his seat belt to get out of the car—he was trapped. Rescuers arrived two hours later, yet they found him alive. **How come?**

3 A man rode into town on Friday. He stayed for three nights and then left on Friday. **How come?**

4 Bobby lives with his parents in Seattle. Last week, while his parents were out, Bobby's neighbor Susie came over to spend the evening. At 8 o'clock precisely she went out to buy a soda from the corner store five minutes' walk away. One minute after she left, two men burst into the house and, ignoring Bobby, took the TV set, the stereo, and a computer. Bobby had never seen the men before and they had no legal right to remove the equipment – yet he did nothing to stop them. In fact, he didn't even act surprised by their behavior. **How come?**

5 A man leaves the hospital and begins to walk home. On his journey he passes a pay phone that begins to ring. Instead of answering it he punches the air and runs all the way home cheering. **Why?**

6 When a fire broke out in an airplane, a panicking passenger opened the emergency hatch and threw himself out, even though he had no parachute. When the paramedics found him, he was alive and well. **How come?**

6 **SPEAKING EXCHANGE** Now choose the problem you are most interested in and read its explanation. (1. page 142; 2. page 139; 3. page 138; 4. page 140; 5. page 141; 6. page 137)

1. Make two *Yes/No* questions to ask about each of the other problems.

> *Was the policeman asleep? Were the teenagers invisible in some way?*

2. **Group Work** Ask your questions to other students who know the explanations for the other problems. Then suggest explanations for each of the other problems.

> *The teenagers might have been the policeman's children.*

114

UNIT 10
Mind matters

Warm Up

1 **Group Work** What is happening in each picture? How are they connected? Discuss.

2a **Pair Work** Match the quotes below with the photos and explain what you think the underlined phrases mean.

　　_____ 1. "Politicians rely on the <u>power of persuasion</u> to get votes."

　　_____ 2. "I gave up eating all sweet things using nothing but <u>willpower</u>."

　　_____ 3. "Walking on hot coals is a question of <u>mind over matter</u>."

b In what situations have you used mind over matter, the power of persuasion, and willpower?

3 ▶**2.20** Listen to six people answering these questions. What do the underlined phrases mean? Ask and answer the questions with a partner.

1. Do you ever <u>have premonitions</u>? Do you take them seriously?
2. Have you ever <u>had a feeling of déjà vu</u>? What happened?
3. Are you someone who is usually able to <u>trust your intuition</u>?
4. Do you know anyone who uses <u>his or her sixth sense</u> a lot?
5. Have you ever <u>been unconscious</u>? What happened?
6. Do you think you have any <u>subconscious fears</u>?

Reading

1   **Group Work** What is hypnosis? What do hypnotists usually do to people? Where and why are people often hypnotized? Discuss.

2   Read the article and find the answers to the questions in Exercise 1.

Help Yourself through **Hypnosis**

Do you ever lose yourself reading a book or surfing online? Do you ever completely tune out in front of the TV? Do you ever find yourself in a daze at work or at school? Do you ever drive to your destination and not remember the journey? If you answered yes to any of these questions, then you have experienced hypnosis.

It's a popular misconception that hypnosis is mind control or brainwashing. It's actually just an increased state of focused attention. When guided by a hypnotherapist, it can be an effective way to cure physical and psychological conditions. It can help a person quit smoking, lose weight, or reduce stress. It can also help to overcome phobias and improve self-confidence.

Under hypnosis, a patient is in a relaxed state of mind. This makes the patient more receptive to the statements a hypnotherapist makes. Depending on a patient's goals, the hypnotherapist repeats positive, encouraging words, such as "You love to exercise every day," or, "You have the confidence to accomplish anything."

One dramatic success story is Angela Pitman, an American woman who underwent hypnotherapy in order to lose weight. While under hypnosis, Pitman was convinced that she had actually had an expensive procedure called "Lap Band surgery," in which the size of the patient's stomach is reduced. "Afterwards, I started eating smaller portions," said Pitman. "If I ate too much, I'd feel sick. Before hypnotherapy I had tried to lose weight myself. But nothing ever worked. I've lost 75 pounds, and I feel so much better about myself." Pitman gained many of the benefits from the actual surgery without risking any of its potential side effects.

While having a hypnotherapist to guide you through hypnosis is ideal, it is also possible to hypnotize yourself to reach certain goals. First, think of a clear, specific statement, such as, "I am not afraid of spiders." Find a quiet place, get comfortable, and close your eyes. Breathe slowly and let all the tension leave your body. Imagine a peaceful scene. Assure yourself that you are very safe. Then repeat your statement to yourself: "I am not afraid of spiders, I am not afraid of spiders, I am not afraid of spiders . . ." When you are ready to return from your relaxed state, count backward from five and slowly open your eyes. Notice how good you feel.

If you have any issues you need to work through, you may want to seriously consider this alternative therapy. Hypnosis is not about a mysterious man swinging a pocket watch in front of you, controlling you, and commanding you to cluck like a chicken or do other embarrassing things. It's a unique therapy that can change your perception of things around you and improve your well-being.

3   Read the article again. Mark the statements below true (*T*), false (*F*), or don't know (*?*).

    _____ **1.** Many people experience hypnosis without realizing it.

    _____ **2.** The majority of hypnotherapy patients are trying to lose weight.

    _____ **3.** A patient under hypnosis is more likely to believe what the therapist says.

    _____ **4.** Angela Pitman had surgery while under hypnosis.

    _____ **5.** Hypnotizing yourself is better than going to a hypnotherapist.

    _____ **6.** Count backward from five to return from hypnosis.

4   **Group Work** Discuss the questions.

    1. How did the article change your opinion of hypnosis?

    2. Have you (or has anyone you know) ever been hypnotized? Give details.

    3. Would you like to be hypnotized? Why or why not? What would you ask for help with?

Grammar | reflexive pronouns

5 Read the rules in the Active Grammar box. Complete the reflexive pronouns.

Active Grammar

	Subject pronouns	Reflexive pronouns
Singular	I	1. _____
	you	*yourself*
	he	2. _____
	she	*herself*
	it	3. _____
Plural	we	4. _____
	you	5. _____
	they	6. _____

Rules

a. Reflexive pronouns are commonly used to talk about actions where the subject and object are the same. The reflexive pronoun is essential to the grammar of the sentence.

Do you ever <u>lose yourself</u> reading a book?

b. Reflexive pronouns can also be used for emphasis when we mean "that person or thing—nobody or nothing else." The reflexive pronoun is not essential to the grammar of the sentence but is added for emphasis.

Before hypnotherapy, I had tried to lose weight <u>myself</u>.

See Reference page 136

6 Match each example below with its rule in the Active Grammar box.

_____ 1. I cut myself while I was cooking.

_____ 2. Emily herself said she's not very good at math.

_____ 3. They blamed themselves for the accident.

_____ 4. I spoke to the boss himself.

_____ 5. You should put yourself in my position and try to understand.

_____ 6. She didn't go to the hairdresser; she cut her hair herself.

7 Complete these sentences with a reflexive pronoun or an object pronoun.

1. I _____ have never been hypnotized but I know people who have been.

2. The yoga teacher taught _____ to meditate by thinking about our breathing.

3. A friend gave _____ a book about acupuncture for my birthday.

4. He's so forgetful – he's always locking _____ out of his house.

5. Some people are so selfish. They only think about _____.

6. I'm so happy you like the house. We designed it _____.

7. I'd like to speak to Ms. Johnson _____, not her receptionist.

8. Oh, no, you're bleeding. How did you hurt _____?

Speaking

8 **Group Work** Do you agree with these statements? Compare your views with other students.

1. Most people can cure themselves of a phobia (**Ex:** fear of spiders) or an addiction (**Ex:** smoking) without getting help from a professional.

2. One of the best ways of learning is being with other students and teaching each other.

3. Both the parents and the children should be punished if the child repeatedly skips school.

Listening

9 ▶2.21 Listen to three people talking about hypnosis. Mark the statement that best summarizes each person's opinion. One statement cannot be used.

_____ **a.** He or she has benefited personally from hypnosis.

_____ **b.** He or she admires hypnotists for what they have achieved.

_____ **c.** He or she thinks that going to hypnotists is often a waste of money.

_____ **d.** He or she thinks it's good for some but wouldn't try it personally.

10 Listen again and complete these verb phrases about belief and opinion. Look at Audioscript 2.21 on page 158 to check your answers.

1. If it works for some people, *I'm in _____ of* it.
2. *I've always _____ that* those people are just good showmen.
3. *I have my _____ about* how much it can actually do for people in the long-run.
4. *I'm _____ that* hypnosis has any effect at all.
5. *I'm _____* people paying for a service and getting nothing real in return.
6. *I _____* hypnosis actually works for anyone.
7. *I'm _____* that it was the hypnosis that helped me.
8. *I _____* I would've had to quit by now.

Speaking

11 **Pair Work** Discuss your opinions about the topics below. Use the How To box and the verb phrases in Exercise 10 to help you.

- hypnosis
- vegetarianism
- marriage
- military service
- using cell phones in public places

> **How To:**
>
> ## Ask about other people's views
>
> *How do you feel about . . . ?*
>
> *What are your views on . . . ?*
>
> *What do you think of . . . ?*
>
> *Are you for or against . . . ?*
>
> *Do you have any strong feelings about . . . ?*

12 **Group Work** Choose a topic from Exercise 11 and give your group a one-minute talk on your opinions. Use the instructions below to help you.

- Explain your experience with the topic and/or why it interests you.
- Give arguments for or any positive points about the topic.
- Give arguments against or any negative points about the topic.
- Give your conclusion and/or summarize your personal views.

Write arguments for and against a point of view ✓ CAN DO

GRAMMAR gerunds and infinitives

Listening

1 **Pair Work** What are the people in each picture doing? What do you think each person's goal is? Discuss.

2 ▶2.22 Listen to a radio interview about advertising and supermarkets. Complete the information.

> **Persuasion**
> 1. Where persuasion takes place: _television,_____
> 2. Large amounts of money spent on: _____
>
> **Supermarkets**
> 3. Two ways to relax customers: _____
> 4. Why discount reward cards are good for supermarkets:
> _____
>
> **Advertising**
> 5. Two types of ads: _____
> 6. Ads for clothes: _____
> 7. Ads for insurance: _____
> 8. Ads for luxury cars: _____
> 9. Ads that use celeebrities: _____

3 **Group Work** In what ways do you think you are influenced by advertising? Discuss.

Vocabulary | advertising

4 Circle the correct choice to complete each sentence.
1. Do you have any favorite _advertising/advertisements_?
2. What are three of the best-known _target markets/brands_ of clothing in your country?
3. Would you like to work in _commercials/marketing_?
4. Do you think you would be good at thinking up _hype/slogans_?
5. What do you usually do during _commercials/marketing_ on TV?
6. Have you ever bought anything through a _target market/classified ad_?
7. Which movie has had a lot of _classified ads/hype_ recently?
8. What do you think the _hype/target market_ is for large cars that can seat eight people?

Grammar | gerunds and infinitives

5a ▶2.23 Circle the correct choices to complete the example sentences in the Active Grammar box. Then listen and check your answers.

Active Grammar

Examples

1. They **persuade** us buying / to buy things we may not want.
2. We **keep** using / to use discount reward cards at the same supermarket.
3. Ads for clothes often **want** making / to make us feel that we belong.
4. I **try** resisting / to resist buying expensive designer clothes, but it's difficult!
5. You could **try** leaving / to leave your credit card at home if you don't want to spend so much.

Rules

verb + gerund	keep
verb + infinitive	
verb + object + infinitive	
verb + gerund OR verb + infinitive with a different meaning	

See Reference page 136

b Write the verbs in bold in the Active Grammar box in the correct place in the chart. Then add the verbs in the box below.

> hope   avoid   allow   arrange   suggest   encourage
> stop   agree   regret   advise   practice   remember

6 Look at these pairs of sentences. What is the difference in meaning between the underlined phrases in each pair?

1. a. The TV remote control wouldn't work, so I <u>tried changing</u> the batteries.
   b. I <u>tried to change</u> the batteries in the remote control but I couldn't open it.
2. a. Did you <u>remember to buy</u> some shampoo when you were out?
   b. I <u>remember buying</u> some more shampoo, but now I can't find it.
3. a. I <u>regret to tell</u> you that you failed your final exam.
   b. I <u>regret telling</u> her that I failed my final exam.
4. a. The news was on, but we <u>stopped watching</u> when the ads came on.
   b. We were having lunch, but we <u>stopped to watch</u> the news.

7 Use the word in parentheses to complete the second sentence in each pair so it has the same meaning as the first.

1. "Why don't we go to the movies?" he said. (suggested)
   He _____ to the movies.
2. "You should get a job in advertising," she said to me. (encouraged)
   She _____ a job in advertising.
3. I made an attempt to speak to her on the phone, but she was out. (tried)
   I _____ to her on the phone, but she was out.
4. "OK. I'll give you a ride to the airport," he said. (agreed)
   He _____ me a ride to the airport.

Speaking

8 Talk to different students in the class and find someone who:

- wasn't allowed to watch TV as a child.
- regrets not studying harder as a child.
- hopes to go abroad next year.
- remembers what they were doing on December 31st, 1999.

Writing

9a Choose one of the statements below or something else you feel strongly about. Write arguments for and against the statement.

- Teenagers should not be allowed to wear designer clothes or shoes at school.
- Small, local stores are better for the community than large supermarkets.
- Background music and TV screens should be banned in public places, such as cafés, waiting rooms, stores, etc.

b Write an essay about the statement you chose in Exercise 9a. Use your notes and the following paragraph plan:

Paragraph 1: Introduction—general statement about the issue

Paragraph 2: Arguments for the statement

Paragraph 3: Arguments against the statement

Paragraph 4: Conclusion—briefly summarize your opinion

LESSON **3** **Talk about regrets and resolutions/ promises to change**
CAN DO ✓
GRAMMAR mixed conditionals

Reading

1 Look at the photo below and answer the questions.
1. Have you ever heard of Temple Grandin?
2. What (if anything) do you know about her?

2 Read the article and answer this question: How does her thinking process differ from that of most people?

Temple Grandin

In 1950, at the age of two, Temple Grandin was diagnosed with autism, a genetic condition with no cure in which a person has great difficulty with communication and social interaction. She appeared to live in her own world, a world that others had great difficulty penetrating. She was hypersensitive to sounds and preferred <u>whispering</u> to loud speech. Noises that others hardly noticed were painful and distressing to her. She reacted by suddenly <u>shrieking</u> loudly in the middle of a public place for reasons her parents couldn't understand, or she would <u>be at a loss for words</u> when others tried to engage her in conversation.

As a child, Grandin was constantly teased for being different. Other children would make fun of her, calling her "tape recorder" as she <u>mumbled</u> to herself and kept repeating things over and over again. Sometimes she might <u>blurt out</u> her thoughts at an inappropriate time, <u>interrupting</u> her parents or teachers while they were talking.

Her mind developed quite differently from that of other children. Most children learn how to apply abstract concepts as they move through childhood. For example, if their parents tell them to "be nice" to other kids, they understand what that means. But Grandin struggled with such concepts. She needed concrete examples before she could understand. If her mother told her to be nice to someone, she couldn't understand because it was vague. However, if her mother explained that she shouldn't hit another child because that child may hit her back, she understood. If her father explained that it would be "nice" to bring flowers to the elderly neighbor who lived next door, that made sense to her. She could then have a mental picture of what "being nice" meant.

Grandin explains that she is a visual thinker who thinks in pictures and sounds. She compares her brain to an Internet search engine that matches images to words. Just as typing "love" into a search engine might get a picture of a mother and child, or a photo of the author of "Love Story," or a picture of the Beatles, who performed the song "All You Need Is Love." Her mind goes through the same process. By seeing these images, she understands what love means.

Grandin was fortunate that her parents were able to get her special attention when she was growing up, and she credits her teachers with helping her develop her special abilities. Because she is a visual thinker and has trouble with abstract concepts, she believes that the way she perceives the world is similar to the way animals do. She relates more easily to animals than she does to other people. Her insights eventually earned her a doctorate in animal science. She began to study the conditions of cattle being taken to the slaughterhouse, picturing the experience from the animals' point of view. Her suggested innovations for a more humane approach to slaughter, which lowered animals' fears and anxieties, were adopted by cattle ranchers throughout the southwestern US.

Grandin eventually secured a teaching position at Colorado State University and is a regular lecturer on both animal behavior and the unique challenges and benefits of autism. She has written several memoirs, including *Emergence* and *The Way I See It,* and was featured in a book by Oliver Sacks, *An Anthropologist on Mars.* In 2010, Grandin was the subject of an awarding-winning HBO movie, *Temple Grandin,* starring Claire Danes. Will Temple Grandin retire now that she is a celebrity? Not likely. She says that her work gives meaning to her life.

3 Read the article again and write a question for each answer.

1. When she was two years old.

> "When was she diagnosed with Autism?"

2. It's a genetic disorder in which a person has difficulty with communication and social interaction.
3. Because she mumbled to herself and kept repeating things.
4. An Internet search engine.
5. Because she relates to animals better than she does to other people.
6. Lecturing on animal behavior and the challenges and benefits of autism.

4 **Pair Work** Discuss the questions.

1. If there were a cure for autism, do you think Grandin would want to be cured so her mind would work like the minds of most people? Why or why not?
2. How would you describe your thinking process? Do you think more in pictures or in words? Do you have an easy time with abstract concepts or do you prefer concrete examples?

Vocabulary | verbs for different ways of speaking

5 **Group Work** Work in two groups. What do the words and phrases in the chart mean? Find their meanings. Then explain them to the other group.

Group A	Group B
whisper	mumble
shriek	interrupt
blurt out	speak your mind
be at a loss for words	snap at (someone)

6a Complete the quotes with the correct form of the words and phrases from Exercise 5.

1. "I told a co-worker that I'd been using one of those self-help CDs to help deal with my stress. Then, in the middle of a business meeting, he suddenly _____ everything I'd told him. Honestly, I _____ – I was so shocked I didn't know what to say."

2. "I went to the movies last weekend and the people behind me were _____ to each other throughout the whole movie. They didn't seem to notice that they were annoying everyone else. In the end, I finally _____ them and they stopped, but by that time the movie was nearly over."

3. "My cousin has been staying with me for the last week. I have to say she's kind of irritating. She's really loud, and every time I say anything she _____ with laughter. The other thing she does is constantly _____ people when they're in the middle of a conversation. I'll be really glad when she goes!"

4. "I gave my first presentation at work yesterday and it went OK. But at the end one of my co-workers told me that I had been _____ and he couldn't really hear me. He's the kind of person who isn't afraid to _____ and I was a little upset at first. I guess it's useful feedback though."

b ▶2.24 Listen and check your answers.

7 **Pair Work** Choose three of the words or phrases from Exercise 5. Tell your partner about different situations in which you or someone else spoke in each of these ways.

Grammar | mixed conditionals

8a Match the examples with the rules in the Active Grammar box.

b Look at the examples again. Does each clause refer to the past, present, or future?

Active Grammar

Examples

_____ 1. *If she works really hard, she'll pass her exams.*

_____ 2. *If I won a lot of money, I'd give up my job.*

_____ 3. *If she had studied harder, she would be in college now.*

_____ 4. *If she didn't study as hard as she does, she would have failed the test.*

_____ 5. *If he had memorized the verbs, he wouldn't have failed the test.*

Rules

a. past unreal conditional = *If* + past perfect, *would have* + past participle

b. real conditional = *If* + simple present, *will* + verb

c. mixed conditional = *If* + past perfect, *would* + verb OR *If* + simple past, *would have* + past participle

d. present unreal conditional = *If* + simple past, *would* + verb

Modal verbs (*can*, *could*, *might*, etc.) can be used in conditionals instead of *will* and *would*.

See Reference page 136

9 Correct the grammar mistake in each sentence.

1. If I had more time, I'll go and study English abroad.
2. If parents shouted at their children, their children become aggressive.
3. I speak English fluently now if I'd learned it as a child.
4. If you'll repeat a word enough times, you'll probably remember it.
5. If I'd attended more classes, I would passed my exams.
6. I'd have a better job if I passed my exam.
7. If you try to read more books in English, your vocabulary improved.

Speaking

10 Which of the sentences in Exercise 9 do you think are true? Tell a partner.

11a Look at the sentences in Exercise 9. Which are regrets? Which are resolutions?

b **Pair Work** Tell a partner about two regrets or resolutions in your language learning or your school/work life.

Review

1 Complete each sentence with the correct form of a verb from the box and a reflexive pronoun.

> enjoy   express   hurt   teach   burn

1. Don't touch the iron. You'll _____.
2. She's a good speaker. She _____ very clearly.
3. Jack had to go to the doctor because he _____ while he was playing football this morning.
4. Thank you for the party. We really _____.
5. He _____ how to play the guitar.

2 Correct the mistakes in the sentences.

1. We encourage all students doing some volunteer work.
2. I've arranged visiting my grandparents on Saturday.
3. I remember to go to the park every day after school when I was a child.
4. He persuaded me joining the new gym with him.
5. My teacher suggested to learn ten new spellings every week.
6. He advised to get us some rest before the exam.

3 Complete each sentence with the correct form of the verb in parentheses. There is sometimes more than one correct answer.

1. If you _____ (not go) to bed so late, you wouldn't be so tired.
2. Dogs _____ (behave) very well if you train them properly.
3. You'd feel a lot better if you _____ (do) more exercise.
4. If I _____ (bring) enough money, I would have paid for your dinner.
5. He'll miss the beginning of the movie if he _____ (not arrive) soon.
6. What _____ (you/do) if you lost your passport?
7. I _____ (lie) on a beach now if I'd booked that vacation.

4 Complete each sentence with the correct form of a word from the box. One of the words cannot be used.

> hype   brand   slogan   interrupt   premonition
> blurt   shriek   mumble   intuition   convince

1. Don't believe all the _____ about that new movie. It's not that good.
2. Can you let me finish what I'm saying without _____ me all the time?
3. The surprise was spoiled because he _____ out the whole plan before I could stop him.
4. Don't worry about other people. Trust your _____ and do what you want.
5. I don't really care what _____ of jeans I wear as long as they're comfortable.
6. I'm not going in a car today. I had a _____ about being in a car accident.
7. I'm _____ that recycling is essential for helping the environment.
8. Could you stop _____? I can't understand you.
9. It's the car company whose _____ is, "We try harder."

Communication | express personal preferences

5 **Pair Work** Complete the questionnaire and make notes about your answers. Then compare answers with a partner.

What are your personal preferences?

1. What would you most like to spend your time doing when you're on vacation?
   a. playing sports
   b. doing nothing
   c. reading a good book
   d. talking to local people
   e. doing a crossword puzzle
   f. other _____

2. When you're learning a language, which of these appeals to you most?
   a. speaking without worrying about mistakes
   b. immersing yourself totally in the country
   c. analyzing grammatical rules
   d. going where the language is spoken

3. Which one of these would you be most interested in doing as part of your work?
   a. working together in a team
   b. doing something practical
   c. writing a story or poem
   d. doing scientific research
   e. being outdoors
   f. other _____

4. When you're working in a group, which one of these are you most likely to do?
   a. be the "entertainer" who makes things fun
   b. take control of any money or numbers issues
   c. keep the group focused on reaching its goal
   d. wonder what other people are thinking
   e. speak on behalf of the group
   f. other _____

5. Which of these statements describe you?
   a. I'm interested in science.
   b. I enjoy a good discussion.
   c. I enjoy dancing.
   d. I like telling stories.
   e. I like trying to figure people out.
   f. other _____

6. Which of these jobs would you most like to have?
   a. artist
   b. nurse
   c. lawyer
   d. teacher
   e. politician
   f. astronaut
   g. journalist
   h. psychologist
   i. other _____

6 **SPEAKING EXCHANGE** Compare your notes with the descriptions on page 141 of the Speaking Exchange. Then discuss these questions in groups.

1. Which description do you think you are most like?
2. Which description do you think your partner is most like?
3. Do you and your partner think/learn in a similar or a different way?

Unit 1 Reference

Tag questions

- Use tag questions in speech and informal writing to check information or ask for agreement.

- Negative tag questions are usually put after affirmative sentences and affirmative tags after negative sentences.

  It's warm today, **isn't it**?

  He doesn't like me, **does he**?

- If the main clause has an auxiliary verb, such as *is*, *can*, etc., it is repeated in the tag question.

  You **can**'t play tennis this evening, **can** you?

- If the main clause has no auxiliary, the tag question is a form of the verb *do*.

  They went to Australia last Christmas, **didn't they**?

- In speech, use intonation to show the meaning of the tag question. If the tag is a real question (we want to know something and are not sure of the answer), use a rising intonation. If the tag is not a real question (we already think we know the answer), use a falling intonation.

- The tag question for *I am* is *aren't I*.

  I'm wrong, **aren't I**?

- After negative words like *never*, *no*, *hardly*, etc., use a positive tag question.

  You never want to go out to clubs, **do you**?

- After *nothing*, use *it* in tag questions.

  Nothing happened, did **it**?

- After *nobody*, *somebody*, *everybody*, etc., use *they* in tag questions.

  Nobody wants to go out tonight, do **they**?

Pronouns using *any/every/ no/some*

- *Any* and *every* can both be used to talk in general about all the members of a group. *Any* looks at things one at a time. *Every* looks at all things together.

  Don't you have **any**thing to do?

  There's enough food for **every**one.

- *Any* can also mean "It doesn't matter which one."

  A: Which bag should I bring?

  B: It doesn't matter. **Any**thing is fine.

- *Nothing* means *not anything*.

  There's **nothing** we can do to change his mind.

Modals of speculation

- Use *could*, *may*, or *might* to talk about present or future possibility.

  A: Where's Jean?

  B: I'm not sure, but she **might be** in the garden.

  A: I think there will be an election before the end of the year.

  B: You **could be** right.

- Use *can* to talk about more general or theoretical possibility.

  The sea **can get** rough here with almost no warning.

- Use *must* to say that you believe something is certain.

  You haven't had anything to eat all day. You **must be** starving.

- Use *can't* to say that you believe something is not possible.

  They **can't know** many people. They've only just moved here.

Unit Vocabulary

Relationships

acquaintance	step-sister
make a good impression	half-sister
to click (with someone)	co-worker
to have a lot in common	close friend
to be on the same wavelength	wife
to see eye to eye (with someone)	partner

Adjectives/Nouns

artistic/art	jealous/jealousy
lonely/loneliness	responsible/responsibility
successful/success	important/importance
skillful/skill	frustrated/frustration

Noises

ring	scream	creak	bang	thud
shout	bark	snore	crash	

Unit 2 Reference

Review of future forms: *will* and *be going to*

For plans and intentions

- Use *will* to talk about a decision made at the time of speaking (including offers and promises).

  *I think **I'll go** shopping after lunch.*

  *I don't think **I'll have** anything to eat.*

- Use *be going to* to talk about a plan or intention in which no details have been decided.

  ***I'm going to study** law, but I'm not sure where yet.*

- Use the present continuous to talk about a future arrangement when details about time, place, etc., have been decided.

  ***I'm meeting** Sonia after my interview in the café.*

For predictions

- Use *will* to make predictions based on what you know or believe. *Think*, *hope*, *believe*, etc., are often used with *will* in this case.

  *I think Ben **will be** the new school president.*

- Use *be going to* to make predictions based on what you can see or hear now.

  *Be careful! You**'re going to fall** off that chair if you lean back like that!*

Future continuous and future perfect

- Use the **future continuous** to talk about something in progress at a definite time in the future.

  Form: *will/won't* + *be* + present participle

  *Don't call me tonight. **I'll be watching** the game.*

- Use the **future continuous** to ask about someone's plans, especially if you want something or you want them to do something.

  ***Will** you **be using** the car on Saturday?*

- Use the **future perfect** to talk about something which will be completed before a definite time in the future.

  Form: *will/won't* + *have* + past participle

  *She **won't have finished** her essay by Friday.*

- The **future perfect** is often used with time phrases with *by*, for example, *by that time*, *by this time next week*, *by tomorrow*, *by then*, *by the end of the trip*, etc.

(just) in case

- Use *in case* to explain why somebody did something. When talking about the past, the verb that follows *in case* can be simple past or past perfect.

  *We took our swimsuits **in case there was** a **pool**.*

- When talking about the future, the verb that follows *in case* is normally in the present. Use the present, future, or a modal verb in the other clause.

  *You should insure your bicycle **in case someone steals it**.*

- Use *just in case* to add emphasis.

  *I'm going to apologize again **just in case** she's still angry with me.*

- Use *just in case* at the end of a sentence to talk about precautions in general (rather than specific situations).

  *I'll take some extra money with me **just in case**.*

Unit Vocabulary

Jobs

journalist	civil engineer
surgeon	social worker	physical therapist

Personality traits for jobs

have an eye for detail	be a good listener
be good with numbers	be a people person
have a "can do" attitude	be a team player
stay calm under pressure	be a self-starter
be able to meet tight deadlines	
bring out the best in other people	

Verb phrases about work

work part-time	do volunteer work
be laid off	retire early
be fired	quit your job
work flextime	work the night shift

After work activities

take a night class	visit chat rooms
work late at the office	socialize with friends

keep up with (your email . . .)

study for a (law, business, . . .) degree online

spend quality time with (your children, family, . . .)

Unit 3 Reference

Review of past forms

- Use the **simple past** to talk about completed actions in the past.

  *We **got up** early and **caught** the 11 o'clock train.*

- Use the **past continuous** to talk about actions in progress at a particular time in the past.

  Form: *was/were* + present participle

  *I **was walking** to work when I **tripped** and fell.*

- Use the **past perfect** to talk about completed actions that happened before another action in the past.

  Form: *had* + past participle

  *I**'d just finished** my lunch when the doorbell **rang**.*

- Use the **past perfect continuous** to talk about actions or situations which continued up to the past moment being talked about.

  Form: *had* + *been* + present participle

  *Before they **moved**, they **had been living** in Australia.*

Articles: *a/an/the/Ø*

Use the definite article *the*:

1. with inventions and species of animals. ***The** giant panda is an endangered species.*
2. with national groups. ***the** British, **the** Ancient Greeks*
3. when there is only one of something. ***the** sun*
4. with rivers, oceans, and seas. ***the** Mediterranean Sea*
5. with superlatives. *China is **the** most interesting place I've been.*
6. with particular nouns when it is clear what is being referred to. *Can you turn off **the** light, please?*
7. with previously mentioned nouns. *Would you like an apple or a banana? **The** banana is very ripe.*

Use the indefinite article *a/an*:

1. with jobs. ***a** teacher, **an** engineer*
2. with singular count nouns (mentioned for the first time or when it doesn't matter which one). *I'd like **an** apple.*

Use no article (Ø):

1. with most streets, villages, towns, cities, countries, lakes, and mountains. *Italy, Mount Fuji*

   But for countries and groups of islands/mountains in the plural, use "the." ***the** Netherlands*.
2. with noncount, plural, and abstract nouns used in their general sense. *Accommodation is difficult to find.*

Adjectives and adverbs

- Adjectives are used to describe nouns. They usually come directly before the noun.

  *I live in a really **beautiful** city.*

- Adverbs (and adverbial phrases) are used to modify verbs, adjectives, and other adverbs.

- Many adverbs end in *-y*, but some words ending in *-y* are adjectives, not adverbs. *friendly, lively, lonely, silly*

  There are also many adverbs which do not end in *-y*. *late, fast, fine, hard, high, well*

  Sometimes the adjective and adverb have the same form: *fast, hard, fine, early, daily, late*

  *He worked really **hard**.   This chair is too **hard**.*

Position of adverbs

The position of adverbs in a sentence can vary.

- **At the beginning of a sentence**

  Connecting and time adverbs (the adverb is not the main focus)

- **In the middle of a sentence (before the main verb)**

  Adverbs of certainty and completeness, of indefinite frequency, of comment, and some adverbs of manner (the adverb is not the main focus)

- **At the end of a sentence**

  Adverbs of manner, place, and time

Unit Vocabulary

Age

modern	ancient	antique
traditional	elderly	

Time expressions

throughout	during
in (1997)	while
since then	from that point on
after that	up until that point
until	at that time

Materials

leather	denim	metal	wool	silk
porcelain	plastic	cotton	wood	

Describing objects

soft	stretchy	shiny	smooth
rough	furry	slippery	itchy

Verb phrases with *take*

take off	take to	take in
take part in	take over	take it in stride

Unit 4 Reference

Conditionals with *if*

- Use the **real conditional** to talk about a possible situation in the future.

  Form: *If* + simple present/present continuous/present perfect, future/present continuous/imperative + verb

  The *if* clause can come first or second. When the *if* clause is first, end that clause with a comma.
  If you need help, ask me.
  We're going to get very wet if it rains.

- Use the **present unreal conditional** to talk about unreal or imagined situations in the present/future.

  Form: *If* + past simple/past continuous, *would* (or *'d*) + verb
  If I lived in the country, I'd do a lot more walking.

- When less certain, use *might* instead of *would*.
  If someone gave me a lot of money, I might take a year off work.

- Also, use the **present unreal conditional** to give advice.
  I'd buy a good English–English dictionary if I were you.

- Use the **past unreal conditional** to talk about past situations that did not happen.

  Form: *If* + past perfect, *would have* + past participle
  If she had studied more, she would have passed the exam.

Modals: obligation

- Use *must/must not* to talk about present and future strong obligations that come from an outside authority.
  All visitors must sign in.

- Use *have to/have got to* to talk about strong present and future obligations that often come from outside the speaker.
  You've got to show your ID before they will let you in this club.

- Use *don't have to* or *don't need to* to talk about a lack of obligation in the present or future.
  You don't have to come shopping with me if you don't want to.

- Use *should* (or *ought to*) to talk about obligations and duties in the future, present, or past, and to give advice.
  I really should go and visit my cousins in Wales.

- Use *should* + *have* + past participle to criticize your own or other people's behavior in the past.
  I shouldn't have spoken to Brian like that.

- Use *supposed to* to talk about what people have to do according to rules or about what is expected to happen.
  You're supposed to wear a tie to work.

- Use *had to* to talk about past and reported obligations.
  When I was in school we all had to wear uniforms.

Emphasis

- Use repetition.
  She's a very, very nice person.

- Add an emphasizing word. *so, such, really, just*
  I was so pleased to meet your sister.
  They are such a nice couple.

- Use the structure: *It is/was . . . which/that . . .*
  It's the kitchen that I particularly like about that house.

- Add an appropriate form of *do*.
  I do wish you could stay a little longer.

Unit Vocabulary

Risk/Achievement

risk	gamble	opportunity	at stake
vast	chance	ambition	big
dream	hazard	substantial	

Outdoor activities

mountain climbing	paddle	summit
rock climbing	camping	foothold
whitewater rafting	kayaking	rope
sleeping bag	rappelling	waves
pitch a tent	harness	rapids
take in the view	handhold	hang on

Phrasal verbs with *out*

find out	run out (of)	turn out
pass out	put out	sort out
back out	make out	

Unit 5 Reference

Past routines: *used to/would/ get used to*

- Use *used to* to talk about past habits and states that do not happen now. In the negative and question forms, *use* does not end with a *d*.

  I **used to catch** the bus to work, but now I go by bike.

  She **didn't use to be** nearly so ambitious.

  Did you **use to enjoy** traveling for your job?

- Use *would* to talk about past habits but not past states.

  When we were little, we **would watch** cartoons on TV.

  We **used to live** in Miami. (NOT: ~~We would live in Miami.~~)

- Use *get used to* to describe the process of becoming accustomed to a new situation.

  We're **getting used to living** in a small town in the country, but it's still a little strange.

- Use *be used to* to say when you have become accustomed to a new situation.

  She's **used to being** her own boss.

- With *be/get used to*, the spelling is always *used* with a *d*.

Expressing degrees of ability

- Use *can* to talk about present or "general" ability.

  She **can speak** Russian very well.

- Use *will be able to* to talk about future ability.

  She**'ll be able to run** faster by next year.

- Use *could* or *was/were able to* to talk about past or general ability.

  She **was able to communicate** effectively in Arabic after working in Egypt for a year.

- Use *was/were able to, managed to,* or *succeeded in* (+ -*ing*) to say what someone could do on a particular occasion.

  They **were able to get** into the house by forcing open the back door.

  She **managed to pay off** all her debts by working in the evenings and on weekends.

  She **succeeded in paying off** all her debts by working overtime.

although/however/ nevertheless

- Use all of these linking words to show that what you are saying is surprising or unexpected in relation to something else you know to be true.

  Form: *Although* + clause, clause

  Although she was half an hour late, they decided to wait a little longer.

  Form: clause, *although* + clause

  They decided to wait a bit longer, **although** she was half an hour late.

- *Though* can be used as a shortened form of *although*. It is more common in informal speech.

- Use *even though* to emphasize a contrast.

  Even though I was very angry with him, I didn't say anything.

- Use *however* and *nevertheless* to show contrast.

  Form: sentence + *However/Nevertheless,* + clause (*Nevertheless* is formal.)

  She was half an hour late. **However,** they decided to wait a bit longer.

  You have not been with this company long. **Nevertheless,** I am still going to promote you.

Unit Vocabulary

Memory

remember	memory	souvenir
memorable	remind	reminisce
nostalgic	forgetful	

Describing appearance

1. Hair

straight	curly	wavy
spiky	dyed	going a bit bald

2. Face

wrinkles	clean-shaven
chubby	round

3. Build

muscular	stocky
slim	a bit overweight

4. General

good-looking	scruffy	attractive
elegant	tanned	

Describing feelings

suspicious	uneasy	curious	shocked
annoyed	optimistic	relieved	

Unit 6 Reference

Present perfect vs. present perfect continuous

- Use the **present perfect** to talk about an action or experience in the past when the time is not important or not known.
  I've visited several countries in South America.

- Use the **present perfect** to describe an action that started in the past and continues in the present, when focusing on the finished action or on the number of times the action has been completed.
  I've lived here since last January.

- Use the **present perfect continuous** when focusing on the activity itself.
  He's been playing tennis for three hours.

- Use the **present perfect** to describe an action that happened in the past but has a result in the present.
  The mail has come. There's a letter for you.

- *Just* means a short time ago. It usually comes between *has/have* and the past participle.
  I've just seen Mariana.

- *Already* shows that something happened sooner than expected. It usually comes between *has/have* and the past participle or at the end of the sentence.
  I've already done the shopping.

- *Yet* shows that the speaker expected something to happen before now. It is used at the end of negatives and questions.
  Have you finished that email yet?
  She hasn't replied to the invitation yet.

Direct and indirect questions

Direct questions

- There are two main types of direct questions: *Yes/No* questions and *Wh-* questions.
  Are you going to Danka's party on Saturday?
  Where did she learn to speak such good Spanish?

- Subject questions are used when the question word (**Ex:** *who*) refers to the subject of the sentence. When a *wh-* word replaces the subject in a question, do not use the auxiliary verb.
  The teacher told us to go. → Who told you to go?

Indirect questions

- Use indirect questions when you want to be polite, such as when you don't know someone. Use the word order of positive statements. Use *if* or *whether* for indirect *Yes/No* questions.
  Can you tell me where the nearest bank is?
  I'd like to know if this bus goes to Oxford.

Making comparisons

- Add *-er* and *-est* to form the comparatives and superlatives of one-syllable adjectives and adverbs, two-syllable adjectives, and adverbs ending in *y*.

- For two syllable adjectives ending in *y*, form the comparative and superlative by removing the *y* and adding *-ier* or *-iest*.

- Use *more* and *most* to form the comparatives and superlatives of adjectives and adverbs with two or more syllables.

- You can also use (*not*) *as . . . as* to make comparisons.
  I can't play the piano as well as Michael.

- *Very* is not used to modify comparatives, but the following are:
  for a small difference—*a bit, a little, slightly*
  for a larger difference—*far, much, very much, a lot*
  I'm feeling a lot better today.

Unit Vocabulary

Phrases about exploration

to go as a solo traveler	to wander around
to be bitten by the travel bug	
to experience culture shock	
to go/be taken into uncharted territory	

Adjective pairs ending in -ed/-ing

fascinated/fascinating	daunted/daunting
challenged/challenging	petrified/petrifying
disgusted/disgusting	annoyed/annoying
inspired/inspiring	worried/worrying

Weather

cool	chilly	subzero temperatures
mild	clear	to drizzle/drizzle
to pour	breeze	sweltering
overcast	sunny	changeable

Verb phrases about moving or traveling

emigrate	live abroad	be off
leave home	roam around	
set off	see someone off	

Unit 7 Reference

Count and noncount nouns

- Count nouns are words like *banana* or *hotel*. They can use a singular or plural form of the verb.
  *That's **a** great **hotel**! They're great **hotels**!*

- Noncount nouns are words like *food, information,* or *equipment*. They use a singular form of the verb.
  *There **isn't** much food left.*
  Common noncount nouns: advice, behavior, equipment, food, furniture, health, information, knowledge, luggage, news, research, traffic, travel, trouble, weather, work
  Common nouns that can be count or noncount: chicken, chocolate, coffee, egg, glass, hair, iron, paper, room, space, time

- Use *a/an, few, a few, some, any, many, a lot of, lots of* before count nouns.
  *I haven't roasted **any potatoes**.*

- Use *little, a little, some, any, much, a lot of, lots of* before noncount nouns.
  *There wasn't **much traffic** this morning.*

- *Few* and *little* (without *a*) are used to talk about negative ideas.
  *She has **few friends** and is quite lonely.*

- *A few* and *a little* are used to talk about more positive ideas.
  *Could I have coffee with **a little milk,** please?*

Passive forms

- Use active forms when the subject is the person or thing that does the action.
  I bought a really fantastic party dress on eBay.

- Use passive forms when who or what causes the action is unknown or unimportant, or to put new information or longer expressions later in the sentence.
  The dog was found three days after it went missing.

- Passive forms are often used in more formal speech and in news stories, scientific, and academic writing.

- Use *by* to say who did the action.
  *A Picasso painting was bought **by a billionaire**.*

- Use the passive in any tense and with modal verbs.
  Form: verb *to be* + past participle
  *We **haven't been given** the exam results yet.*

Causative forms: *have/get (something) done*

Form: *have* (or *get*) + object + past participle

Use *to have* (or *get*) *something done*:

- to talk about arranging for something to be done by someone else.
  *I **have my hair dyed** once every six months.*

- to talk about things that happen to us or to describe an "experience."
  *I **had my bike stolen** last week.*

- There is another use of *get* + object + past participle (NOT ~~have~~) which is used to mean "finish doing something."
  *I need to **get my homework done**.*

Unit Vocabulary

Words and phrases about excess

extravagant	excessive	a luxury
extra-large	to spoil someone	overpriced
far-fetched	to go on a spending spree	

Food and cooking

a saucepan	an oven	a range	salty
a frying pan	a plate	a dish	sweet
to scramble	parsley	to grill	sour
a vegetarian	to bake	a plate	raw
a vegetable	to roast	to fry	rare
to chop	to boil	to stir	beef
cabbage	to slice	to beat	bitter
a peach	to grate	spicy	
a wooden spoon			

Verb phrases about money

to bid for something	to get a refund
to get a discount	to get a bargain
to haggle for something	to get a receipt
to be able to afford something	to be worth it

Animals and animal idioms

fly	wings	bull	horse	fin
cat	duck	fish	feathers	dog
bat	eagle	horns	spider	tail
fur	whale	paws	hooves	bug
beak	claws	bear	whiskers	talons

to be as blind as a bat
to take the bull by the horns
straight from the horse's mouth

Unit 8 Reference

Stating preferences

It's time . . .

- "It's time I did something" is used to mean "I should have done something already or at least started it."

  It's time you did your homework.

  Form: *It's time* + subject + past tense

I'd rather . . .

- "I'd rather you did/didn't do something" is used to say what you'd prefer someone else to do.

  I'd rather you didn't smoke in here.

  Form: subject + *would rather* + object + past tense (+ *than* . . .)

- "I'd rather do/not do something" is used to talk about what you'd prefer to do.

  I'd rather not spend all day lying on the beach.

  Form: subject + *would rather* + verb (+ *than* . . .)

I'd better . . .

- "I'd better do/not do something" is used to talk about something when it is advisable to do it in the present or future.

  I'd better fix that window as soon as I can.

  Form: subject + *had better* + verb

Reported speech

- Use "reported" or "indirect" speech to tell people what somebody said or thought.

  1. Make the tense of the verb one "step" further back into the past.

     "I want to go out." → She said (that) she **wanted to go out.**

  2. Modal verbs also change.

     "Can you help me paint the kitchen?" → She asked me **if I could help** her paint the kitchen.

  3. Subject and object pronouns change.

     "I will give it to you soon." → He said **he** would give it to me soon.

  4. References to particular times also change.

     *"The books will be delivered **tomorrow**."* → She said the books would be delivered **the next day**.

  5. Word order changes.

     *"What **are you doing** this weekend?"* → He asked me **what we were doing** this weekend.

  6. Use *if* (or *whether*) when reporting *Yes/No* questions.

"Did you enjoy the movie?" → He asked me **if** I had enjoyed the movie.

Reporting verbs

- *Say* and *explain* are followed by (*that*).

  She **explained that** John was ill and couldn't come.

- *Tell* is followed by verb + object + (*that*).

  He **told us that** we needed to show identification.

- *Ask*, *remind,* and *warn* are followed by object + infinitive.

  We **reminded him to mail** the letter.

- *Promise* and *decide* are followed by infinitive.

  We **decided to stay** at home and watch TV.

- *Admit* and *suggest* are followed by gerund.

  He **admitted liking** her a lot.

Adjectives and adverbs: *hard* and *hardly*

- *Hard* as an adjective means firm and difficult to cut or break. *The mattress is too **hard**.*

- *Hard* as an adverb means using a lot of effort or force. *She's been working **hard** all day.*

- *Hardly* is an adverb which means *almost not* or *very little*. *I **hardly** know the people in my class.*

- *Hardly* is often used with *anything, anyone, anywhere,* and *ever*. *We **hardly** ever go out in the evening.*

Unit Vocabulary

Words and phrases about success and failure

best-seller	go under	give it a try
have had their day	give up	be up to snuff

Personality

proactive	headstrong	selfish
manipulative	outgoing	open
opinionated	easy-going	witty
to be a complete doormat		single-minded
to be the center of attention		to be down-to-earth
to be really high maintenance		to be a party animal

Adverbs: intensifiers/gradable and nongradable adjectives

important—vital	extremely	really
upset—devastated	absolutely	very
hungry—starving	big—huge	
tired—exhausted	happy—ecstatic	

Unit 9 Reference

Dependent clauses: sequencing

- Use *Having* + past participle or *After* + present participle to show the order of events when telling a story or describing a series of events.

  Having discussed *the problem for several hours, we decided to go out for something to eat.*

  After explaining *to her boss why she needed a raise, she told him that she was thinking of leaving the company.*

- Other examples with a similar structure include:

  Before painting *the room, she had to strip off the old wallpaper.*

  On entering *the room, he noticed that all the windows were open.*

  While cleaning *the room, she discovered a locked diary.*

Past modals of deduction: *must/might/can't have*

- Use *must* to say that you believe something is certain.

- Use *might* to say something is a possibility.

- Use *can't* to say that you believe something is not possible.

- For the past, use *must/might/can't have* + past participle. This is the same for *I/you/he/we/they*.

  You **must have enjoyed** *your vacation in Australia.*

  I think I **might have left** *my wallet in that store.*

  She hasn't called me so she **can't have gotten** *my message.*

- *Might have* + past participle can also refer to the present or future when a time expression clarifies the context.

  I'll give him a call but he **may have left** *by now.*

  By this time next year I **might have moved** *to Brussels.*

- It is also possible to use *may* instead of *might* and *couldn't* instead of *can't*.

  She **may have stopped** *to get some gas.*

  They **couldn't have gone** *swimming. They didn't take any towels.*

Relative clauses

Defining relative clauses

- **Defining relative clauses** define or identify the person, thing, time, place, or reason. They cannot be left out. No commas are used before or after the defining relative clause.

  Tim is the teacher **who/whom I told you about***.*

  That's the street **where I grew up***.*

- *That* can be used instead of *who*.

  The woman **that/who** *I share an office with has been in the company for years.*

- The relative pronoun can be left out if it is the object of the verb in the relative clause.

  Simon bought the jacket **(that)** *we saw when we went shopping last weekend.*

Nondefining relative clauses

- **Nondefining relative clauses** give extra information which can be left out. Commas are used before and after non-defining relative clauses unless they end a sentence.

  I loaned my new bike, **which I really like***, to my brother.*

  Cairo, **where I lived for several years***, is a fascinating city.*

- *Who* and *which* cannot be replaced by *that*.

Unit Vocabulary

Words and phrases about crime and punishment

robbery	thief	community service
speeding	road rage	intimidation
witness	fingerprints	

Insurance and court cases

sue (someone)	appeal
file (a lawsuit)	premium
convict (someone of)	arson
sentence (someone to)	fraud

Introducing and telling a funny story

Did you hear the story about . . .	You're kidding!
Have you heard the one about . . .	How ridiculous!
So, here's what happened . . .	Unbelievable!
But that's not all . . .	No way!
And then . . .	

Compound adjectives

middle-aged	one-way	single-minded
left-handed	part-time	last-minute
brand-new	so-called	time-consuming
homemade		

Unit 10 Reference

Reflexive pronouns

- **Singular:** *myself/yourself/himself/herself/itself*
  Plural: *ourselves/yourselves/themselves*
- Use reflexive pronouns to talk about actions where the subject and object are the same person.
  I cut myself while I was cooking.
- Reflexive pronouns can also be used for emphasis when we mean "that person or thing, and nobody or nothing else."
  They built that house themselves.

Gerunds and infinitives

Certain verbs are followed by particular structures:

- Verb + gerund: *enjoy, avoid, imagine, consider, finish, miss, practice, involve, suggest*
  Does the job involve working in the evenings?
- Verb + infinitive: *want, seem, offer, decide, hope, afford, agree, arrange, promise, refuse, manage*
  He offered to give me a ride to town.
- Verb + object + infinitive: *persuade, convince, encourage, allow, advise*
  I encouraged her to work as hard as she could.
- Verb + gerund OR verb + infinitive with a different meaning: *remember, regret, try, stop, go on*
  I stopped talking to Sam. (I was talking to Sam and then I stopped.)
  I stopped to talk to Sam. (I stopped what I was doing in order to talk to Sam.)

Conditionals

- Use the **real conditional** to talk about future possibility.

  Form: *If* + simple present or present continuous or present perfect, *will/going to* present continuous
  If you're going to the party tomorrow, I'll see you there.
- Use the **present unreal conditional** to talk about present or future unreal or imagined situations.

  Form: *If* + simple past/past continuous, *would/could/should/might* + verb
  He'd be much more healthy if he didn't smoke.

- Use the past unreal conditional to talk about past unreal situations with a past result.

  Form: *If* + past perfect, *would have/could have/should have/might have* + past participle
  If you hadn't been so rude, he wouldn't have walked out.
- Use **mixed conditionals** with an *if* clause referring to the past and a main clause referring to the present/future.

  Form: *If* + past perfect, *would* (or *'d*) + verb
  If we hadn't missed the plane, we'd be in Spain now.
- You can also use **mixed conditionals** with an *if* clause referring to the present/future and a main clause referring to the past.
  If you didn't want to come to the movie tomorrow, I wouldn't have bothered getting you a ticket.

Unit Vocabulary

Words and phrases about the mind

subconscious (fears)	willpower
to trust your intuition	your sixth sense
to be unconscious	mind over matter
to have a premonition	
the power of persuasion	
to have a feeling of déjà vu	

Verb phrases about beliefs

be in favor of	suspect
be skeptical that	doubt
have your doubts about	be against
have always believed that	be convinced

Advertising

advertisement	advertising	slogan
classified ad	marketing	hype
target market	commercial	brand

Verbs for different ways of speaking

whisper	blurt out	be at a loss for words
shriek	interrupt	speak your mind
mumble	snap at someone	

Speaking Exchange

Unit 2 | Page 26, Exercise 3

3 Mma Makutsi looked at her and then looked down at the typewriter keyboard. She opened a drawer, peered inside, and then closed it. At that moment a hen came into the room from the yard outside and pecked at something on the floor. "Get out," shouted Mma Makutsi. "No chickens in here!" At ten o'clock Mma Makutsi got up from her desk and went into the back room to make the tea. She had been asked to make bush tea, which was Mma Ramotswe's favorite, and she soon brought two cups back. She had a tin of condensed milk in her handbag, and she took this out and poured a small amount into each cup. Then they drank their tea, watching a small boy at the edge of the road throwing stones at a skeletal dog.

At eleven o'clock they had another cup of tea, and at twelve Mma Ramotswe rose to her feet and announced that she was going to walk down the road to the shops to buy herself some perfume. Mma Makutsi was to stay behind in case the telephone rang and in case any clients came in. Mma Ramotswe smiled as she said this. There would be no clients, of course. And she would be closed at the end of the month. Did Mma Makutsi understand what a disastrous job she had obtained for herself? A woman with an average of ninety-seven percent deserved better than this.

Mma Ramotswe was standing at the counter of the shop looking at a bottle of perfume when Mma Makutsi hurtled through the door. "Mma Ramotswe," she panted. "A client. There is a client in the office. It is a big case. A missing man. Come quickly. There is no time to lose."

Unit 4 | Page 52, Exercise 10

Student A

Unit 9 | Page 114, Exercise 6

6. Explanation
The airplane was on the ground when he leaped.

Unit 6 | Page 73, Exercise 12b

Student B

Camel trips at DakhlaOasis *Egypt*

Price: $160 per person per night

Where?
Dakhla Oasis is about 850 km from Cairo. The hotel is situated at the top of pink cliffs that surround the oasis below. Within the oasis, there are beautiful fields and gardens full of grapes, olive trees, date palms, figs, apricots, and citrus fruits. Beyond the oasis, there are the incredible sand dunes of the Sahara Desert.

Accommodations
Dakhla has 32 large rooms, all with private bathrooms. The rooms are simple but tastefully furnished in the local style. They all have fans and also heaters for the cold winter nights. Some rooms have a terrace with spectacular views of the nearby mountain range. The restaurant serves delicious local food including the traditional falafel.

Activities
There are camel trips and walking tours available from half a day to 3-plus days. These go across the sand dunes of the desert and also up into the mountains. The guides will help you set up the tents and prepare a delicious barbecue dinner on the campfire with homemade bread, baked in the sand.

Unit 2 | Page 30, Exercise 6a

Seattle Center for Business Studies

BA in Business Studies: Full-time, Part-time, or Online Learning: our flexible mode of study allows you to combine online learning with university-based study.

We offer excellent facilities and instruction to anyone who is committed to taking initiative and studying to his or her full potential.

Many places available for mature students and overseas students.

For more information and to apply, contact:
Dr. Anne Owen, Director of Studies
Seattle Center for Business Studies
129 Pine Street, Seattle, WA 98127

Nursing Degree—Miami

Our program is a full time, 3-year course leading to a BSN degree and license as a Registered Nurse. Half the course is classroom or private study and the remaining time is experience-based. Right from the start, students will be working with patients, with appropriate support, and this will involve working some evenings, nights, and weekends. The training will be demanding. However, the potential personal rewards can also be great.

You will need to have a high school diploma and to be at least 18 years old to sign up for the course.

Unit 9 | Page 106, Exercise 10

Story 1

At 5 A.M. one September morning, two would-be robbers from Edmonton, Canada, raided a small gas station in Vancouver. After locking the attendant in the bathroom, they made their getaway with a few hundred dollars. Coming from Edmonton, they didn't know their way around Vancouver, and 20 minutes later they drove up at the same gas station to ask directions.

The attendant, Mr. Karnail Dhillon, having just escaped from the bathroom, was alarmed to see the two robbers coming into the store again. "They wanted me to tell them the way to Port Moody," he said. "I guess they didn't recognize me or the gas station."

He was just calling the police when the pair came back again to say that they couldn't get their car to start. While they were waiting for a mechanic to help them, the police arrived and arrested them.

Unit 9 | Page 114, Exercise 6

3. **Explanation**
   He was riding a horse named Friday . . .

Unit 4 | Page 52, Exercise 10

Student B

Unit 6 | Page 73, Exercise 12b

Student A

Bird watching in Mexico at
Yucatan Ecolodge

Price: $100 per person per night

Where? Yucatan Ecolodge is a 5-hour drive from Cancun with wonderful views of the Gulf of Mexico. The area is famous for its varied plant and animal life, especially birds.

Accommodations Stay in a comfortable bungalow with a balcony as well as bedroom, living room, and bathroom. There are fans but no air conditioning. Meals include a tasty Mexican breakfast and a four-course candle-lit dinner with fresh food and seafood. There is also a game room and a swimming pool for you to enjoy.

Activities Available tours include bird watching, trips to caves in the area, and moonlight safaris. There is also a small Natural History Museum, offering an overall view of the flora and fauna surrounding the hotel.

Unit 3 | Page 38, Exercise 3

Student A

Letters to the Editor

In last week's edition, Mark Wright longs for "the good old days." An international traveler, he claims that today everything looks the same no matter what continent he is on. He implies that there are no individual cultures and that national identities are disappearing. I strongly disagree with him and am shocked by his wildly inappropriate negativity. How can he fail to see and appreciate the incredible diversity in the world today?

In the past people tended to be stereotyped by nationality or where they lived. With a more international view, today people are less specifically pigeon-holed by where they come from. Being Chinese, Mexican, or Canadian no longer defines you. It's only part of who you are. Now it's commonplace for any person to eat from the endless menu of international cuisine, go on vacation anywhere from Burma to Bolivia, and have friends from around the world.

In my opinion, this diversity and availability is a good thing. Yes, identical chain restaurants keep popping up globally. But that does not mean you *have to* drink frappuccinos or eat Big Macs. You can choose to have sushi, curry chicken, Pad Thai, or a falafel instead. There were hardly this many choices in Wright's "good old days"!

-Marcia Kohl, Boston, MA

Unit 6 | Page 78, Exercise 7a

You love your creature comforts

You love your vacations but you prefer a touch of home wherever you go. Creature comforts mean a lot to you. Trekking through the desert with a camel for company is probably not your idea of a great vacation. You prefer to get lots of rest and lots of sun.

You love a bit of adventure

You're a bit of an adventurer compared to some tourists. You hate lying around sunbathing, but prefer something different, such as whitewater rafting. However, you also prefer to sleep in a nice bed in a good hotel after a long day's adventure.

You love to be independent

You're a true independent traveler who probably avoids package vacations and is rarely seen in a big resort in Cancun. You love exploring far-flung countries and mixing with the locals. And you've probably got shelves full of photos and interesting souvenirs.

You're a real explorer

You are a real explorer who loves to get lost in places where no tourist has gone before. You love meeting the locals, hate bumping into anyone who speaks your language, and don't mind sleeping in the open with the local wildlife for company.

Unit 9 | Page 114, Exercise 6

2. **Explanation**

The water in the river only came up to the man's chest.

Unit 3 | Page 38, Exercise 3
Student B

Letters to the Editor

I must respond to Mark Wright's article "The good old days" from last week. I agree with him <u>fully</u> on the sameness of today's world—this being the inevitable downside to globalization. Nothing irks me more than the identical clothes people wear and gadgets they carry. Not to mention chain stores and restaurants. <u>However</u>, his argument that the old days were better is simplifying things too much.

In my opinion, our world today is much richer and more exciting than in <u>the old days</u>. Thanks to the Internet, we have instant access to international music, movies, newspapers, and magazines—that is how I was able to read and respond to Wright's article from across the world in Korea. The Internet gives us access to foreign languages like never before. To say that English is taking over the world is imprecise. Yes, large numbers of people now speak English. A global English facilitates communication and has major advantages for global business, scientific research, and tourism. But other world languages are doing very <u>well</u>. And no one is looking for a single world language to take over.

Also contributing to our exciting world today is the constant intertwining of cultures. A Brazilian designer working in Asia will <u>usually</u> create different clothes than he would <u>back home</u>. Food from a Chinese restaurant in Britain will taste different than in China, or even New York. Some people might even prefer it. Branded goods are also influenced by cultures with McDonalds selling beer in Germany, lamb in India, and rice burgers in Hong Kong.

With the luxury to travel as much as he does, I have a few words of advice for Mr. Wright: Why stay at the Hilton in every town? Experience the local hotels, which will more likely offer authentic cuisine and give you a richer cultural experience. And on your next trip look past the uniformity and seek out the differences. You will see how interesting and diverse the world indeed is <u>today</u>.

–Chang-Ho Lee, Seoul, Korea

Unit 9 | Page 114, Exercise 6

4. **Explanation**

Because Bobby was only 9 months old . . .

Unit 4 | Page 54, Exercise 5

How to play

1. Play in groups of three to five.
2. Make a set of 15 question cards for the game using the topics or grammar from this unit.

> *How would you feel about doing something "extreme" (like sailing alone across an ocean), where your life might be in danger?*

3. Each player puts a game piece on Start. When it's your turn, take a question card and answer the question. If you answer well and keep speaking for at least one minute, throw the die and move again. If you land on a ladder, go up it, and if you land on a rope, go down it.
4. The winner is the player who reaches Finish first.

Unit 3 | Page 33, Exercise 6a

Student B

Sunday:

Juliet's father promises that Juliet will marry Paris (the son of the Prince of Verona).

Romeo and Juliet meet, fall in love, and decide to marry.

Tuesday:

Juliet is told she will marry Paris the next day.

Juliet takes a "sleeping potion" to pretend to be dead.

Thursday:

Juliet wakes up from the effects of the "sleeping potion."

She discovers Romeo is dead and kills herself.

The two families find their two children dead and make peace with each other.

Unit 9 | Page 106, Exercise 10

Story 2

An ambitious burglar broke into a vast mansion on millionaires' row in Bel Air, Los Angeles. He went through the house room by room, putting anything of value that he could see and carry in a large bag he'd brought with him. Having completely filled his bag, he decided it was time to leave.

He started to realize that he wasn't sure of the way out but moved on quickly, through a large dining room, past an indoor gym, and through another room filled with exotic parrots. By now he was beginning to panic. Then, having run through a large library and a small room full of art, he began to get desperate.

He ran up a small spiral staircase to what seemed to be a large bedroom. He knocked on the door and went in. The owners of the house had been asleep in bed but sat up in fright to find a traumatized burglar desperate to find his way out of the maze of rooms. After giving him detailed directions, they called the police, who arrived minutes later and escorted the relieved burglar to the safety of a nearby police station.

Unit 9 | Page 114, Exercise 6

5. **Explanation**

The man had just been cured of deafness, and the ringing phone is final proof that it has been a success.

Unit 4 | Page 46, Exercise 10b

I blog, therefore I am

I'm sure someone's said that before, but hey, I'm new to this. I have been looking through the blogs out there and I knew there were lots, but I didn't realize that there were lots and lots and lots and lots and lots. I wasted hours today going through some of them. I didn't mean to, I just didn't notice where the time had gone. The thing is that most of them have links to other blogs, and it's easy to get carried away. It's curious though—all these people out there putting their thoughts and lives out for everyone to see. In my case, it's just people I don't know who see it, because I haven't told anyone I do this. Which of course leads to the question, why **do** I do this? I have a journal, too, that I write in when I have time, but I find it easier to sit at the computer and type. But why put it up on the Web? It's hard to answer that one. Some people seem to use blogs as a way of keeping family up-to-date or to stay in touch with friends, but there are many people like me who just throw their thoughts out into cyber-space for anyone who feels like reading them. I'm sure that this is a great topic for psychoanalysts everywhere; I wonder what they think?

Posted: Sunday, February 13th at 10:37 P.M.

Unit 10 | Page 126, Exercise 6

Types of thinkers/learners

Linguistic: They like to think in words and use complex ideas. They are sensitive to the different sounds and meanings of words and enjoy the process of learning a foreign language.

Logical-mathematical: They like to understand patterns and the relationships between things. They are good at thinking critically and problem-solving. They like to analyze and understand the rules.

Interpersonal: They like to think about other people and are often peacemakers. They are aware that different people have different views on life and they probably have lots of friends.

Existential: They like to spend time thinking about philosophical issues and don't like to be bothered with trivial questions. They are always asking questions and provoking discussions and debates.

Kinesthetic: They like to think in movements and find it difficult to sit still for long. They are interested in fitness and health and they learn best when they are physically involved.

Unit 9 | Page 106, Exercise 9

Unit 3 | Page 33, Exercise 6a

Student A

Place: Verona, Italy

Background: Capulets (Juliet's family) and Montagues (Romeo's family) are two families with a long-standing history of fighting each other.

Monday: Romeo and Juliet get married.

Wednesday:

Romeo finds out about Juliet and thinks she is dead.

Romeo kills Paris.

Romeo then drinks some poison and kills himself.

Unit 9 | Page 114, Exercise 6

1. **Explanation**

   The teenagers were traveling on the road that crossed the road that the police officer was on. They drove through a green light.

Unit 2 | Page 28, Exercise 9

WANTED

INTERNET AND COMPUTER EXPERT

Internet and computer expert wanted.
Can you help this busy Internet café?
Are you good with computers?
Do you know about the latest developments in Internet technology?
Can you communicate well with all kinds of customers?

If you are the right person for us, we will offer you a good salary and free use of all facilities.

Write to: Jenny Keaton, PepeNet Café, 21 University St., Chicago, IL 60601

Assistant organizer
for social activities

Our English language school is looking for an enthusiastic person to help organize our busy social activities program.

You don't need experience but you do need to be energetic and sociable. You also need to have a good level of English.

The job is part-time with hours to suit you. Good pay rates to be negotiated. We also offer a discount on our English courses to the successful candidate.

Write to: The Secretary, Oakwood School of English, 16 Bridge Street, Boston, MA 02122

Writing Bank

Unit 6 | Page 70, Exercise 10a

Informal emails

1 Read the email. Which of the following best summarizes Mary's experience?

1. She's about to finish an interesting class.
2. She's nearly at the end of an exciting vacation.
3. She's coming to the end of her time in college.
4. She's about to quit a job she's been doing for a long time.

Writing skill | punctuation

2a Look at the email again and find examples of the following:

1. an exclamation point
2. a question mark
3. an apostrophe
4. a dash
5. a period
6. a comma

b Match the punctuation above with the correct explanations below.

_____ **a.** used to show the end of a sentence

_____ **b.** used at the end of a sentence to show it is a question

_____ **c.** used at the end of a sentence, often to show excitement, surprise, or other strong emotions

_____ **d.** used in writing to show pauses in speech, especially in lists, between adjectives, and around clauses

_____ **e.** used to show missing letters in contractions and with the possessive _s_

_____ **f.** used in informal writing to add an extra thought or idea to a sentence

Name, date, and email address are included at the top, so don't write them in the main part of the email.

Use an informal greeting with or without the person's name.

Use informal language, including contractions (Ex: _I've_), informal words, and exclamation points.

From: Mary Ryland
Date: 07.12.12 19:34
To: leila@hotmail.com
Subject: elephant orphanage
Attach: elephant2.JPG (285 KB)

Hi Leila,

Wow! Where do I start? Did I tell you about this amazing project I'm doing before I go to college? I've been on vacation in Sri Lanka for three months working in an elephant orphanage! It's the first time I've been anywhere like this – and although I was a bit daunted at first, now I love it!

We don't work all the time – there's plenty of time to have a real vacation, too. It's been great to experience a different culture and to see the places I've only read about in books. The best part is meeting so many friendly people, and it's fascinating being so close to the elephants. I'm attaching a photo of me washing one of the babies.

I only have ten more days to go. I'm looking forward to seeing you all, but I don't want to leave this place.

See you soon!

Lots of love,

Mary

Useful Phrases

Opening phrases	_Hi (Leila),_ **Hello** _(Leila),_ **Dear** _(Leila),_
Giving news	_Did I tell you about . . . ?_ _It's the first time I've . . ._ _It's been great to . . ._
Attaching photos	_I'm attaching a photo of . . ._ _I'm sending you a photo of . . ._
Closing phrases	_I'm looking forward to seeing you . . ._ _Lots of love, Best wishes,_ _All the best,_

143

Unit 7 | Page 85, Exercise 10

Formal letters

1 Read the letter and answer the questions.

> 1. What are the three problems the customer is complaining about?
> 2. What does she want?

> Use *Dear Sir or Madam:* if you don't know the name of the person you are writing to. Use *Dear Mr./Mrs. Smith*, if you know the name.

Writing skill | formal and informal language

2 Look at the letter again. Is the language used formal or informal? Give two examples from the letter.

3 Mark the sentences formal *(F)* or informal *(I)*.

> ____ 1. It would be great to hear from you soon.
>
> ____ 2. I would be grateful if a full refund could be sent as soon as possible.
>
> ____ 3. I look forward to hearing from you at your earliest convenience.
>
> ____ 4. Love, Jenny
>
> ____ 5. I'm writing to tell you about something I bought recently.
>
> ____ 6. Dear Ms. Harrison,
>
> ____ 7. I am writing with reference to the service I received at your restaurant last week.
>
> ____ 8. Dear Anna,
>
> ____ 9. You know how I feel about all this, don't you?
>
> ____ 10. Sincerely, Julio Manzanares
>
> ____ 11. I am sure that you will understand why I feel so annoyed about this situation.
>
> ____ 12. Could you give me the money back, please?

> Write the name and/or title and address of the person you are writing to.

> Write your address here. Don't write your name.

55 Chestnut Avenue
Pomona CA, 90187

February 15, 2012

> Write the date here.

Customer Service
Film Express
214 W. 40th Street
New York, NY 10013

Dear Sir or Madam:

I am writing to complain about two DVDs I bought recently on the Internet from your company and about how I was treated by a member of the staff when I called to complain.

First, I ordered them on January 6th and I was promised they would arrive in three days, but they weren't sent to me for over two weeks. Then, when they arrived and I opened the box, I was shocked to see that one of them was broken, as they clearly hadn't been packaged correctly.

Second, when I called to complain, I was very disappointed by the way I was treated. The staff member who I spoke to was extremely rude and did not offer me any form of refund or replacement.

I would be grateful if you could send me a replacement DVD as soon as possible, or if this is not possible, I would like a full refund. Thank you for your help with this matter.

Sincerely,

Diana Jones

Diana Jones – customer number: FE3428890/3

email: jonesd@youmail.com

> Use formal language. Don't use contractions (I would like . . . NOT: I'd like).

> Include any relevant reference numbers and email addresses at the end of the letter.

Useful Phrases

First lines	*I am writing in reference to . . .* *I am writing to complain about . . .* *I am writing in order to . . .*
Ways of complaining	*I was promised that . . . but . . .* *I was shocked to see/find that . . .* *I was very disappointed by . . .* *The items clearly hadn't been packaged correctly and were damaged.* *The service I received was not of the standard I would expect from your company.*
Last lines	*I would be grateful if you could send me a full refund/a replacement as soon as possible.* *I would like a full refund/a replacement.* *I look forward to hearing from you at your earliest convenience.* *Thanks you for your help with this matter.* *Thank you in advance.*

Reports

1   Read the report below. Which of the topics in Exercise 8, page 100 is it about?

Writing skill | paragraphs

2   What is the purpose of each paragraph in the report? Can you give each a short heading?

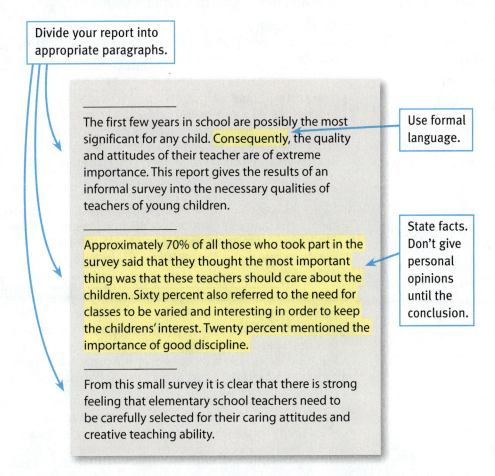

Divide your report into appropriate paragraphs.

Use formal language.

The first few years in school are possibly the most significant for any child. Consequently, the quality and attitudes of their teacher are of extreme importance. This report gives the results of an informal survey into the necessary qualities of teachers of young children.

Approximately 70% of all those who took part in the survey said that they thought the most important thing was that these teachers should care about the children. Sixty percent also referred to the need for classes to be varied and interesting in order to keep the childrens' interest. Twenty percent mentioned the importance of good discipline.

State facts. Don't give personal opinions until the conclusion.

From this small survey it is clear that there is strong feeling that elementary school teachers need to be carefully selected for their caring attitudes and creative teaching ability.

Useful Phrases

Introduction	*This report gives the results of . . ./is intended to . . .*
Reporting results	*Approximately 70% of all those who took part in the survey . . .*
Conclusion	*From this survey it is clear that . . .*

Articles

1 Find five different pieces of information between the article and the interview in Exercise 8, page 112.

Writing skill | referencing words

2a Find these underlined words in the article and say what they refer to.

1. there (line 3)
2. they (line 7)
3. this (line 9)
4. it (line 11)
5. she (line 13)
6. them (line 18)

b How can using pronouns like those above improve an article?

> Think of an interesting title.

The American "Sherlock Holmes"

1 Deep in the heart of the United States, far from Baker Street in London, lives a man named "Sherlock Holmes." In May of this year, I tracked him down <u>there</u> and had the chance to ask him a few questions that I'd been wondering about.

> Give some background or context to the title.

5 It turns out that Holmes's parents (he prefers to be called "Sherlock" by his friends and family) were great lovers of the work of Conan Doyle. He has memories from his earliest childhood of how <u>they</u> used to read the stories to him. And apparently, they always knew that if they were going to have a boy, they would give him <u>this</u> name. They wanted him to feel special.

> Use informal language.

10 Early on, Holmes used to get quite angry about people's reactions to his name, but he says he's more relaxed about <u>it</u> now. There was a time in San Francisco when a store clerk looked at his I.D. card and thought he must be the real, original Sherlock Holmes. <u>She</u> looked like she'd seen a ghost.

> Give examples of the points you make to interest your reader.

15 Oddly enough, Holmes says that people look to him sometimes to solve problems or mysteries. Luckily, he's done some magic himself, so he understands how some of the tricks on TV are done. On one occasion the police called him to help <u>them</u> out with a case they couldn't solve. Fortunately, he was able to find some clues on a computer that helped
20 them figure out what had happened to the missing person.

Meeting the American "Sherlock Holmes" was quite an experience. I'm not sure that I would want to be named after such a famous person, but from what I saw he has coped with it extremely well. As far as I'm concerned, parents need to think long and hard about the consequences of the names
25 they give their children for their future lives!

> Express your opinion.

Useful Phrases

Interest your reader	*Oddly enough . . .*
	To my surprise . . .
	Unbelievably . . .
Give examples	*There was a time when . . .*
	On one occasion . . .
Give your opinion	*As far as I'm concerned . . .*
	In my opinion . . .

Phrasal Verbs

A phrasal verb consists of two or more words: a verb + a particle (an adverb or a preposition) [+ a preposition]. The meaning of a phrasal verb is usually very different from the meaning of the verb alone. For example, the phrasal verbs *look up* (search for in a book or other source) and *look after* (care for) have very different meanings from *look*.

Some phrasal verbs are intransitive (they cannot take an object). The majority are transitive (they take an object). Sometimes the object can come after the particle or after the verb. For example, <u>hand in</u> your papers / <u>hand</u> your papers <u>in</u> / <u>hand</u> them <u>in</u>. These phrasal verbs are known as *separable*. With other phrasal verbs the words in the phrase cannot be separated; they are known as *inseparable*.

Some common phrasal verbs

Separable	
Ask out	ask someone on a date
Bring up	1) raise children 2) mention a subject
Call back	return a phone call
Call off	cancel
Call up	make a phone call
Figure out	find the solution
Fill in	give detailed information
Fill out	writing information on a form
Fill up	fill completely
Give back	return
Hand out	give to each person in a group; distribute
Hold up	keep waiting
Look over	examine carefully
Look up	search for information in a book or other source
Make up	Invent (a story)
Pick up	1) lift 2) collect in a car
Put away	put something where it belongs
Put back	return to the place it was found
Put off	Delay doing something you don't want to do; procrastinate
Shut off	turn off; stop
Show up	make someone feel stupid or bad
Split up	to end a relationship
Take back	return
Tear down	destroy
Try on	put something on to check the fit
Turn around	change direction
Turn down	refuse
Turn in	1) produce a great result 2) tell the police about a criminal 3) go to bed
Turn up	increase the volume
Work out	resolve a problem

Inseparable	
Catch on	1) understand 2) become popular
Come across	find by chance
Come by	visit
Come from	born in a place; originate
Come up with	invent or create something
Cut back/down on	use less; reduce
Fit in	be accepted by others
Get along with	have a friendly relationship
Get away from	escape
Get away with	go unnoticed or unpunished
Get in	enter
Get over	recover
Get up	get out of bed
Give up	stop trying
Go on	1) continue 2) happen
Go for	choose
Go through	1) experience 2) spend 3) check 4) be approved
Grow up	become an adult
Hang up	end a phone conversation
Keep out of	stay away from; not be involved
Make off with	steal
Make up	apologize after a quarrel
Look into	investigate
Look forward to	anticipate
Look up to	admire
Put up with	tolerate
See to	deal with someone or something
Take after	look or behave like a relative
Turn up	appear suddenly
Work out	exercise

Audioscript

UNIT 1 Making connections

▶ 1.02 (Page 9)

1. Hi, Allie. It's Keith. I'm calling about tonight. Um . . . Jackie and Steve were supposed to come, but I just heard they can't make it. Steve's dad is in the hospital. Anyway, I was wondering if you still want to go to the movie or not. We could do something else if you want. I don't mind. Give me a call on my cell and let me know, OK? Talk to you soon. Bye.

2. This message is for James Stevenson from the Global Bank Fraud Detection Department. On October 26th, a charge for $8,300 was made to his credit card account ending in 2126. We need him to confirm this charge before we can go ahead and authorize the payment. Please have him call Tony Jenkins at 1-800-555-3843 as soon as possible. Thank you.

3. Hello? I'm calling for Brian Jarvis. I saw your ad on Craig's list for a four-year old VW Jetta for sale. I would definitely be interested in coming over to look at it. Could you give me a call sometime? The best number for me during the day is 718-555-3750. That's my work number and just ask for Sarah Shaffer. I'm looking forward to your call. Thanks.

▶ 1.03 (Page 9)

A: So, what about you? Do you have any friends that you're really close to?
B: Hmm, that's a tricky one. I don't think so. I suppose I have a few people that I get along really well with, but we're not best friends like you and Angela. Maybe it's a guy thing.
A: Well, yeah, like I said, Angela and I have been best friends since we were kids.
B: So what makes her so special?
A: I guess it's that I can tell her everything that's going on with me. We text each other constantly.
B: Yeah, that's different for me. I mean, I have close friends like Jim, and Paula, and Alex, but they're very different people, so I usually talk to them about different things.
A: Like what?
B: Well, for instance, Jim's known me all my life. He knows my whole family, so whenever there are family problems, he's the person I talk to about them. Now, Paula and I have gotten close only in the last couple of years, but we've both had some pretty tough relationships so we talk about that stuff.
A: So Paula's the person you talk to about your love life stuff?
B: Right.
A: And Alex?
B: And Alex . . . well, I guess he's more like my career counselor. Whenever I get upset about work or have to make work decisions, he always has good suggestions.
A: But it wasn't always like that, was it? I remember when you were growing up you had a best friend.
B: Yeah, Doug. But we kind of lost touch when we both went off to college.
A: Do you ever talk to him now?
B: No, not really. Since then, it's pretty much been like this—a few close friends, but no best friend.

▶ 1.04 (Page 10)

A: So, Mike, you've been with the company for nearly a year now, haven't you?
B: Yes, that's right. I started last April.
A: And you feel pretty happy here, don't you?
B: Absolutely. It's a good job and the people here are really great.
A: Good to hear. So, are you clear about your targets for this year?
B: Yes, I think so. We have to increase sales by 15%, don't we?
A: That's right. If we do, everyone gets a 20% bonus. That will make *everyone* happy, won't it?
B: Definitely.
A: Now, let's talk about punctuality. You have trouble getting here on time, don't you?
B: Uh, well, I can explain that . . .

▶ 1.05 (Page 11)

Being in a large family usually means learning to "juggle" several tasks at once—making dinner while helping children with homework, bandaging a knee, keeping an eye on the games outside, and lending a caring ear.

However, in addition to normal family life, the Boehmers juggle clubs, rings, torches, balls, and anything else they can get their hands on. It all started when Larry Boehmer's job as a pipeline worker took him away from his wife, Judy, and his then four children. He had a lot of spare time on his hands. Judy said that when their son Adam was in the first grade, he came home one day and said he'd seen a video about circus performers at school. Adam wanted to know if his dad could do anything like that.

This was all the motivation Larry needed, and he decided to spend his evenings in his motel room learning to juggle. And here is a man who once he puts his mind to something, usually finishes it. Then at home, when his children saw him practicing, they wanted to join in. Larry is a big family man so he was only too happy to let them.

Larry and three of the children gave their first family performance at an amusement park. From there it just got better and better. And today they are the largest family of jugglers in the world.

According to Judy, they didn't plan on this happening. When the kids saw each other juggling, they picked up on different things. One would do rings, another would do clubs, tumbling, or the unicycle. Before they knew it, everybody was doing something.

Larry insists that his children's talents aren't inherited; it's simply a matter of practice and perseverance. He says that it's not in the genes. It's a skill that anybody can do. According to Larry, most people who try to learn juggling give up too soon, but he thinks almost anybody can learn. Larry believes that everyone has a specialty but perfecting it takes a lot of practice. In the end though, doing the shows is the fun part.

▶ 1.06 (Page 13)

A: So, the article claims that children's birth order plays a huge role in who they are and what they'll become when they grow up. What are your thoughts on this?
B: Well, I couldn't agree more. I think first born children always have a harder time than the other kids. Parents have more rules because they expect so much more.
A: I see your point, but I'm not sure if I agree with that. In my family, and in others I know, parents were really careful to treat all the kids the same. I mean, you're not a very good parent if you treat each child differently.
B: I don't think that's completely true. You can be an excellent parent, but once you've had experience raising a child, well, things change—you approach things differently—and that definitely has an affect on your kids.
A: Yeah, I think there's some truth in that, you know, that parents get better and better the more children they have.
B: Well, that's certainly what my oldest sister says!

▶ 1.09 (Page 16)

1.
A: Hi, it's me. Listen I'm really sorry I'm late, but my meeting ran over. My boss just went on and on. Anyway, I'm on my way, and I won't be long, I promise.
B: How much longer do you think you'll be?
A: Half an hour max—I promise. I know we said three o'clock but really there was nothing I could do . . .

2.
A: So, how's it going?
B: Fine, fine. Everyone's having a really good time.
A: But with this rain, you probably haven't been able to get out much.
B: Well, no, we haven't, but it's a great old house and the kids love exploring the attic. They've also got games to play and things to do inside. You know, it's actually been OK.
A: They say the weather should clear up in the next few days.
B: Yeah, I hope so. The kids want to do some hiking. There's supposed to be some really nice country around here.

3.
A: So, what do you feel like doing?
B: Well, first, I need to finish this essay.
A: OK. Then what?
B: I don't know. Do you feel like getting something to eat or . . . ?
A: Not really. There are a couple of movies I'd like to see.
B: Are they playing around here?
A: Yeah, I think so. Would you be up for that?
B: Well, it depends which ones.

4.
A: So, we've talked it over, and now we're going to meet up on Friday.
B: OK, but what went wrong today?

A: Well, I thought we had it all set up, but he said he was expecting an email from me to confirm.

B: So, you didn't send him one?

A: Well, no. I mean as far as I was concerned . . .

5.

A: Hi. Jenny?

B: Yep. Oh, Hi, Dave. Where are you? You're really late!

A: Yeah, well, I got started a little late, and I had to make a few detours along the way.

B: So, is everything OK?

A: Yeah. Everything's fine. Now, you did say you were on Vermont Drive, didn't you?

B: No, not Vermont Drive—Vermont Street. Where exactly are you?

A: Uh, I'm not totally sure but I'm in a busy area. I think I'm near Park Mall.

B: Park Mall? But that's halfway across town. What are you doing there?

▶ 1.10 (Page 18)

A: . . . so, have you come across, Genes Reunited on the web?

B: Genes what?

A: Genes Reunited. You know, it's like Friends Reunited only this is a website where you can try and find old relatives to add to your family tree.

B: Oh. Then no, I haven't, but I'd like to. I always thought I'd like to know a little more about my family history.

A: Well, then this is just the thing you're looking for. It's great. I know because I've started putting together my own family tree.

B: So, how far back have you gone?

A: Well, I'm pretty confident about as far back as my great-grandparents, Clara and John.

B: Wow, you didn't actually know them, did you?

A: No, unfortunately, they died in the 1970s. Totally devoted to each other, and of course they'd been through two World Wars together.

B: Yeah, that generation went through a lot, didn't it? Do you know when they were born?

A: Yeah, I do. My great-grandfather, John, was born right at the turn of the century in 1900, and my great-grandmother, Clara, was born just a year before that: in 1899.

B: Cool. How many children did they have?

A: Just two: Laura and Ben. Both were born around 1930 I think.

B: So, Laura's your grandmother. I've heard you talk about her, haven't I?

A: Um-hmm, yeah, that's right. She lives upstate. I go and visit her about once a month.

B: Oh, is her husband still alive?

A: Bill? No, he died a couple of years ago. So, she's on her own now.

B: How many kids did they have?

A: Laura and Bill had 3 kids: my mom Rachel, and my Aunt Sue, and Aunt Deborah.

B: Gosh, 3 girls.

A: Yep . . . but they're all very different.

B: Really? How so?

A: I've never told you about Aunt Sue?

B: I don't think so.

A: Well she was—is—an anthropologist. She's the family adventurer. She's spent most of her life with a tribe somewhere in Africa, studying the language and culture, religion and so on. She's supposed to be an expert on the place.

B: And speaking of adventurers, wasn't there some stuff about your grandmother's brother?

A: Oh, yeah, Uncle Ben. Well that's all kind of mysterious. No one will talk about him. Apparently, when he was in his early 20s, he just took off and nobody ever heard from him again. I'm sure there was a big blow-up, but I've never been able to find out exactly what happened.

B: Hmm, must have been bad if no one will talk about him.

A: Yeah, pretty weird, huh?

B: Yeah.

A: So then my mom and dad had just me.

B: I bet being an only child is great.

A: Uh, sometimes. It could be kind of lonely, too. But at least I've got some cousins. Aunt Deborah had a son and a daughter, Leon and Esther. Esther's a year or so older than me, and I'm a couple of years older than Leon. We really get along. We used to be pretty close. I saw them a lot as a kid because Aunt Deborah and her husband split up when the kids were little, and they used to come over for all the holidays.

B: What about now? Are you still close?

A: Well, Esther met a doctor while she was traveling around in New Zealand after she graduated. So she decided to move there to be with him. And Leon spends his summers working as a scuba diving instructor in Jamaica, and he spends his winters teaching skiing at a resort in Colorado.

B: Hard life.

A: Yeah, tell me about it.

UNIT 2 Making a living

▶ 1.11 (Page 22)

1.

A: Hi Julia. What's the matter? You look a little upset.

B: Oh, I don't know. I'm so fed up with work at the moment. It's so stressful here and I'm working longer and longer hours. I'm feeling totally overworked and underpaid.

A: I know. It's been bad for a while.

B: In fact, I'm thinking about quitting.

A: Really? What would you do instead?

B: I don't know. Anything for a change. I'd love to just do some volunteer work abroad or something different.

A: You should do some research on the Internet.

B: Yes. That's a good idea. In fact, I think I'll go to the library now and do it there. It's my lunch break and I've got at least half an hour.

A: Good idea! Let me know how it goes.

2.

C: How are you, Simon? What have you been doing?

D: Oh I'm fine. I've been making plans. I'm really excited.

C: Oh? Really? What's going on?

D: I've decided I'm going to quit my job and go back to school. I'm planning to get trained to do something completely different.

C: Really? What are you going to do?

D: Well, I've always wanted to be a vet. And life's too short. I want to go ahead and do it now!

C: Well, good luck!

3.

E: Hi, Maria. Do you want to grab some dinner tonight?

C: I can't, sorry. I've got an interview tomorrow.

E: An interview? What for? I thought you liked working from home.

C: Well, it's been OK, and I guess I like the flexible hours and not having to commute and stuff. But to be honest, I'm feeling a little isolated.

E: Yeah, I know what you mean.

C: Anyway, I'm meeting them at eight-thirty tomorrow morning, so I can't be out late.

E: Oh, well, good luck. I hope you get it.

4.

G: I think I'm going to try and look for another job.

H: Why? Don't you like where you are?

G: Yeah, it's OK. But I want to be promoted . . . and there are lots of other people here who'll get those jobs before me.

H: Oh, come on, you don't know that.

G: Sure I do. I think they'll make Sarah the sales manager. She's really good and she's been here forever.

H: OK, but what about assistant manager?

G: David's going to be assistant manager. I heard him talking to Jim about it.

H: Oh, I didn't know that. I see what you mean.

▶ 1.12 (Page 22)

1. That's a good idea. I think I'll go to the library now and do it there.

2. I've decided I'm going to quit my job and go back to school.

3. I'm meeting them at eight-thirty tomorrow morning.

4. I think they'll make Sarah the sales manager. She's really good and she's been here forever.

5. David is going to be assistant manager. I heard him talking to Jim about it.

▶ 1.13 (Page 23)

I'm standing in the extraordinary Rock Gardens of Chandigarh in India where I've spent the morning talking to Nek Chand, the visionary artist who created these gardens. Chand is a small, elderly man with a wrinkled face and gray hair, and he is extremely modest about his work. I tried to find out what made him create these gardens, but all he told me was that one day he started, and then he continued—day after day for 19 years. His modest manner, however, hides an incredible story.

Nek Chand was the son of a poor farmer, and in 1958 he started work as a government road inspector. At the time, Chandigarh was being designed and built by a famous Swiss architect who used a lot of concrete. Chand was fascinated by the process of design and construction using concrete, and decided to build his own "kingdom." He started to collect rocks and other bits of garbage from the building sites. Secretly, he took these things to a wooded area outside the city and began to build his garden. This had to be done in secret because Chand was building on land that belonged to the government.

First, he made the walls and paths and the buildings. Then he moved on to the second phase—creating over 5,000 sculptures. These sculptures include an incredible range of different kinds of figures—people, animals, birds, and many other bizarre and wonderful creatures. Each figure is different, and each one is made from material that had been thrown away. Chand recycles anything he can find – old bicycles, bricks, chunks of concrete, broken plates, old sinks, power plugs and other electrical equipment, small rocks and the list goes on and on.

Chand worked on the rock garden, his "secret kingdom" every day after work and every weekend for 18 years. Every minute of his free time was filled by working on this huge project that nobody else knew anything about. Then after 18 years, the garden was discovered by accident. At first, Chand was afraid that it would be destroyed, since it was built illegally on government-owned land. But quickly, people became interested in it, and the government realized that the garden might make a good tourist attraction. They paid Chand a small salary to work on the project full-time and one year later the Rock Garden officially opened.

Now, it is one of India's most popular tourist attractions, with 5,000 visitors every day. His huge achievement doesn't seem to have changed Chand at all. He told me that he was just doing his job. Everyone has a job they do, and this is his job. He says his life is utterly routine—every day he eats, he sleeps, and he works. Tomorrow morning, he will be doing the same thing he's doing today. Same with the day after that. He says it makes him happy, just doing it. Which is a good thing, because soon, he will have spent half a century "just doing it".

▶ **1.14** (Page 25)

As part of our efforts to improve the work/life balance of the people who work here, we've done a small survey of 20 of our employees. Everyone in the survey was between 21 and 30 years old. One of the things we wanted to find out was how people spend their time when they're not working. And these are the results.

First, nearly half the group regularly works late at the office. In fact, 9 out of 20 people stay late at work at least three times every week. However, hardly any of them thought this was a bad thing; only 3 of them, in fact. 25% of the group had done volunteer work at some time in their lives, but only 10% were doing it now.

Next, classes. The group as a whole was very interested in taking classes or doing activities at night. The vast majority say they take at least one night class, mostly art or language classes. Only a small minority would like to take more night classes, though. So it's not surprising that a lot of people are either taking, or have taken, some kind of online classes, mostly to expand their career opportunities by getting a degree or learning new skills.

Everyone said that a good way of relaxing was watching TV or a DVD, but nobody liked doing this every evening. Only a few people said they turned their computer on every evening, with visiting chat rooms being the most popular online activity.

The majority of the group preferred being with friends or family to being on their own as a way of relaxing. 60% said they found it easy to unwind after work but the vast majority of people said they would like to change their work/life balance. Most said they want to work less and make more time for themselves.

▶ **1.15** (Page 30)

1.
A: Hello, you must be Karen Goodman.
B: Uh, yes. Hello!
A: Hello, Karen. Nice to meet you. My name's Michael Harrison. Please, have a seat.
B: Thank you.
A: So, thank you for applying for the job and coming to the interview today. First, I'd like to ask you about your experience. In your letter, you say you've worked in an office before. Tell me about that.
B: Um, well, actually, that was a while ago.
A: OK. Well, what did you do there?
B: Nothing much really. I was just an assistant—you know, answering the phone and stuff.

2.
C: Ah! There you are.
D: Oh my gosh. I'm so sorry.
C: Let's see. You're John, aren't you? John Scott?
D: Yes, that's right.
C: Well, come in John. I'm Peter Manning, and I'll be interviewing you today. I'm the current Chair of the Economics Department here. Very nice to meet you. Thank you for coming.
D: I'm really very sorry. I thought it would be a much quicker trip. The traffic was terrible, and then once I got here, I couldn't find the building.
C: OK. Uh, can I start by asking you about your reasons for applying to the program? What do you think you'd get from studying economics at this particular university?

3.
E: All right. Why don't we move on, Leo? You've talked about your experience up to now. So, I'd like to know about your plans for the future, after you've gotten your degree here. Where do you see yourself in five years?
C: Uh, I'm not really sure what I want to do after that. I mean, I'd love to study here. I think I'd get a lot out of it, and I'm sure

I'd bring a lot to the table, you know, but, um, after that, well, I don't know right now. I haven't really thought about it.
E: Do you see the hospitality industry as a long-term thing in your life or just something for the short-term?
C: Well . . . hmm. I'm thinking just short-term for now. I really haven't thought much about the future. The thing is I don't know how I'm going to feel. I guess I ought to think further down the road but . . .

4.
G: Well, thank you very much for talking to me today, Linda. We're coming to the end of the interview now, so is there anything that you'd like to ask me before you leave?
H: Yes, I do have a question, if that's OK.
G: Of course. Fire away.
H: Well, I was wondering how you handle promotions. I mean, I want to have a real career in the field of journalism and I'd like to know what kind of opportunities for advancement there might be.
G: That's a good question. We're very interested in the professional development of our staff and offer many opportunities for further training and promotion within the company. The right person might be promoted to a position such as senior editor, and of course, we're always looking for people to manage completely new magazines. Anything else?
H: Could you tell me when you're going to make your decision?
G: I've got some other candidates I'll be interviewing over the coming days, but I'm sure you'll hear from us soon.
H: Thank you very much.

▶ **1.16** (Page 30)

1. Thank you for applying for the job and coming to the interview today.
2. I'd like to ask you about your experience.
3. You say you've worked in an office before. Tell me about that.
4. I'm Peter Manning, and I'll be interviewing you today.
5. Can I start by asking you about your reasons for applying to the program?
6. Where do you see yourself in five years?

UNIT 3 Lessons from history

▶ **1.17** (Page 33)

Until the 3rd century BC, Carthage had been a powerful city which controlled most of the Mediterranean Sea. For the previous few hundred years, the Carthaginians had been trading with people in India and the Mediterranean area. There had been many battles between the Romans and the Carthaginians to try to control the area. Although, Carthage had taken control of many important places, they hadn't managed to take Sicily, the island on their doorstep. So, when the Romans won total control of Sicily, Carthage decided to attack Rome.

The leader of the attack was a brilliant young general named Hannibal. He had 40 war elephants, all trained to charge at the enemy. As Hannibal's army was marching northward toward the Alps, soldiers from Spain and other areas joined them. The icy mountains were difficult to cross, however, and by the time they reached Italy in 218 BC, many of his soldiers and elephants had died. They famously won three battles, but in the end the Romans were stronger and they took the city of Carthage and won the war.

▶ **1.18** (Page 35)

1.
A: Brrr! It's really cold today, isn't it?
B: Yeah. Do you want to borrow my sweater?
A: Well, thanks, but the thing is, I can't wear wool because it makes me so itchy. To tell you the truth, I know this sounds very stuck-up of me, but the only thing I'm really comfortable in is silk.
B: No, no, I know exactly what you mean. I don't have anything silk with me, of course, but I've got a cotton jacket in the back of my car.

2.
A: Hey, I like your jeans.
B: Thanks. They're nice, aren't they? I bought them yesterday. I really like how it has all these metal zippers and things. It makes me look pretty tough, eh?
A: Yeah, that look is big right now.
B: Mmm-hmm. The only problem is all these metal things kind of poke at you. And I love the fit, but it's pretty uncomfortable.
B: You think that's bad—I had a pair of leather jeans once. They looked great, but I could hardly breathe!

3.
A: I bought my nephew a really nice toy train made of wood for his birthday but I don't think he ever plays with it.
B: Oh? Really? Why not?
A: Oh I don't know . . . I love wooden toys . . . but I think most kids prefer plastic ones . . . you know, the adults like wood, but the children want plastic—or better still, computer games.

▶ **1.19** (Page 36)

A: Hello, welcome to today's edition of *Then and Now*. Today we're talking about an incredible country, with a fascinating culture and a long history going back over 5,000 years. China is incredibly rich in art and culture, and its food and traditions are well-known around the world. But two aspects of China are perhaps less well-known. First, this vast country has a long history of inventing things. Second, in recent years, China has started to flourish as an important global economy with ultra-modern cities and many booming industries. Today we've got China expert, Sandra Celaya here to tell us all about this flourishing land of invention. Hello, Sandra.
B: Hello.
A: Well, this show is called *Then and Now* . . . so let's start with "then": China's

history and this idea of umm . . . a "land of invention." Well, I knew that the Chinese invented paper, but I must admit, I didn't know that they invented so many other important things. Before we talk about those, can you remind us about the story of paper?
B: Yes. It was in 105 AD that papermaking was perfected in China. Actually, the first paper was made of silk. Well, it was really the waste from silk making, which they pulped up to make paper.
A: And paper had an enormous impact on China, didn't it?
B: Yes, with paper, and then printing, it meant people could get information much more easily.
A: So, what else did the Chinese invent?
B: Well, a number of simple but important things . . . I think one of the simplest inventions was the wheelbarrow, invented around 220 AD, which meant that large loads could be carried by just one person. And the Chinese invented a host of other things that we take for granted today, like silk, porcelain, the kite, and even the umbrella!
A: And we have the Chinese to thank for fireworks, don't we?
B: Yes, that's right. In the 8th century, the Chinese discovered gunpowder. And by the 10th century, it was being used to make fireworks, guns, rockets, and bombs, so it eventually had a huge influence on the whole world. Another major invention was a machine for making cast iron, which they first developed in the 6th century BC.
A: Wow! That really is a long time ago. That must have made a big difference to people's lives, too.
B: That's right. A lot of iron was used for agricultural tools, so production really increased after that . . . which brings us quite nicely to the present—to the "Now"—to present-day China.
A: Is agriculture production big in China now?
B: Well, yes, there's a lot of agriculture, about 10% of the economy is based on agriculture, you know, things like rice, tea, cotton, and fish. But it's certainly not just countryside and agriculture. There are some huge, modern cities like Shanghai and industry is huge in China now. It accounts for about 46% of the nation's economy. Steel production is a large part of that and is expanding all the time.
A: That's certainly a booming industry. So what other industries are important in China now?
B: Well, as you know, so many of the things people buy are made in China. Industrial production accounts for about half of China's economic wealth, including such consumer items as toys, clothes, shoes, cars, and electronics, as well as the heavier industrial products like iron and steel. China is the number one exporter of steel in the world.

▶ **1.20** (Page 37)

A: So, what do you think?
B: Well, I think the first one is easy. I mean, we have to decide on the three most important inventions ever. So,

for the first one, do you agree that the computer is definitely the most important?
A: Well, maybe. But isn't it true that we wouldn't have computers without electricity? So, really I think that the invention of the light bulb and discovering how to use electricity is incredibly important. What about you?
B: Hmm. I guess you're right. How do you feel about television then?
A: It's similar to the computer really. I mean, again, we wouldn't have television without electricity, right?
B: OK. So should we say the light bulb for the first one?
A: Yes, fine. And what else do you think is important?

▶ **1.21** (Page 42)

A: Hi, Kevin. How's it going?
B: Oh, hi! Pretty good, but I'm a little tired.
A: Oh? Are you busy these days?
B: Well, yeah. I'm taking a class, didn't I tell you?
A: No. I didn't know.
B: It's mostly online, but there's one day a week on campus. It's a lot of work.
A: Why?
B: It's a long story, but I'm trying to get certified in Spanish.
A: Spanish? But I thought you hated Spanish!
B: Well, yeah—it was definitely my worst subject in school. My brain just isn't wired for languages, and I didn't understand a thing.
A: So why do you want to do it now?
B: I don't want to, but I need to. You know, looking back, I wish I'd studied harder at school and just learned Spanish then, because I really need it now. I want to change careers and become a teacher.
A: A Spanish teacher?!
B: No. I want to be a math teacher, but they have this new requirement that you have to know some Spanish if you want to teach in the city.
A: Really? That doesn't seem fair . . .
B: Well, there are a lot of kids here who only speak Spanish at home. And anyway, those are the rules. Now that I'm older and wiser, I realize that staying in school and studying harder would have given me more opportunities in life.
A: I guess you're right. They say hindsight is 20/20. When you're young, you can't see the point of some things that turn out to be important when you're older. I mean, how were you to know that doing well in Spanish back then, would help you become a math teacher now?
B: I know.

UNIT **4** Taking risks

▶ **1.22** (Page 47)

1. There were six of us paddling together and fighting the rapids just trying to hang on. It was amazing! We flipped over twice! The first time was terrifying, but the second time was actually kind of fun.

2. You use every muscle in your body: legs, arms, fingers, toes, and everything in between. You do everything you can to hang on, you know, clinging to these tiny handholds, just to keep moving up. It's a mental challenge too because you have to figure out the best way to make a path from one foothold to the next.

3. When I reached the summit, I forgot my exhaustion and took in the gorgeous view. I felt like I was on top of the world! Of course, then we had to get all the way back down, which took hours. And I thought going down was a lot harder on my knees, too.

4. I usually don't mind all that stuff – carrying all my stuff on my back and hiking out to the middle of nowhere and everything. But this time everything took longer than we planned and we had to pitch a tent in the dark, and that was no fun. Then it rained all night, and my sleeping bag got soaked. And then I couldn't start a fire to heat food and stay warm. But I survived.

5. Climbing up wasn't too hard, but getting back down was the scariest thing I've ever done. Luckily, I completely trusted my partner below. But even so, I was checking the ropes and harnesses like every five seconds to make sure they could hold us up.

6. Well, it was a lot harder than it looked! And it was pretty windy at first, so the waves were really big for a lake. I tipped over a bunch of times, at first. Anyway, by the end of the day, I got the hang of it. My arms and shoulders were killing me, but I'm proud to say I made it all the way around the lake. I think that's probably about four or five miles.

▶ **1.23** (Page 49)

One of the best things we did on vacation was to go whitewater rafting. At first I was pretty nervous, especially when they told us we had to sign something which said we wouldn't hold the company responsible if we got injured or died! Anyway, before we started off, the guy in charge of our raft told us we had to wear lifejackets. I was surprised that we didn't have to wear any kind of helmet. We were also supposed to wear sneakers, but I'd forgotten mine so I had to wear my sandals. Once we got going though, I calmed down and the whole thing was fantastic! There were eight of us in the raft and there really were a lot of rapids. It was kind of like being on a roller coaster. At one point, I almost fell in.

The one thing I'm sorry about is that I didn't get any photos. I should have taken my camera, but I was afraid I would drop it in the water.

▶ **1.24** (Page 50)

A: So . . . did you go ahead and download it?
B: Yeah, I said I would, didn't I?
A: Yeah, but sometimes you say you'll do things that you don't.
B: ok. Sometimes. But this time I did.
A: And . . . ?
B: You were right. It was pretty good.
A: Pretty good!? Come on! It was much better than that. I think it's the best movie that I've seen in a long time.

B: Really? You know, I do like Clint Eastwood, but I guess I've never really been that into movies about boxing.
A: I hear you, but it's not really about boxing.
B: Isn't it? All the characters are boxing coaches, boxers, or ex-boxers. The main character is an ex-boxer who runs a boxing gym and the other main character wants to be a boxing champ.
A: That's true, but there's a lot more to it than that. There are lots of other themes running through the movie.
B: Hmm, such as . . . ?
A: Well, risk, for one.
B: What do you mean?
A: Well, remember at the beginning of the movie, one of Clint Eastwood's best boxers leaves him just as he has a chance to make it to the big time?
B: Oh yeah, that's right. He goes off with another manager, right?
A: Yep—after years of training in the gym with the Clint Eastwood character. And the reason he leaves is because Clint won't take a risk with him.
B: That's right. He won't put him in a big championship fight because he's afraid the boxer will get hurt. The other manager will, so the fighter goes with him.
A: Exactly—the Clint character plays it safe. He's just too cautious. And then this young female boxer turns up. She'd been working in a café but dreaming of being a champion.
B: But I thought he didn't want to take her on because she was a woman or a "girlie" as he put it, not because it was a risk.
A: Well, yeah, at first. But when she actually turns out to be really good, he's faced with another risk.
B: Ah. You mean, he'll train her into something great and then she'll leave him.
A: Exactly, and that's what almost happens.
B: Right—but she sticks with Clint in the end.
A: Yes. And he takes a kind of emotional risk too.
B: Hmm—you mean about getting involved with her as a person?
A: Exactly. Remember how he keeps writing to his daughter and how she never writes back?
B: Yeah, I never figured what that was all about. Obviously there's some story— something happened that we never really find out about.
A: Yeah, well, they become emotionally connected. The female boxer ends up becoming a substitute daughter to him and given what happened with his real daughter, that's a big risk he's taking too.
B: Yeah, yeah. I see what you mean. I hadn't really looked at it like that before, but now that you say it, I see what you mean.

▶ **1.25** (Page 52)

Well, obviously both pictures are of someone doing the same thing but in very different situations. I guess the first guy

is one of those people who's really into risk-taking—you know, extreme sports and stuff. Not like the second guy!

So, they're both ironing. In the first picture, I can see a man ironing some kind of white shirt. It's got long sleeves and it looks like a T-shirt or a sweatshirt or something. But the ironing board is balanced on top of a high jagged rock that rises up straight from the sea. I can't imagine how he got there with the ironing board and how he manages to stay there himself without falling into the rocks in the sea below. It's amazing.

On the other hand, the second picture is of a much more ordinary situation. A middle-aged man is doing the ironing in his kitchen – his wife might be out at work. He is also looking after his children but not very well. Strangely, the guy in the first picture looks more relaxed than the man in the second picture, even though it must be very dangerous. Maybe it's because he loves rock climbing and the sea and he doesn't have to look after any children. I know I hate ironing but I am also scared of heights and climbing, so I wouldn't like to be in either situation.

UNIT 5 Looking back

▶ **1.26** (Page 59)

A: Oh! I'd forgotten about this photo. Wow! This brings back a few memories.
B: Is that when you lived in Vermont?
A: Yeah, that's right. That's where my parents lived for years and where I grew up. It was this big old house. We rented one floor of it, but the rest of it was empty, and we had this big old yard, pretty much to ourselves.
B: Is that you on the sled?
A: Yep. Haven't changed a bit, right? That's Betty pulling the sled. Have I ever told you about Betty?
B: Um, maybe. Remind me.
A: Well, my mom went back to teaching when I was about two, so she hired Betty to come in and watch me for most of the day. I guess she was kind of like a nanny—but a young, very pretty nanny. The idea was that she'd just be around for a few months. But Mom started teaching summer school too, so she ended up staying until I was almost seven. She was really important to me. I'm still in touch with her and her family.
B: Wow! That's awesome.
A: Yeah. This is one of my favorite photos of her. She was really cool. That's probably a big reason why I have such great memories of my childhood. She was really a lot of fun. We were always doing interesting things, but at the same time you couldn't mess with her. When she told you to do something, you did it. No arguing—that was for sure.
B: She sounds great. So, what kind of kid were you? I bet you were a troublemaker.
A: Me? No! I was a model child. Believe it or not, I was pretty advanced for my age in a lot of ways.
B: Oh, yeah? Like what?
A: Well, according to my mom, I had already said my first words by the time I was eight months, and I was able to walk, more or less, by ten months.

B: Whoa!

A: And I was pretty musical, for a kid. I could play simple tunes on the piano pretty well before I was four, which I hear is quite early.

B: (laughs) So where did it all go wrong?

A: Yeah, I know. I guess I just peaked too soon.

▶ 1.27 **(Page 60)**

My little brother, Chris, and I have always been pretty competitive, even as little kids. I remember one Christmas, we both got bikes, and he could ride his on his own before I could. He was only five and I was almost seven. I got so mad! But at least I was better at swimming. I was able to swim pretty well by the time I was eight. Not Chris. He's always been kind of scared of the water, but I've always loved it. Even now he's not really comfortable in the water. I mean, he can swim, but he doesn't really like it, so he's not great at it.

What else? Oh, yeah, our grandpa was a great chess player, so we got into that at one point – I think we were about thirteen or fourteen. Anyway, I was really good at it—so good in fact that Chris has never managed to beat me—not even once. The last time he lost, he said he'd never play me again. And guess what? He never has!

And a couple of years ago, we both took up skiing. Chris loves it and he's great at it—a real natural. I'm just OK—but I'm getting better. In fact, the last time we were out, I was able to go down my first black slope without falling down. The black trails are for advanced skiers, so I was really proud of that.

▶ 1.28 **(Page 61)**

A: . . . and I think this photo must have been taken about the same year as the one with the sled.

B: So, who are all these people? That's got to be you sitting on the ground with the dogs, right?

A: Yep. Taking it easy, as usual. And that's my dad on the left, then there's my mom. And that's Aunt Joan on the far right. She was my father's older sister and next to her is her husband, Uncle Pierre. This photo's actually taken outside the hotel that my aunt and uncle had just outside Montreal. It was like a three-hour-drive from Vermont, so we used to go and stay with them a lot in the summer.

B: Did you bring Betty?

A: No, Betty never came with us. She didn't need to, because my parents were there to watch me.

B: How did you like staying at the hotel?

A: Oh, the hotel was great. As a kid I found it really exciting. At home in the summer, I'd get really bored. There wasn't much to do, but at the hotel there were endless possibilities. I used to go around everywhere exploring. There were woods out back, and of course the river wasn't far at all. And sometimes, I remember, I'd go in the kitchen and the cook would let me try some of the desserts! But no, overall, it was the best. Way more fun than just hanging around at home!

B: And how did you like the dogs?

A: They were a lot of fun. They became like my best friends and they used to come exploring with me. I was always really sad to leave them when we had to go home.

▶ 1.29 **(Page 62)**

1. This year hasn't been great, but I'm sure things will be better next year.

2. Kate? Kate, thank goodness you're home. I've been so worried.

3. Listen, I think we're lost, and we shouldn't be walking around here late at night. I'm not sure it's that safe here.

4. Would you look at this! An email just showed up in my inbox from my last boss. I wonder what this could be about.

5. Well, of course, he said that was why he came home so late, but you don't believe him, do you?

6. You're always late! Why can't you be on time for once in your life?

7. She said what? No! I don't believe it! That's terrible!

▶ 1.30 **(Page 64)**

Hmm, where shall I start? Well, the basic story is that a girl named Catherine, is left this box by her mother, who died when Catherine was just a baby. Catherine discovers the box when she's the same age as her mother was when she died. Inside the box are eleven objects, like a red hat, part of a map, and the like. All of them are meaningless at first, but when Catherine begins to look over each object, she discovers new things, not only about her mother, but also about herself. And so through these objects Catherine learns that her mother was not the sweet and innocent woman that everyone likes to remember her as.

So, what did I think of it? Well, overall, I really enjoyed it—it's an interesting idea for a story—and I thought it was very well-written. Not only that, but there are lots of things about Catherine's life that I can totally relate to. The events were different, but the feelings and thoughts reminded me so much of my own life that I found myself constantly underlining parts of the story.

On the other hand, at times I found it a little slow. I wanted to know about the objects, and it seemed to take forever to find out what they were all about. Still, apart from that one small thing, it was an easy read, and I'd definitely recommend it.

▶ 1.31 **(Page 66)**

Well, first of all it's very important to make sure that your time capsule container is going to last for a very long time obviously! So, it mustn't rust, it mustn't leak and it must be very hard-wearing. We were told to avoid any kinds of plastics and go for a material like aluminum or stainless steel.

We put in various books, newspapers, and photographs—all of which I still think were a good idea. With books and papers, it's important to make sure they're printed on the highest quality paper—so they don't deteriorate any faster than absolutely necessary.

One mistake we made was to put in color photographs. I mean, photographs are very good information carriers across time and cultures, but apparently, black and white photographs are much more stable and long-lasting than color prints, so that's something worth bearing in mind.

The other thing which we should have thought about was that some kinds of technology become redundant. We put in an old video tape and they probably won't be able to view that when the capsule finally gets opened. So, it's probably best not to include any items that require any technology or equipment to use . . . other than eye and hand.

Finally, and again, pretty obviously I guess, do make sure that the outside of the capsule is clearly labeled using a permanent marker pen saying what it is and any necessary instructions.

UNIT 6 Exploring the world

▶ 1.32 **(Page 70)**

1.
A: Do you like camping?

B: I hate it! I went once, and I was petrified because I kept hearing animals. I even found pitching my tent pretty daunting.

2.
A: Are you scared of flying?

B: Not really. I went up in a small airplane. I was a little worried at first because it was pretty bumpy. But in the end I found the whole experience really inspiring.

3.
A: How do you feel about eating food you've never tried before?

B: Well, the other day, a friend of mine got me to try snails. I was annoyed with him because he didn't tell me what they were. Well, when I found out, I was nearly sick to my stomach! They were really disgusting!

4.
A: How would you feel about a job that involved working with animals?

B: Actually, I've just spent the summer holidays working at a monkey sanctuary, and I loved it. Monkeys are fascinating when you get to know them. Catching them to give them medicine was pretty challenging, but it was all very rewarding.

▶ 1.33 **(Page 71)**

1. The summer is generally hot and very humid and quite uncomfortable. It's often overcast, too, and there is no breeze to cool things down. It's very different in the winter, when it's cool and the sky is clear.

2. I'm a not a big fan of temperate weather – you know, when it never gets very hot or cold. It's just boring. I like my weather to change and be dramatic. Like when you get these sweltering days and then there's a big thunderstorm with lightning and there's a big downpour for hours. Or when it's like an oven in the day and you get subzero temperatures at night.

3. The weather here is very <u>changeable</u>. In the summer, the days are generally <u>sunny</u> or <u>partly cloudy</u>, but they can be rainy, too, especially in June. And the nights are sometimes a little <u>chilly</u> but not really cold. In the winter, it seems to <u>drizzle</u> a lot and the sky is always <u>gray</u>.

▶ **1.34** **(Page 71)**

1. The weather here isn't usually very hot or very cold.
2. I got completely soaked even though it rained for just five minutes.
3. The sky was full of clouds, and the sun didn't come out all day.
4. I was glad I'd brought a jacket to wear at night.
5. I can't stand it when you get one of those gentle rains that goes on for hours and hours.
6. What a terrible camping trip! We were freezing all the time, even in our extra-thick sleeping bags.
7. If I were you, I'd bring sunscreen and a raincoat. You never know what the weather will be like here.
8. It was a wonderful place—blue skies and the light was really good for taking photos.

▶ **1.35** **(Page 72)**

A: Hello everyone. I think we'll get started since it's already a few minutes past 7:30. Let me introduce Jamie. He's our Bhutan expert. He's spent a substantial amount of time in this wonderful country, and I'm sure he'll be able to help you with whatever questions you have. So Jamie, I'll turn it over to you.
B: Hello. Thank you. Please feel free to ask whatever you want and if I can't answer anything, well, I'll say so! So, fire away. Yes?
C: Um. Yes. When is the best time to go?
B: Well, in the winter it can get up to about 15 degrees Celsius, that's about 59 degrees Fahrenheit, in the daytime, but you often get subzero temperatures at night. There is a lot of snow in winter, and that can make traveling difficult. It's hot in the summer, sometimes really sweltering, but it rains a lot, too. So, in my experience, the best seasons to visit are the spring and the fall. Spring is beautiful with flowers and beautiful sunny days. And the fall is great too—the temperatures are perfect—it's not too hot or too cold, and there are clear views of the Himalayas. Yes . . . ?
D: What activities do you recommend?
B: One of the most popular activities for visitors to Bhutan is going trekking in the Himalayas. The high mountains and deep valleys are spectacular. You don't see many people either. You can sometimes walk for days before coming to the next village. You can see a huge variety of plant life that ranges from dense forests to tiny mountain flowers. I've been many times. You won't be disappointed, I can assure you!
D: Thank you.
B: Excuse me, I'd like to know if we need to take anything special in the way of clothes or gear.
B: Yes, good question. The changeable

climate means that you will need a wide range of clothes, including rain gear and good hiking boots. And the sun can be very strong, especially up in the mountains, so you'll need a hat and sunglasses. I'd also recommend warm clothes for the evenings. It can get pretty chilly, even in the summer.
D: Would we need to carry our own equipment on a trek?
B: No. In Bhutan, trekking is only done in organized groups, and they provide yaks that carry your luggage, the food, and all the camping equipment—which is all provided by the way.
D: That's a relief!
B: I've always found them to be very well-equipped and helpful.
D: And who goes with the trekking group? I mean do they provide a guide?
B: Oh yeah, there's always a guide who speaks English and a cook and other assistants to help make the trek run smoothly. They're all very friendly. You really don't need to worry about getting lost or anything.
C: And what about the food? What's the food like?
B: Mmm. Well, it's interesting. The Bhutanese eat a lot of meat, dairy, vegetables, and rice. The national dish is a fabulous chili pepper and cheese stew called Emadatse. Hot chili peppers are very common ingredients in Bhutanese cooking, and you'll find that a lot of their dishes are very spicy. I love the food. Yes, sir?
D: I'm thinking of going in the fall. Do you know if there are any interesting festivals at that time?
B: Well, the dates of festivals vary according to the moon, but this year there are some festivals in fall, although The most popular one for tourists is held in Thimphu, the capital, and this year it's in October. People dress in really colorful traditional clothes, and there is a lot of music and dancing, including masked sword dances. All the festivals are important religious events for the people to offer thanks to their gods.
D: I've seen pictures of strings of flags in the mountains. Can you tell me what they are?
B: They're prayer flags. Each flag has a sutra or Buddhist prayer written on it. The Bhutanese are very religious. They believe that when the wind blows through the flags, it carries the good wishes from the prayers all across the land.

UNIT 7 Indulging yourself

▶ **2.02** **(Page 82)**

Well, we have a really big dinner on Thanksgiving in our family, like most families in the US. It's great, but we always end up eating too much and feeling too full! Our traditional Thanksgiving dinner is a whole roasted turkey with stuffing—that's this delicious stuff that you stuff inside the turkey. It's made with bread crumbs, celery, spices, and other stuff, depending on the family. Stuffing recipes vary between

families—different people in the US make it in slightly different ways, but that's the way our family does it. And then there are a lot of side dishes like mashed potatoes, green beans, gravy, and of course, cranberry sauce. For dessert we always have ice cream and pumpkin pie. I love pumpkin pie!

My favorite part of the meal is the mashed potatoes. My mom has a special way of cooking them to make them taste really delicious. First, you wash them, cut them into pieces, and boil them for about 20 minutes or so. Then you put them in a big bowl and add lots of salt, pepper, butter, milk, cream cheese . . . anything creamy! The secret is to add lots of real butter. Then you smash them until everything is mixed together and then whip it until the potatoes are soft and fluffy.

▶ **2.03** **(Page 83)**

And now, entertainment news. More celebrity items and movie memorabilia are going under the gavel. In the last few years, some items have hit the headlines after they were sold at auctions for absurdly high prices.

Back in 2001, the white bikini worn by Ursula Andress in the James Bond movie *Dr. No* was put up for auction. The actress reportedly decided to sell the two-piece suit after she discovered it in the attic at her home. Andress is now in her sixties, but she became famous overnight in 1962 when she played the first "Bond girl" in the first James Bond movie. The bikini was bought for $61,000 by Robert Earl, the co-founder of Planet Hollywood.

More recently, the red leather jacket worn by Michael Jackson in the music video *Thriller!* was auctioned off for a whopping one point eight million dollars! Before the auction, experts thought the jacket would go for as high as $400,000, which is a very high price, but no one expected it would sell for almost 2 million dollars!

Of course, traditional auctions are not the only way to bid for things. Thousands of people now buy and sell things on eBay, the popular Internet auction site. And sometimes the most incredible things go for extraordinary prices! Three of Marilyn Monroe's chest x-rays were sold at a recent auction for $45,000. But one of the most bizarre sales involved a piece of gum that had been chewed by pop star Britney Spears. The seller said he found the gum on the sidewalk outside a hotel when he saw Britney spit it out. The description that went with the gum on the Internet read: "It is completely preserved as you can see, with Britney's teeth marks highly visible! This is the chance to own a piece of pop history—right from the mouth of the princess of pop herself!" There is no guarantee that the gum is authentic, but potential buyers can contact the seller directly and then use their own judgment to decide.

It is not only celebrity items that have been making news on eBay. Three boys in Texas got a nasty surprise last Christmas after their father had given them constant warnings about their bad behavior. He had bought them 700 dollars worth of video games for Christmas. But when there was no improvement in their behavior, the father auctioned off their Christmas presents on eBay. He sold the items for $1,700 and gave the money to the local church.

So, it seems that almost anything can be bought and sold and that ridiculously high prices will sometimes be paid for completely ridiculous items.

▶ **2.04** **(Page 88)**

A. feathers   B. wings   C. beak   D. talons
E. fur   F. tail   G. paws   H. whiskers
I. horns   J. hooves   K. fins

▶ **2.05** **(Page 88)**

1. I didn't just hear about Kim's party from someone else—she told me herself. It was straight from the horse's mouth.
2. I've got to tell John the bad news but I feel really bad about it. I'll just have to take the bull by the horns and do it.
3. I need glasses for most things nowadays. I'm as blind as a bat without them!

▶ **2.06** **(Page 90)**

Conversation 1

A: Good evening. Do you have a reservation?
B: Yes, we have a reservation for two for Morrison.
A: Madison. Um, I don't see anything under that name.
B: Um . . . no, it's Morrison.
A: Sorry. Morrison, ah, yes. If you'd like to follow me . . .
B: Thank you . . .
C: Can I get you something to drink?
B: Yes, please. A bottle of mineral water— sparkling, please.
C: Certainly, Sir.
C: Are you ready to order?
B: Yes, I think so.
C: Ma'am?
B: I'll have the steak.
C: How would you like it?
B: Rare, please.
C: Rare. Thank you. And for you, sir?
B: I'll have the grilled tuna, please.
C: Um . . . Sorry, sir. We're all out of the tuna.
B: Oh! OK, then. I'll have the swordfish.
C: Um, I'm terribly sorry sir, but there's no swordfish either.
B: Oh! Is there any fish on the menu today?
C: Yes, there's the grilled sea bass.
B: I'll have that then, please. And I'll have potatoes with it, please.
C: I'm terribly sorry, but we've run out of potatoes. We had trouble with deliveries today. But we have a nice rice pilaf you can have with it.
B: Well, all right, but I'm not very happy about all this.

Conversation 2

A: Can I help you?
B: Oh, yes . . . I'd like to try these on, please.
A: Yes of course. What size are you?
B: Umm well, usually a US size seven but sometimes an eight.
A: A seven is a size 38 and an eight is a 39.
B: Good. Could I try both?
A: Yes, that's fine. I'll bring both for you. I won't be a minute. Was it black you wanted?

B: Yes.
A: OK, fine. Would you like to take a seat over there? OK. I have a black in size 38, but not in 39. I've brought a brown in size 39 for you to try on.
B: Thanks. I'll try the 38 first.
A: Oh, they look really nice on you. How do they feel?
B: I really like them but they feel kind of tight. I think I'll try the 39s, but I don't like brown.
B: Uh-hmm. Oh, yeah. These are better. Mmm. The 39s fit better, but I really don't like the color. Are you sure you don't have any black 39s?
A: I can go check if you'd like.
B: Yes, please. I really think I prefer the black.
A: No, I'm sorry—only brown in 39.
B: Oh! Can you call one of your other stores and see if they have any? I don't like the brown . . . they won't go with any of my clothes.
A: Yes, of course.

Conversation 3

A: Good morning. I'd like to make an appointment with Tina to have my hair done, please.
B: Yes, of course. When would you like to come in?
A: Do you have anything for tomorrow morning before noon?
B: Um, yes, there's a ten-thirty, an eleven-fifteen, or an eleven forty-five.
A: Oh, ten-thirty's good, thanks.
B: Fine, ten-thirty. That's with Tina. And what would you like to have done? Just a cut and blow-dry?
A: Well, a cut and blow-dry yes, but I'd also like to have some highlights done. In fact, I was thinking of getting multicolored highlights this time. Would that be possible?
B: Oooh yes. That sounds fun! Great. We'll see you tomorrow at 10:30.
A: Thank you. Bye.

UNIT 8 Aiming for success

▶ **2.07** **(Page 91)**

1. If the business continues to lose money, it will probably go under and have to close.
2. His book's been an instant best-seller. Everybody's talking about it.
3. Just because you failed this exam doesn't mean you should give up. You can always retake it in October.
4. I think these reality TV shows have had their day. No one watches them anymore.
5. I'm afraid your work really isn't up to snuff. You'll just have to redo it.
6. I'm not sure that pushing the car will help start it, but you can give it a try.

▶ **2.08** **(Page 93)**

A: . . . so, generally things are going fine. We've talked about your work attitude, which is very good. Over the three years that you've worked here, you've shown a consistently professional approach to your work.

B: Thank you. I have say that I've really enjoyed it. Testing computer games is a lot of fun, and my co-workers are very helpful and supportive.
A: OK. So, the next part of this appraisal is to think about your future. What do you see yourself doing next?
B: Well, as I said, I've really enjoyed the game testing work that I've been doing, but I feel that it's time I moved up. I mean, I think I'd like to have a little more responsibility.
A: Yes, I think that's something we need to think about. You've shown some good leadership skills. How would you feel about becoming a team leader? You know, then you'd be supervising a team of game testers and making sure everything gets done right.
B: Well, yes, I'd love to, but to tell the truth, I'm not sure I have the right skills. Would there be any management training?
A: Sure. We have some excellent sessions that we run in-house. I think taking some of them would give you more confidence. In fact, there's one coming up next week and there's another in a couple of months. I'd rather you did the first one, though, so that we don't waste any more time. What do you think?
B: Well, yes. I'd be very interested. It'd be great to get training started as soon as possible. I'd rather not wait for two months, if that's OK with you.
A: OK. Great. In that case, I'd better get your name on the list right away for the one next week. Let me just check with Mikiko now. Excuse me, for a minute.

▶ **2.09** **(Page 93)**

1. I think I'd rather you did the first course.
2. I feel that it's time I moved up.
3. I'd rather not wait for two months.
4. I'd better get your name on the list right away.

▶ **2.10** **(Page 93)**

C: Hi, Will. How did your appraisal go?
B: It went well, thanks. My boss thinks it's time I took more responsibility and maybe even became a team leader.
C: Oh, that's good.
B: Yeah. I was thinking of looking for a new job, but now I think I'd rather stay here.
C: I'd love it if you were our team leader. I'd much rather have you in charge than someone we don't know.
B: Thanks. Listen, I've got a meeting in five minutes. I'd better go. See you later.

▶ **2.11** **(Page 94)**

1. She isn't very strict, and she hardly ever gets upset or worried.
2. He's the kind of person who has a goal and works hard to achieve it.
3. She's determined to do what she wants, and she won't take advice from anyone.
4. He has a way with words—he uses words in clever, funny ways.
5. She's a people-person—she really enjoys meeting and talking to people.
6. He's one of those people who's always honest and doesn't keep secrets from anyone.

7. He has very strong views about a lot of things and talks about them in a way that annoys people.
8. She's the kind of person who cares only about herself. She never thinks about other people.
9. He's good at making things happen. He doesn't just react to things, you know?
10. She's one of those people who is good at secretly controlling or tricking people to get what she wants.

▶ **2.12** (Page 96)

1. I want to be the best player on the field.
2. I won the race easily.
3. I'm not going to practice today.
4. You can succeed if you're confident.
5. Why are you feeling so negative?
6. Will you help me tomorrow?

▶ **2.13** (Page 102)

A: . . . and our next caller is Julie. So, what's on your mind, Julie?
B: Well . . . guys, Chris. Guys are always on my mind.
A: Ah. Now where have I heard that before?
B: I know, I know, but it feels like I've tried everything, and I'm just not getting anywhere.
A: So what exactly do you mean when you say you've tried everything?
B: Well, there was this guy I really liked a couple of months ago at work. We used to joke around the office a lot and had lunch together a few times. I'd text him now and then. At first, it all seemed to be going pretty well. But then all of sudden, he seemed to just start avoiding me.
A: What, like overnight?
B: Well, I don't know if it was that sudden, but it was pretty strange.
A: And nothing had really changed?
B: No. Well, like I said, I had been texting him a lot.
A: What kind of things were you texting?
B: Oh, nothing much. Just silly things. You know, like telling him I thought he was really cute, and stuff like that.
A: Anything else?
B: Well, I did send him a card or two, and some flowers, and I made a cake for his birthday and brought it to his office. With some balloons.
A: To the office?
B: Yeah, well, I don't know. Do you think that was a little over the top?
A: So, Martina, you said you're an athlete?
C: Yeah, well, I do a lot of long-distance running—you know marathons and stuff.
A: Oh yeah, so what exactly were you calling about?
C: Well, just recently, I had this race, you know, a really big one, it was on TV and everything and, I . . . well, how can I put this? I, I just couldn't do it.
A: What do you mean you "couldn't do it"?
C: Well, it was really hot, but about half-way, I was falling behind the leaders, and I just had to stop—which is really unusual for me. And then, I just couldn't get going again, and so I just gave up.
A: I see.

C: And since then, I've lost all my confidence. I'm thinking I may have to give up running altogether. But really, it's been my life up to now.
A: That sounds really difficult. Have you talked to anyone about how you're feeling?
C: Well, yes. I work with a sports psychologist, but she's just telling me to . . .
A: So Tim, what would you like to talk about today?
D: My job, I guess.
A: OK, go ahead.
D: Well. I've been at my company for a while now, and, well, I kind of feel like I've gotten stuck.
A: Stuck?
D: Yeah, stuck—I'm not going anywhere. The thing is other people who started around the same time as me have gotten promoted and moved up the ladder, but I'm still doing exactly the same job as when I started.
A: Mmm-hmm. And you feel like you've been doing well at your current job?
D: Well, yeah. For the most part. I guess there have been one or two problems, but that happens to everyone, right? I mean, I had some trouble with one of my clients, but that wasn't really my fault. They weren't interested in dealing with anyone who wasn't at least a Vice President. They thought they were too good for someone like me who's just a manager. Anyway, they didn't renew their contract with us, so I got into a little trouble about that. And then I've been warned a few times about coming in late.
A: So, are you late for work pretty often?
D: Yeah, well, I guess so.
A: Just how often, Tim?
D: Well, maybe a couple of times a week.
A: What—every week?
D: Pretty much, I guess. It's just that I'm a heavy sleeper and I never hear my alarm clock. I've tried different kinds but it doesn't seem to make any difference . . .

UNIT **9** Crime solvers

▶ **2.14** (Page 105)

A: Did I tell you about this really funny lawyer story that a friend of mine emailed me the other day?
B: No.
A: Well, the way it goes is that there's this lawyer in North Carolina, I think, or somewhere in the southern US. Anyway, he buys this box of really rare and very, very expensive cigars . . .
B: OK.
A: And because they're so expensive, he decides to insure them . . . against fire and stuff like that.
B: Fair enough.
A: Yes, except that, he smoked his complete collection of these fantastic cigars within a month, and before he'd even made his first payment on the insurance policy, the lawyer filed a claim with the insurance company.
B: You mean he wanted the insurance company to pay him? Why?

A: Well, in his claim, the lawyer stated that the cigars were lost "in a series of small fires."
B: How ridiculous!
A: And of course, the insurance company refused to pay since you know, they weren't really lost in a fire. The guy had just smoked them. And then, the lawyer sued the insurance company—and get this—he won!
B: What?
A: And so the company had to pay the claim.
B: No! You're kidding.
A: But that's not all! So the insurance company accepted the decision and wrote the guy a check for $15,000. But here's the best part!
B: Go on! I bet this will be good.
A: After he cashed the check, the guy was arrested! The insurance company had him charged with 24 counts of arson! And based on his own insurance claim, the lawyer was convicted of deliberately burning his insured property.
B: I don't believe it.
A: Yeah. And so he was sentenced to 24 months in jail and a $24,000 fine. Isn't that great?
B: No way! Is that really true?
A: I guess so. Bill said he saw it on the news.
B: Unbelievable!

▶ **2.15** (Page 107)

A: Did you see these photos in the paper? It says they're of someone who was in the middle of stealing computer equipment from someone's house . . .
B: Really? So, how did they manage to do that?
A: I'm not sure. I suppose they must have fixed up some kind of security camera.
B: What? Inside their own house?
A: Yeah. That would be pretty unusual. Do you think the thief realized he was being caught on camera?
B: He can't have done, can he? Otherwise, he'd have taken the camera too!

▶ **2.16** (Page 107)

1. We don't know who took the money. There were a lot of people in the office during the day and it might have been any of them.
2. I wonder why Pete didn't turn up to do his community service. He can't have forgotten about it. I reminded him yesterday.
3. I'm not sure where Jo is. She might have gone over to Sally's. They're working on a school project together.
4. How did you know about the surprise party? Someone must have told you!
5. You can't have spent your whole paycheck already. You only got paid yesterday!
6. I can't have left my keys at home. I remember feeling them in my jacket pocket when I got on the bus.
7. She can't have finished her homework yet. She only started it a few minutes ago.
8. I lost one of my gloves. I might have dropped it on the way to work.

. . . and finally, a burglar was given an eleven month prison sentence today after admitting to breaking into a local home and stealing thousands of dollars worth of computer equipment.

The homeowner, Denise Gray, who had been burglarized once before, set up a webcam that would start recording as soon as it detected movement in the room. So even though the burglar stole the computer and webcam, the images had already been sent over the Internet to a private email address.

After the trial, the police officer in charge of the case commented that after the break-in was discovered, Ms. Gray simply gave them the email address, and they were able to watch several minutes of footage and identify the thief, who was well known to the police. When the thief denied breaking in to the property the police simply showed him the footage. The webcam made their job easy. The officer said it was a real pleasure to see the thief's expression when they showed him the pictures.

A: Sherlock Holmes, I must ask you first . . . How is it that you have the same name as Sherlock Holmes, the great detective?

B: Please, call me "Holmes"—that's what my friends and family call me—well, you see, my parents were great fans of the original Conan Doyle stories. Both parents, my father especially, would spend hours reading the adventures to me—even as a child.

A: Really!?

B: Yes . . . and when I was born, they discussed a number of first names. They wanted to give their son a name that was uncommon—but also that represented something special. They didn't take long to decide on "Sherlock Holmes" as he was their favorite literary figure—and they knew no one would forget me once they'd heard my name. And boy, were they right!

A: So, how do people in general react when you introduce yourself to them?

B: Well, I get all kinds of reactions really—everything from the usual "Where's Dr. Watson?" type comments to people just thinking I'm being funny.

A: I can imagine. And do you mind?

B: No, not at all. I never have. I think, the best reaction was one time when I was in San Francisco, and I went into an electronics store to buy a TV. The clerk behind the counter was a young lady around 18 or so. When she saw the name on my credit card, she must have stared at it for about 10 full seconds. Then she looked up at me and she said, in all sincerity, "I didn't know you were real! Wait 'til I tell my friends I saw the real Sherlock Holmes!"

A: No!

B: Yes! You could have knocked her over with a feather. The expression on her face looked like she'd seen a ghost. It was very amusing.

A: Given your name, do you feel that you have any special talent or ability to solve mysteries in everyday life?

B: Well, I will say that having that name does mean that people often turn to me if anything unusual happens. For example, if I'm watching TV with a friend or family member and a magician comes on and does some kind of trick—all eyes turn to me to explain how it's done.

A: Really? How funny!

B: It's not as if I've ever been interested in magic. Anyway, about two years ago, an old family friend suddenly disappeared from work with about $7,000. His mother hadn't heard from him for days. Even though we hadn't been in touch for years, she called me after the local police said they couldn't help. To keep her calm, I met her at her son's house, pulled out my flashlight and magnifying glass, and slowly went through the house looking for clues.

A: And did you actually find any?

B: Well, fortunately, he hadn't deleted his email messages from his computer. The emails seemed to suggest that he'd deliberately taken the money to leave town and live in a warmer climate, which was what I told his mother. In the end, it turned out that he realized he couldn't really start a new life on only $7,000 and he returned to face the justice system. It was hard for him, but I was pleased to have worked out what happened!

A: Just like your namesake.

Nick Leeson's life started as a classic rags-to-riches story. He was born into a working class family and left school with almost no qualifications. Nonetheless, in the early 1980s, he got a series of clerical jobs with different banks, ending up with Barings, a well-known investment bank, where he did well and received rapid promotion.

Before long, he was making millions for Barings by betting on the future direction of the Japanese stock exchange. His bosses back in London were delighted with his large profits and put more and more trust in him. By the end of 1993, he had made more than £10m—about 10% of the total profit of the bank for that year. However, what the bank didn't know was that Leeson had a special account where he was hiding his losses.

By December '94 the losses hidden in that account totaled $512 million. As the losses grew, Leeson requested extra funds to continue trading, hoping to get himself out of the mess by more deals. In the end, Leeson managed to lose the bank one point three billion dollars of the bank's money and effectively destroyed Barings

As the direct result of his actions, he had wiped out the 233 year old Barings investment Bank, who proudly counted the Queen as a client. Investors saw their savings wiped out, and some 1,200 of Leeson's fellow employees lost their jobs.

What became of Leeson? After going on the run, the world's most wanted man, on the cover of every newspaper, checked in a flight to Europe using his own name and hiding beneath a baseball cap. The German authorities were alerted and the police were there to arrest Leeson as he touched down. In December 1995 a court in Singapore sentenced him to six and a half years. In jail, he is said to have spent a lot of time doing exercise and he also, apparently, found God.

He was released early, in the summer of 1999 and, after his return to the UK, found that he was effectively homeless and without a job. Leeson though, has managed to bounce back and make the most of his experiences. He has made an estimated £50,000 from his book, and the fee for selling his story to the newspapers is reported to be about three times that amount. The story has also been turned into a movie called *Rogue Trader*, starring Ewan McGregor.

UNIT 10 Mind matters

1. Once I had a premonition that something awful was going to happen to an old school friend of mine, Carola, who'd moved to Australia and I hadn't seen for ages. I somehow knew something was going to happen and then later that day, another friend of mine phoned to say that Carola had had an accident and was in hospital. A few other things like that have happened recently, so nowadays I take my premonitions a bit more seriously than I used to . . .

2. It was really weird. The other day, I was at my brother's 30th birthday party and was talking to some people there. And then in the middle of the conversation, I suddenly had a really strong feeling of déjà vu. I just felt that the whole thing, you know, the place, the people—the exact conversation—had all happened before in exactly the same way. It made me feel really strange for a couple of minutes.

3. I think more and more, I'm learning to trust my intuition when I have decisions to make about—whatever—like deciding which job to apply for, or knowing which road to turn on if I get lost, or knowing when someone's lying to me. I find if I start analyzing things and trying to figure it out, I get confused. But if I go with my gut feeling, without thinking about things too much, I'm usually right.

4. My cousins are twins and they have always been incredibly close. Even now that they're older, they still have a sixth sense about each other. They always seem to know when something happens to the other one, even if they're miles apart. One of them knows if something important has happened to the other one, especially if they're in trouble or if one of them has been hurt.

5. I've only been unconscious once in my life and that was when I was playing football in the park with some friends. We used to play every Sunday, and I really enjoyed it, but I got hurt a lot. One day, I was knocked unconscious by someone. You know, I still don't really know how it happened. I just remember waking up, lying on the grass looking up at a group of about twenty people all staring down at me, and I didn't have a clue what was going on.

6. I think that I'm a very single-minded person. I mean, I really drive myself hard to succeed at everything I do. That can be a problem sometimes. I've been wondering why I make myself work so hard and get so stressed out about things, and I think it's maybe because I have a subconscious fear of failure. I think that deep down, without really being aware of it most of the time, I'm really scared of failing—I don't know why. Maybe it's because I'm the oldest child in my family, and I had a lot of responsibility growing up.

▶ **2.21** **(Page 118)**

1.
A: How do you feel about hypnotherapy?
B: Well, I know some people swear by it, so that's something. It sounds as if a lot of patients leave pretty satisfied. I don't really get how it works, and I don't think it would really work on someone like me, but that doesn't matter. If it works for some people, I'm in favor of it. I wouldn't try it myself, though.

2.
A: What are your views on hypnosis? Do you have any strong feelings about it?
C: Yes, I do. I've always believed that those people are just good showmen. To my mind, it's all a bunch of nonsense—those hypnotherapists are just good at being nice to people, so they're a little bit happier at the time. But, I have my doubts about how much it can actually do for people in the long-run. I'm skeptical that hypnosis has any effect at all, and I'm against people paying for a service and getting nothing real in return. I mean, I doubt hypnosis actually works for anyone.

3.
A: What do you think of hypnosis?
D: Yeah. I'm a big believer myself. I have to say that when I went for a session with a hypnotist, it was fantastic. It saved my job. I mean, I was able to deal with the stress of my job much better after that and I'm convinced that it was the hypnosis that helped me. In fact, if I hadn't gone to the session, I'm sure I would've had to quit by now.

▶ **2.22** **(Page 119)**

A: Welcome to Our Modern World. On our show today, we're talking to Rachel Kim about the power of persuasion. All around us, there are images on television, jingles on the radio, ads in magazines, sound bites on the news, promotions in the malls. They're all hard at work – trying to make us believe something or persuading us to buy something. Fear not, however, Rachel Kim is here to reveal their secrets and show us how to resist all this persuasion. Hello, Rachel. First, persuading people is big business, isn't it? I mean, supermarkets and politicians, advertisers and salespeople, they all take it very seriously, don't they?
B: Yes. They spend a lot of money coming up with psychological tricks to guarantee that even the most cautious among us are open to manipulation.

A: Let's talk about supermarkets. How do they make us buy things we don't necessarily want? What are some of their tricks?
B: Well, the first one is they try to relax us by playing music and by pumping the smell of freshly-baked bread into the store. Research has shown us that the smell of fresh bread makes people buy more.
A: I know I've probably done that without even thinking about it.
B: Exactly. Most of the time, we're completely unaware that it's going on. It's subconscious persuasion.
A: And before the show you mentioned discount reward cards?
B: Yes, well, from the supermarket's point of view, discount reward cards are a huge success story. As customers, we think we're being rewarded for shopping at that particular supermarket. What's really happening, however, is that the store is basically not only tempting us to shop there again, but also getting valuable information about what we're buying.
A: More information to help them figure out how to persuade us to buy even more things.
B: That's right! It's great for market research, but not so great for our privacy.
A: Mmm. So, what about the advertising industry? What secrets can you reveal? How do advertisements persuade us to buy certain products, or watch certain shows?
B: Well, first of all, there's so much of it. These days ads are everywhere from TVs to websites to our cell phones. And no matter how much we think we know about what the advertisers are doing, they still end up winning. Generally, we still fall for the ad and end up buying the product, which, more often than not, is something we don't need.
A: Yes.
B: When you get down to it, there are really only two types of ads: those that appeal to the thinking part of our brain and those that appeal to the emotional part. Generally, ads that appeal to our emotions are usually much more successful. These emotional ads are often based on psychological theories about the mind. By that I mean, advertisers know that images can reach our emotions at a level that we are not aware of and so are much more powerful in persuading us to do things.
A: So, how are emotions used?
B: Well, for instance, ads for clothes often try to make us feel that we belong by showing us how to buy the right clothes to fit in with our peers. And ads for insurance often play on our fears. For example, they might show a car accident in slow motion so we're afraid and suddenly need to feel safe. And self-esteem is an important one too. Many ads for luxury products like expensive cars or watches, work by making us feel good about ourselves so that we feel we deserve to have a luxurious or adventurous lifestyle.
A: Hmm, and celebrities are used a lot too, aren't they?

B: Yes, that's very popular. Celebrities are often used as a quick way of getting the message across. Their success and familiarity makes them feel friendly, interesting, cool, whatever . . . We see our favorite pop star drinking a particular soft drink, and we're immediately persuaded to buy it.

▶ **2.23** **(Page 120)**

1. They persuade us to buy things we may not want.
2. We keep using discount reward cards at the same supermarket.
3. Ads for clothes often want to make us feel that we belong.
4. I try to resist buying expensive designer clothes, but it's difficult!
5. You could try leaving your credit card at home if you don't want to spend so much.

▶ **2.24** **(Page 123)**

1. I told a co-worker that I'd been using one of those self-help CDs to help deal with my stress. Then, in the middle of a business meeting, he suddenly blurted out everything I'd told him. Honestly I was totally at a loss for words—I was so shocked I didn't know what to say.
2. I went to the movies last weekend and the people behind me were whispering to each other throughout the whole movie. They didn't seem to notice that they were annoying everyone else. In the end, I finally snapped at them and they stopped, but by that time the movie was nearly over.
3. My cousin has been staying with me for the last week. I have to say she's kind of irritating. She's really loud and every time I say anything she shrieks with laughter. The other thing she does is constantly interrupt people when they're in the middle of a conversation. I'll be really glad when she goes.
4. I gave my first presentation at work yesterday and it went OK. But at the end, one of my co-workers told me that I had been mumbling and he couldn't really hear me. He's the kind of person who isn't afraid to speak his mind and I was a little upset at first. I guess it's useful feedback though.